30P

The Best of British Festivals

Music · Food · Theatre · Comedy · Dance · Literature · Art ·
Carnivals · and much, much more...

Barney Jeffries

THE BEST OF BRITISH FESTIVALS

Summersdale Publishers Ltd
46 West Street
Chichester
West Sussex
PO19 1RP
UK

www.summersdale.com

Printed and bound in Great Britain

ISBN: 978-1-84024-656-8

Contents

Introduction

Throughout history, in every corner of the world, people have held festivals. Whether it's worshipping the sun god at the solstice, giving thanks for the harvest or initiating young warriors into the tribe, the need to come together, to mark an occasion, to celebrate is hardwired in the human psyche, in the rhythms of our lives. We need festivals.

In Britain, we have a fantastic variety to choose from. Some date back hundreds of years; some are just setting out. Some attract visitors and participants from all over the world; some are all about the local community. Some make headline news while others are well-kept secrets. Many are unique; many are just plain weird. There are huge festivals and tiny festivals, festivals that last one night and festivals that last all summer, countercultural festivals and festivals sponsored by multinational corporations. Our shopping centres and TV shows may suggest a country of clone towns and lowest-common-denominator culture, but our festivals tell a very different story.

It helps that Britain isn't a single nation. It's not even three nations. England, Scotland and Wales all have their traditional festivals, but so too do the ancient kingdoms of Cornwall and the Isle of Man. There are festivals keeping alive the culture and language of Northumbria, festivals celebrating our Roman and Viking heritage, and the exuberant festivals brought by more recent immigrants from the Caribbean, India, China and elsewhere. While much of our cultural life is centred around the big cities, festivals thrive in far-flung places. More often than not, they take place in historic settings or beautiful surroundings. Travelling to festivals is a great way to explore the highlights and hidden treasures of this island.

We've tried to reflect this tremendous diversity in this book. At these festivals, you'll find music, dancing, beer, costumes, tents, processions, funfair rides, face painting, idyllic locations, traction engines, organic falafel stands, morris dancers, bonfires, vintage cars, drumming circles, horse racing, sculptures in unusual places, hotdogs, hot air balloons, giant puppets, sailing ships, street theatre, floral displays, mud, ancient customs, fire-eaters, sheepdogs, literary readings, races, kites, stand-up comedians, ice creams, souped-up Beetles, aerobatics displays, Punch and Judy shows and a whole lot more besides. It's fair to say there's something for everyone.

An evening of Monteverdi in an ancient church on the Gower Peninsula may not resemble a mad weekend of open-air clubbing at Creamfields. Champagne-sipping aristocrats at Henley don't have much in common with mud-splattered tent dwellers at T in the Park, and it's a long way from Padstow's pagan hobby horses to the experimental digital art of Manchester's Futuresonic. All of them, though, share something special. It's that festival feeling.

You know it when you feel it. It's the feeling of being outside the stresses and the structures of everyday reality. It's the buzz. It's the atmosphere, the mood of celebration. It's the sense of community that makes you strike up conversations with strangers. It's the possibility of a different way of living. And you wish it could continue.

It doesn't, of course. Monday morning comes around and mundane reality returns. A life that was all festivals and no work would be unworkable; but a life that was all work and no festivals would be unliveable.

Festivals come and go, and dates and venues can change from year to year. Arrangements alter, sometimes at the last minute. We've tried to provide as much accurate information as possible, but please check out the details with the festival organisers before you make any plans.

Key to the symbols in this book

| FREE | = | entry is free of charge, though voluntary donations may be encouraged in some cases |

| £ | = | up to £10 |

| £ £ | = | £11 to £20 |

| £ £ £ | = | £21 to £50 |

| £ £ £ £ | = | £51 to 100 |

| £ £ £ £ £ | = | £100+ |

| £? | = | these festivals are priced per event and the cost will depend on how many events you choose to attend |

| ▲ | = | there is on-site camping |

| 👤 | = | you can bring your children along |

Map of Britain
showing regions

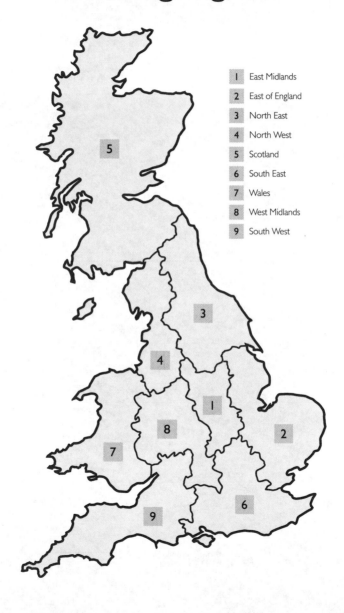

1 East Midlands
2 East of England
3 North East
4 North West
5 Scotland
6 South East
7 Wales
8 West Midlands
9 South West

East Midlands

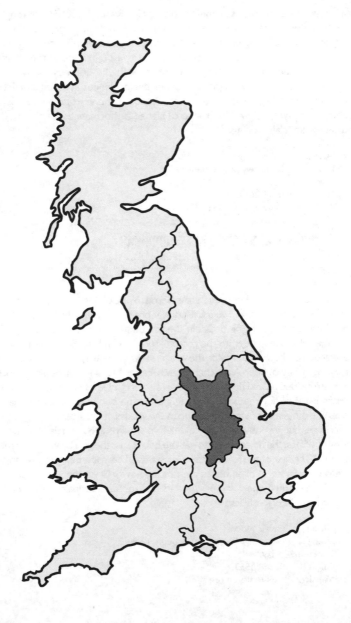

Leicester Comedy Festival

The UK's longest-running comedy festival

Leicester boasts the longest-running comedy festival in the country, dating way back to – don't laugh – 1994. Since then, it has hosted performances from everyone who's anyone on the stand-up circuit, and continues to programme the hottest talent around. It's not just about the big names in the theatres, though. You can spot the stars of tomorrow in the comedy clubs, sketch showcases, improvisation nights and other performances in a range of venues across Leicestershire. There's also the chance to hone your own skills at a workshop or symposium. The range of signed performances for the hard-of-hearing is especially strong.

When:	February
Where:	Leicester, various venues
Duration:	10 days
Tel:	0116 261 6812
Website:	www.comedy-festival.co.uk

Bottle Kicking and Hare Pie Scrambling

The first rule of bottle kicking is: there are no rules...

The village of Hallaton in Leicestershire is home to one of Britain's strangest sporting events. The story goes that two local ladies were saved from a bull when a bolting hare distracted the charging beast. In thanks, they donated several acres of land (known as Hare Crop Leys) to the rector – on the condition that after the Easter Monday service, he should provide the villagers with two hare pies, two dozen penny loaves and plenty of beer. After church each Easter Monday, a hare pie and penny loaves are divided up and thrown for villagers to 'scramble' after. They then process to Hare Pie Bank for the Bottle Kicking game. The bottles are in fact small beer barrels and the game is ostensibly between the villages of Hallaton and neighbouring Medbourne, but anyone is free to join in. Two streams about a mile apart provide natural goal lines, the object being to get the barrel past the goal by whatever means necessary. The first of the few official rules states, 'There are no rules, and anyway, there is no referee.' Broken bones are not unknown. Once the game is over, the 'bottles' are cracked open, and participants and spectators repair to the pub for a fitting end to a ferociously festive day.

When:	Easter Monday
Where:	Hallaton, Market Harborough, Leics.
Duration:	1 day
Tel:	01858 555305
Website:	www.hallaton.org

Darbar South Asian Music Festival

Britain's best festival of Indian classical music

£ £ £ £ £

Leicester's Darbar has quickly established itself as the UK's leading festival of South Asian music. There are morning, afternoon and evening concerts, mainly at The Phoenix, featuring some of the finest musicians from India, the UK and worldwide. Together they represent around 20 different classical music traditions, with sitars, tablas and vocal virtuosity figuring prominently. Indian classical music is a living tradition, so expect centuries-old ragas overlaid with modern instruments and a vibrant fusion of styles.

When:	First weekend of April (Fri–Sun)
Where:	Leicester
Duration:	3 days
Tel:	0116 266 0946
Website:	www.darbar.org.uk

Gatecrasher Summer Sound System

Rave till dawn at this mammoth dance fest

£ £ £ £ £

This is a truly massive dance festival, attracting the biggest live acts and superstar DJs on the scene. With 20 live bands and 200 DJs across 20 arenas catering for all sorts, there's something to put a grin on the face of every one of the 60,000 punters. There's camping on site, including VIP and boutique options, although as with most dance festivals, don't expect to crash out before dawn – the music keeps pumping till 6 a.m. Away from the music, there are white-knuckle rides, 24-hour shopping and plenty of food and drink stalls. Although there is car parking on site (including spots for campervans), you're better off picking up a shuttle bus from the train stations in Northampton, Banbury or Milton Keynes. Gatecrasher is strictly over-18s only; if you look fresh-faced, bring ID.

When:	Spring Bank Holiday weekend (Sat/Sun)
Where:	Turweston Aerodrome, Brackley, Northants.
Duration.	2 days
Website:	www.gatecrasher.com

Off the Tracks

So nice they hold it twice

£ £ £

Your favourite festival is over for another year, and you can't bear the thought of waiting 12 months for the next one… It's a familiar feeling for many, but Off the Tracks devotees can feel smug: they hold their festival twice a year, and familiar faces return time and again. The music is an eclectic and cosmopolitan mix of global fusion, folk, roots and beats across two stages, as well as acoustic sessions. There's a very popular real ale bar, with 45 ales to choose from, plus plenty of stalls and good food, and a laid back, friendly atmosphere. Ticket prices are lower than for many weekend festivals; you pay a little extra for camping, but there are good facilities including hot showers.

When:	Spring Bank Holiday weekend/weekend after August Bank Holiday (Fri–Sun)
Where:	Donington Park Farmhouse, Isley Walton, nr Castle Donington, Leics.
Duration:	3 days each time
Website:	www.offthetracks.co.uk

Acoustic Festival of Britain

Turn on, tune in, un-plug

£ £ £ £ £

Acoustic guitars don't just mean protest singers or folk bands. The line-up here covers everything from blues to rock, pop to ska, as well as the more-expected singer-songwriters, folk and Celtic musicians. Donovan, Jah Wobble and Marillion are among the artists to have unplugged their amps here. Away from the music, there are real ale and food stalls, fair-trade crafts, juggling and tipi circles. The venue is in beautiful parkland around Catton Hall on the Derbyshire–Staffordshire border, and on-site camping is available.

When:	Spring Bank Holiday weekend (Sat–Mon)
Where:	Catton Hall, Catton, Walton-on-Trent, Derbyshire
Duration:	3 days
Website:	www.acousticfestival.co.uk

Dot-to-Dot Festival

Join up the dots as you party your way around the city

Dot-to-Dot, which began life in Nottingham in 2005, is a different sort of music festival – no stages in fields, no Portaloos. Instead, the bands play in a number of venues across the city from early afternoon till dawn and you can crash out in your own bed after a marathon 16-hour session. One wristband (very reasonably priced considering the acts who play) gets you entry into the various venues. The line-up is decidedly hip, ranging from the latest indie crazes (the likes of The Cribs and Kate Nash played just before hitting the mainstream) to critical darlings (New Young Pony Club, Architecture in Helsinki) and more obscure acts. The Nottingham festival is now preceded by a similar event in Bristol the day before, featuring most of the same artists.

When:	Spring Bank Holiday weekend (Sat/Sun)
Where:	Bristol and Nottingham
Duration:	2 days
Tel:	08713 100000
Website:	www.dottodotfestival.co.uk

Glastonbudget

Keeping the music alive

Queen, U2, Sex Pistols, Nirvana, Oasis, Pink Floyd, The Who, The Police, T-Rex, Red Hot Chilli Peppers and Guns N' Roses on the same bill? Welcome to the parallel world of Glastonbudget. OK, so it's actually the likes of Fake That and Antarctic Monkeys rather than the real things, but Europe's biggest and best tribute band festival is great fun. Accept no imitations.

When:	Spring Bank Holiday weekend
Where:	Turnpost Farm, Wymeswold, Leicestershire
Duration:	3 days
Tel:	0116 269 8807 (Booking)
Website:	www.glastonbudget.co.uk

East Midlands

Big Session

Folk and frolics in the De Montfort's backyard

£ £ £ £ [♀] [▲]

Curated by folk-rock institution the Oysterband, this mammoth folk session takes place over a weekend in the elegant surroundings of Leicester's De Montfort Hall, with indoor and outdoor stages. Top names from the world of contemporary folk and roots perform sets. There are also impromptu sessions, an open-mic space in the beer tent and a ceilidh, so bring your instruments. The festival has previously been awarded the prestigious Red Kite mark and A Greener Festival Award for its level of environmental sustainability.

When:	Second weekend of June
Where:	De Montfort Hall, Leicester
Duration:	3 days
Tel:	0116 233 3111
Website:	www.bigsessionfestival.com

Northampton Carnival

Putting the unity into community

FREE [♀]

Northampton has held a number of midsummer festivals over the years, but this multicultural carnival, reinvented in 2005, has brought a new lease of life. The aim is to 'put the unity back in community' and get as many people as possible involved. Fantastically colourful costumes are based around an annual theme, and floats from other carnivals around the UK add to the atmosphere.

When:	Second Saturday in June
Where:	Northampton town centre
Duration:	1 day
Website:	www.northamptoncarnival.co.uk

Download

Prepare to meet the new monsters of rock

£ £ £ £ £ **A**

Donington Park racetrack in Leicestershire has always been the place to come for heavy rock music. Download, launched in 2003, is the spiritual successor of the Monsters of Rock festival, which ran here from 1980 to 1996 – Iron Maiden were one of Download's first headliners. With punk, ska, emo, hardcore and other genres figuring high on the bill, Download attracts a more diverse crowd than the Dungeons-and-Dragons-playing heavy metal stereotypes. You can also play LaserQuest and human table football in 'The Village'.

When:	Mid-June
Where:	Donington Park, Leics.
Duration:	3 days
Tel:	020 7009 3333
Website:	www.downloadfestival.co.uk

Oakham Festival

Putting Rutland back on the map

£?

This festival aims 'to put Rutland on the map as the host of one of our country's great festivals!' This is particularly ambitious considering Rutland itself was only put back on the map a few years ago. They've got a little way to go, but there's already a diverse arts programme – music, comedy, theatre, dance and visual arts all figure – complemented by events at the Uppingham Fringe, which uses the enviable arts facilities at Uppingham School.

When:	End of June
Where:	Oakham (various venues)/Uppingham School, Rutland
Duration:	10 days
Tel:	01572 723393
Website:	www.oakhamfestival.co.uk

Dove Holes International Jazz and Beer Festival

Welcome to the centre of the jazz universe

For one weekend every year, the village of Dove Holes on the edge of the Peak District National Park becomes the centre of the universe – or at least, it does for a few hundred jazz aficionados. This small, friendly festival nevertheless attracts some big names in the traditional New Orleans jazz world. There's a vibrant atmosphere, not unaided by the extensive range of real ales on offer. Camping is available, and there are good catering facilities in the community hall lounge and other outlets in the village. Dove Holes was voted the ugliest village in Britain in a 2001 BBC poll, but don't let that put you off – it has a great personality.

When:	First weekend of July
Where:	Dove Holes, nr Buxton, Derbyshire
Duration:	3 days
Tel:	01298 814722
Website:	www.dovejazz.co.uk

Oundle International Festival

Organs and open-air opera in Oundle

A major classical and jazz festival with a strong international flavour in a variety of historic venues in and around this pretty Northamptonshire market town. Expect some prestigious performers, celebrity organ recitals and lunchtime and coffee concerts. There's also a good programme of open-air theatre (community opera, Shakespeare, kids' theatre) and lighter entertainment, including the popular outdoor Fireworks Concert.

When:	Mid-July
Where:	Various venues, Oundle, Northants.
Duration:	10 days
Tel:	01780 470297
Website:	www.oundlefestival.org.uk

Buxton Festival

A must for true opera lovers

The Peak District spa town of Buxton is home to an elegant opera house, designed in 1903 by Frank Matcham, the architect behind London's Palladium and Coliseum. Refurbished in 1979, it's now the focal point of one of the most prestigious arts festivals in the UK. Rarely performed operas and works by Handel are particular specialities. There's also a high-calibre programme of other music and literary events: Joanna Trollope, John Simpson and Julian Barnes are among the leading authors who have appeared in the past.

When:	Mid-July
Where:	Buxton, Derbyshire
Duration:	16 days
Tel:	01298 72289
Website:	www.buxtonfestival.co.uk

Buxton Festival Fringe

The biggest Fringe in England (apart from Brighton)

The Fringe started out in 1980 as an alternative to the world-renowned Buxton Festival and has blossomed into a showcase for dance, drama, music, poetry, comedy and much more. The organisers firmly believe that 'art is for all' and their open-handed welcome to all genres has led to some pretty diverse programmes over the years. Many performers use it as a warm-up on their way to Edinburgh.

When:	Mid-July
Where:	Buxton, Derbyshire
Duration:	18 days
Tel:	01298 214184 or 01298 70562
Website:	www.buxtonfringe.org.uk

Bug Jam

An infestation of Beetles

This was the first of a 'New Wave' of VW events when it started up in 1987. The Bugs are, of course, Beetles – and you'll find an incredible variety, from perfectly preserved vintage 1950s models to customised freaks. Campervans and Beach Buggies are also popular. The weekend includes many similar features to VW Action (which takes place in August at the same venue), including 'Run What You Brung' and 'Show and Shine', but tends to attract a younger, madder crowd and louder music – imagine an old skool rave, with Beetles, and you're on the right lines.

When:	Third weekend of July
Where:	Santa Pod Raceway, Wellingborough (M1 J14/14), Northants.
Duration:	3 days
Tel:	01234 782828
Website:	www.bugjam.co.uk

Stainsby Festival

Intimate festival in a picturesque rural location

This intimate folk festival is held in a lovely rural setting, on a greenfield farm site in the hamlet of Stainsby. Celebrating its 40th anniversary in 2008, it's a registered charity run by dedicated volunteers, with all profits ploughed back into the event. There's a good range of music – by no means limited to traditional folk. As well as performances in the colourful marquees, there are workshops (including plenty of activities for children), dancing, singarounds, craft stalls, fire shows and wicker sculptures. Camping is free.

When:	Third weekend of July
Where:	Brunt's Farm, Stainsby, Derbyshire
Duration:	3 days
Tel:	01246 559036
Website:	www.stainsbyfestival.org.uk

Nottingham Riverside Festival

Something for everybody at this free festival

Nottingham City Council lays on an impressive programme of entertainment over this long weekend. There's three days of world and roots music over three stages, pumping out everything from Balkan beats to brass band. Other attractions range from street theatre to steam engines, and there's a cosmopolitan selection of food stalls. There are also many opportunities for people of all ages to get involved, with workshops for circus skills, bhangra dancing, MC-ing and film-making, to name but a few. Saturday night ends with a big fireworks display above the River Trent.

When:	First weekend of August (Fri–Sun)
Where:	Victoria Embankment, Nottingham
Duration:	3 days
Website:	www.nottinghamcity.gov.uk

International Gilbert and Sullivan Festival

Three weeks of musical mayhem

For three weeks following the Buxton Festival and Fringe, the town goes musical mad. Amateur G&S societies from the UK and overseas perform nightly at the Opera House, battling it out for the coveted title of International Champion. There are also productions from professional Gilbert & Sullivan companies each year, and a packed programme of fringe events, including late night cabaret in the Festival Club and outdoor singing in the Pavilion Gardens.

When:	August
Where:	Buxton, Derbyshire
Duration:	3 weeks
Tel:	01422 323252
Website:	www.gs-festival.co.uk

Leicester Caribbean Carnival

A taste of the Caribbean in the Midlands

Multicultural Leicester hosts one of the largest carnivals in the country, with a parade around the city centre leading to a large show in Victoria Park. The parade features a host of floats and mas (masquerade) en masse, plus steel bands, soca, calypso and reggae. The party in the park includes live music, a funfair, craft stalls, workshops and more. There are usually events around the city in the week leading up to carnival.

When:	First Saturday in August
Where:	Victoria Park/City Centre, Leicester
Duration:	1 day
Website:	www.lccarnival.org.uk

Summer Sundae Weekender

A sweet midsummer musical treat

One of the best small festivals around, Summer Sundae has grown from a Sunday-only concert to a three-day festival with five stages and over a hundred bands. Past acts have included Belle and Sebastian, Air and Kate Nash, and there's always a great line-up of alternative music. Though numbers are limited to 6,000, the grounds of De Montfort Hall are beginning to burst at the seams – a section of neighbouring Victoria Park has been colonised for a campsite. If you arrive in Leicester early, look out for lots of gigs around the city as part of the official festival fringe.

When:	Second weekend of August
Where:	De Montfort Hall, Leicester
Duration:	3 days
Tel:	0116 233 3113
Website:	www.summersundae.com

Bloodstock

This one goes up to 11

£ £ £ £

Heavy metal doesn't get much of a look-in at most festivals. Bloodstock, the UK's largest event dedicated to the metallic dark arts, redresses the balance with a vengeance. Run by fans for fans, it was originally an indoor gig at Derby's Assembly Rooms; the open-air festival has run since 2005. Expect seriously loud rock and surprisingly polite punters. Aspiring rock gods should send in a demo for a chance to play at Bloodstock unsigned – or failing that, head for the beer tent at the end of the night for some heavy karaoke.

> **When:** Mid-August
> **Where:** Catton Hall, Derby
> **Duration:** 3 days
> **Website:** www.bloodstock.uk.com

Northampton Balloon Festival

Balloons galore and all the fun of the fair

£

More than seventy hot air balloons colour the skies over Northampton every morning and evening for this three-day festival. Look out for strange flying objects, which have included shopping trolleys, beer cans, vans and a 120-foot FA Cup in the past. Balloon races take place at 6 a.m. and 6 p.m. daily, but there's plenty of entertainment throughout the day, including funfair rides, circus acts, street performers, kids' shows and impressively cheesy live music (Tony Christie and the great Chesney Hawkes have performed in recent years). There are choreographed firework displays to end the night on the Friday and Saturday.

> **When:**   Third weekend of August
> **Where:**   Northampton Racecourse, Northants.
> **Duration:** 3 days
> **Tel:**   01604 838222
> **Website:** www.northamptonballoonfestival.com

Shambala

Down-to-earth, family-friendly fun – expect the unexpected

£ £ £ £ [👤] [⛺]

Shambala has grown over the past few years from 150 friends in a field with a borrowed sound system to several hundred friends in a field with a few sound systems, workshops, mind-blowing site-specific artworks, cafes, circus acts, crazy golf, hot tubs, saunas, medieval sports, gurning championships and carnival parades. It's creative, wild, silly, friendly, fun, green, ideal for (inner) children and full of surprises. It's almost impossible not to walk around with a ridiculous smile on your face all weekend.

When:	August Bank Holiday weekend
Where:	A field, five miles south of Market Harborough, Northants.
Duration:	4 days
Website:	www.shambalafestival.org

VW Action

Vee-Dub be good to me

£ £ £ [👤] [⛺]

Few makes of car inspire the feverish devotion among their disciples that Volkswagen does. Thousands of members of the VW cult roll up in their pride and joy to worship at VW Action. These vehicles receive more love than most children and are admired like supermodels – the coveted 'Europe's most beautiful VW' trophy is just one of the awards for those on show here. There's an awesome array of racing on the drag strip, including the chance to race your own vehicle in the 'Run What You Brung' session, and local VW clubs are encouraged to put on their own events. If that's not enough, there are bands, DJs, a full funfair, fancy dress, movies and a giant 'auto jumble' sale (as well as actual cars for sale). Camping is available, though presumably you'll have brought your VW Campervan anyway.

When:	Last weekend of August
Where:	Santa Pod Raceway, Wellingborough (M1 J14/14), Northants.
Duration:	3 days
Tel:	01279 725252
Website:	www.vwaction.co.uk

> For those who can't get enough of their Vee-Dubs, you'll find similar shenanigans at the one-day London Volksfest at North Weald Airfield, just off the M11, in July. The three-day Big Bang (www.big-bang.co.uk) on the last weekend of April, also at Santa Pod, features more VW worship, drag racing, music, comedy and fun, also incorporating the Campervan and Bus Show. If Golfs are your thing, meanwhile, Santa Pod Raceway hosts a one-day GTi Spring Festival in April and another one in July. See www.vwaction.co.uk or www.santapod.co.uk for more details.

Nottingham Goose Fair

Sadly no geese these days

Once said to be the largest fair in Europe, the Goose Fair has been a fixture in Nottingham for over seven centuries – only bubonic plagues and world wars have ever stopped it. Thousands of geese used to be driven from East Anglia to be sold at the fair, which was also famous for its cheese. Sideshows and merry-making always had their place alongside commerce, and by the beginning of the nineteenth century merry-go-rounds and other rides had become increasingly popular. The fair today has over 500 attractions from roller coasters and big wheels to craft marquees and market stalls, though the closest you'll come to a goose is the Hook-a-Duck stall.

When:	First week of October (Weds–Sat)
Where:	Forest Recreation Ground, Nottingham
Duration:	4 days
Tel:	0844 477 5678 (Tourist Information)
Website:	www.nottinghamgoosefair.co.uk

World Conker Championships

Conkering the world

The village green of Ashton, Northamptonshire, surrounded by horse chestnut trees, provides a fitting setting for the most prestigious event in the international competitive conker calendar. Having grown from humble beginnings in 1965, when a group of regulars in the local pub organised a conker contest as something to do on a rainy day, this is now truly a world event. The world championship title first went overseas in 1976 (to Mexico), and dozens of competitors now represent countries as far-flung as Jamaica, the Philippines, Ukraine and South Africa. The event's quirky fame attracts large crowds, and there are plenty of stalls and sideshows to keep spectators entertained during any lull in the sporting action. If you want to compete, you'll need to book in advance: there are 256 places available in the men's tournament and 64 in the ladies', as well as a junior championship and a team competition. Stringed conkers are provided on the day to stop anyone soaking theirs in vinegar overnight. Proceeds raised are donated to charities for the blind and visually impaired.

When:	Second Sunday of October
Where:	Ashton, Oundle, Northants.
Duration:	1 day
Tel:	01832 272735
Website:	www.worldconkerchampionships.com

Robin Hood Pageant

Head back in time with Nottingham's favourite son

Nottingham Castle, home of Robin Hood's arch-enemy the Sheriff of Nottingham, is the venue for this medieval extravaganza, held over a weekend in October half-term. Meet Robin Hood and his Merry Men, try your hand at archery, cheer on the jousting knights or watch the falconry displays. There's a recreated medieval village, 'living history' exhibitions and traditional crafts, and you'll probably bump into Friar Tuck in the medieval alehouse.

When:	Fourth weekend of October (Sat–Sun)
Where:	Nottingham Castle, Nottingham
Duration:	2 days
Website:	www.nottinghamcity.gov.uk/robin_hood_pageant

East of England

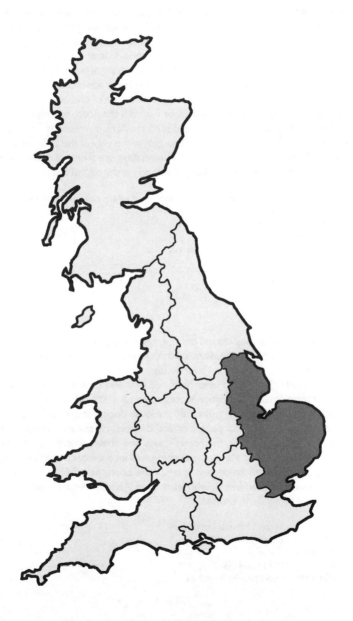

The Haxey Hood

If you thought rugby was hard to follow...

FREE

Twelfth Night (6 January) was traditionally a festive day when people went a little mad, and nowhere do they go madder than in the Lincolnshire village of Haxey. For seven centuries, they've been playing their own peculiar sort of mass rugby game: the Haxey Hood. Play begins when the 'hood' (a leather tube) is thrown into the middle of the scrum or 'sway' – usually numbering around 200 players from the local villages, though anyone can join in, and hundreds more come to watch. The object of the game is to get the hood to the door of one of the four pubs in the parish. Nobody is allowed to throw or run with the hood, so progress is slow as the whole mass of people pushes and pulls in different directions – woe betide anything, from fences to parked cars, that gets in the way of the sway. Reaching a result usually takes two to four hours, and inevitably a great deal of drinking ensues in the chosen pub, which gets to keep the hood for the rest of the year.

When:	6 January (unless this is a Sunday, in which case it will be the preceding Saturday)
Where:	Haxey, Lincs.
Duration:	1 day
Website:	www.wheewall.com/hood

Straw Bear Festival

Bear baiting with no animal cruelty involved

£?

Nobody knows when they started doing it, and nobody knows why either, but at some point in history the people of Whittlesea decided it would be a good idea to cover a man in straw, call him a Straw Bear, put him on a chain and make him dance. The townsfolk would offer beer, tobacco and beef in exchange for this riotous entertainment. The practice continued till 1909, when the local police decided it was a form of begging. In 1980 the locals decided to revive the tradition. The Straw Bear now leads a parade of 250 dancers, musicians and performers, with lots of morris dancing, mummers' plays and street entertainment. There are concerts and barn dances in the evening, and a ceremonial bear-burning the following day (the man inside having taken the costume off first). Whittlesea's bear now has a German friend, who visits from Walldürn near Frankfurt, which holds its own Straw Bear festival.

When:	Second Saturday of January
Where:	Whittlesea, Cambs.
Duration:	3 days
Tel:	01733 204348
Website:	www.strawbear.org.uk

Stamford Mid-Lent Fair

Established before William the Conqueror was born

[£?] [♦]

There are new festivals, long-running festivals and ancient festivals – and then there's Stamford Mid-Lent Fair. One of the largest street fairs in the country, it's been going for over a thousand years, since the days of King Edgar – in fact, so well established that an Act of Parliament would be required to stop it. It's changed a bit, mind, being mostly given over to funfair rides, which look gloriously incongruous as they take over the made-for-costume-drama stone streets. The whole caboodle moves on to Grantham the following week.

When:	Monday–Saturday following Mothering Sunday
Where:	Stamford town centre, Lincs.
Duration:	6 days
Website:	www.stamford.co.uk

Lynn Fiction Festival

A novel way to spend a weekend

[£?]

Small but perfectly formed, the King's Lynn Fiction Festival presents world-famous fiction writers in friendly, intimate surroundings. Previous line-ups read like an A to Z of contemporary novelists: A. L. Kennedy, Adam Thorpe, Ali Smith, Andrea Levy, Andrew O'Hagan… and we're still on A. There's a stimulating series of readings, talks, interviews and discussions of contemporary literary issues. A similarly high-calibre poetry festival takes place in September.

When:	Second weekend of March
Where:	Town Hall, King's Lynn, Norfolk
Duration:	Long weekend
Tel:	01553 691661
Website:	www.lynnlitfests.com

BLOC Weekend

BLOC-rocking beats

Great Yarmouth may not be the first place you associate with cutting-edge electronic music, but for one long weekend Pontin's pulses to sophisticated beats and techno treats. Professor Karl Bartos – one of the original members of krautrock *übermenschen* Kraftwerk – was a notable coup in 2008. There are three indoor venues, and the music goes on till 6 a.m. Lightweights can crash out in comfortable chalet accommodation and watch live footage beamed in on BLOC TV. All the usual holiday camp amenities, from go-karting to arcades, are laid on, but bring a spare duvet – the North Sea coast can be chilly in March.

When:	Third weekend of March (Fri–Sun)
Where:	Pontin's, Great Yarmouth, Norfolk
Duration:	3 days
Tel:	08708 031626
Website:	www.clubbing-uk.com

Stilton Cheese Rolling

Cheesy May Day fun

Curiously, stilton is not and never has been made in Stilton. It was in Leicestershire in 1730 that one Cooper Thornhill came across the distinctive blue-veined cheese, negotiating exclusive marketing rights. Thornhill owned the Bell Inn in Stilton, Cambridgeshire, an important coaching stop on the Great North Road, and it was from here that the cheese's fame spread. Competitive cheese rolling, with a thick slice of English eccentricity, has become an annual tradition in the village. Hundreds of visitors from around the country come to watch the teams trundling their cheeses down the high street. As well as not being from Stilton, the cheese isn't actually a cheese – it's a piece of telegraph pole cut in the shape of a round of stilton. This can make cheese rolling a hazardous sport, and competition is fierce in the men's, women's, children's and disabled heats. Besides the racing, there's a traditional May Queen and Maypole dancing, as well as food stalls, rides, fancy dress and music in the evening.

When:	May Day Bank Holiday Monday
Where:	Stilton, Cambs.
Duration:	1 day
Tel:	01733 241206
Website:	www.stilton.org

East of England

Truckfest

Welcome to truckers' heaven

Not to be confused with Truck Festival (a small music festival on an Oxfordshire farm), Truckfest is 'an articulated extravaganza' that hauls its way to six venues around the country each year. Truckfest Peterborough is by far the biggest – in fact, it's the largest event of its kind anywhere in Europe. For anyone involved in the road haulage industry, it's the event of the year and unquestionably unmissable. But it's far more than just a trade show. Thousands of enthusiasts come to admire new trucks, old trucks, stunt trucks, custom trucks, international trucks, big trucks, bigger trucks, enormous trucks... There are also family camping areas, trade stalls, entertainment and the odd celebrity guest.

When:	First weekend of May
Where:	East of England Showground, Peterborough, Cambs.
Duration:	2 days
Tel:	01775 768661
Website:	www.truckfest.co.uk

Other Trucking Festivals

Truckfest South East
Last weekend of May
Kent County Showground, Detling, Kent

Yorkshire Trucking Spectacular
Second weekend of June
Driffield Showground, East Yorkshire

Truckfest South West
First weekend of July
Bath and West Showground, Shepton Mallet, Somerset

Truckfest Scotland
First weekend of August
Royal Highland Showground, Ingliston, Edinburgh

Truckfest North West
Second weekend of September
Haydock Park Racecourse, Lancs.

MyFest

Social networking goes live

Think most festivals offer ridiculously over-hyped bands for ridiculously over-inflated ticket prices? Then MyFest could be the festival for you. The first and, so far, only festival to feature purely bands with a MySpace profile, it's a chance to discover some great new music (and maybe to meet some of your virtual friends in real life). There's a huge number of bands and singers over three days, and tickets are less than half the price of most weekend festivals. Also to be enjoyed are comedy acts, urban poets, skateboarding demos, free circus skills training, a record fair, fairground rides and yummy food at reasonable prices.

When:	May Day Bank Holiday weekend
Where:	North Weald Airfield, Harlow, Essex
Duration:	3 days
Website:	www.myfest.co.uk

Norfolk and Norwich Festival

An explosion of energy

An energetic and eclectic arts festival, Norfolk and Norwich presents some of the biggest names in classical, jazz and world music. Comedy and dance are also well represented, along with a strong programme of children's theatre, circus and left-field events including breathtaking physical theatre and innovative site-specific works. Open artists' studio, free events and street entertainment add to the festive feel. The festival is centred around Norwich, with venues including the Cathedral, Playhouse and Arts Centre, but events also take place in the surrounding area including Sheringham, Swaffham and Wymondham Abbey.

When:	Early May
Where:	Norwich, various venues
Duration:	2 weeks
Tel:	01603 877750
Website:	www.nnfestival.org.uk

Lincoln Book Festival

Lincoln's literature lovers enjoy a packed programme over this ten-day festival

Leading authors, from popular fiction and literary novelists to non-fiction writers, give readings and talks, and there's also comedy, music, workshops and other events. There's a strong effort to create a bookish buzz throughout the city, especially among children. The annual One Read programme aims to get as many people as possible reading and talking about the same book. *Alice in Wonderland* was a recent selection, with related events including a Mad Hatter's tea party and a screening of Jan Svankmajer's unsettling arthouse film adaptation. Look out for next year's book and people's comments on the lively website.

When:	Mid-May
Where:	Lincoln (various venues)
Duration:	10 days
Tel:	01522 873894
Website:	www.lincolnbookfestival.co.uk

Bury Festival

Outdoor spectaculars in Suffolk

One of East Anglia's leading arts occasions, the Bury St Edmunds Festival features more than seventy events across the city. It kicks off with a big outdoor celebration in the Abbey Gardens, including the traditional Beating Retreat military ceremony and a spectacular concert – recently, an amazing 400 performers filled the stage as the Bury Township Choir was joined by South African group Mbawula. St Edmundsbury Cathedral hosts some high-quality classical concerts, while an eclectic range of musicians perform in the Abbots Ale Marquee. Films, literary events, children's shows, comedy, theatre, dance, street art and street markets, workshops, walks, kite-flying and more add up to a fulfilling festive fortnight.

When:	Mid–late May
Where:	Bury St Edmunds, Suffolk
Duration:	16 days
Tel:	01284 769505
Website:	www.buryfestival.co.uk

Cambridge Beer Festival

Britain's oldest real ale festival

Started in 1974, Cambridge's is the longest-running CAMRA (Campaign for Real Ale) festival in the UK and the third largest – over 70,000 pints are downed each year. There's a special selection of Cambridgeshire and East Anglian ales. Soak up the beer at the famous cheese stall, which has a great spread of traditional cheeses, breads, scotch eggs and the like.

When:	Whitsun/last week of May
Where:	Jesus Green, Cambridge
Duration:	3 days
Website:	www.cambridge-camra.org.uk

Stamford Shakespeare Festival

A summer season of open-air plays in beautiful historic surroundings

Outdoor performances of Shakespeare are a summer tradition, well represented by the Stamford Shakespeare Company. Their summer festival includes two Shakespeare productions and a family show in their purpose-built open-air theatre in the grounds of historic Tolethorpe Hall. The arena provides comfortable seating under an all-weather canopy that will keep you out of reach of any summer showers. If you really want to spoil yourself, splash out on a pre-theatre buffet in the Hall's elegant dining rooms, or order a gourmet picnic and eat al fresco looking out over the Hall's classic English grounds. A perfect way to spend a summer evening.

When:	June–August
Where:	Tolethorpe Hall, Little Casterton, Stamford, Lincs.
Duration:	3 months
Tel:	01780 756133
Website:	www.stamfordshakespeare.co.uk

Aldeburgh Festival

An impressive arts programme at the home of one of Britain's favourite composers

Benjamin Britten founded this festival in 1948 along with singer Peter Pears and librettist Eric Crozier, and it forms the highpoint of a busy year-round programme of musical activity around his former Suffolk home. Classical music tops the bill (several Britten works premiered here), with an emphasis on contemporary work, but the programme also encompasses poetry reading, literature, lectures, drama and visual arts. Venues include Snape Maltings, a large malthouse converted into a concert hall, and Aldeburgh's fifteenth century church, where Britten and his lifelong partner Pears are buried side by side.

When:	June
Where:	Aldeburgh, Suffolk
Duration:	1 month
Tel:	01728 687110 (box office)
Website:	www.aldeburgh.co.uk

The Colchester Medieval Festival and Oyster Fayre

Step back in time and sample some real medieval fare

Colchester held its first History Fayre in 1989 to celebrate the 800th anniversary of the granting of its Royal Charter. The event was so popular that they've repeated it ever since. The Oyster Fayre is a recreation of a medieval fair, set around the fifteenth to sixteenth century. Traders in traditional tents and costumes sell their wares – expect linen and leather, spinning wheels and suits of armour – and artisans show off their crafts. There's dancing, music and mummers' plays, storytelling, archery contests, armed combat and falconry. Traditional food and drinks including mead are available, along with more modern fare, though anachronisms are kept hidden as much as possible.

When:	Second weekend of June
Where:	Lower Castle Park, Colchester, Essex
Duration:	2 days
Tel:	01206 525527
Website:	www.snakeinthegrass.co.uk

East of England Country Show

Fun for farmers, families and friends

One of the country's largest agricultural shows, the East of England Country Show attracts thousands of visitors from across the eastern region. Agricultural events remain at the heart of the show, but you don't need to be a farmer or breeder to appreciate the huge range of livestock on display, with everything from Shetland ponies to Shire horses. There are demonstrations of farm machinery both vintage and modern (Stunt JCB driving, anyone?), country sports and equestrian events. Added to this are a family fun zone, a flower and garden area, all sorts of stands and stalls – come prepared for some serious food shopping – and live music in the evenings. The East of England Showground also hosts a smaller Autumn Show in October and a two-day Christmas Festival, where you can get all your Christmas shopping done over a weekend in mid-November.

When:	Second weekend of June
Where:	East of England Showground, Peterborough
Duration:	3 days
Tel:	01733 234451
Website:	www.eastofengland.org.uk

Thaxted Festival

Holst's legacy lives on in this quaint English town

The light and airy interior of Thaxted's grand parish church – known as 'the Cathedral of Essex' – enjoys exceptional acoustics, and provides a wonderful setting for the annual Thaxted Festival. The first Whitsuntide Festival was organised in 1916 by local resident Gustav Holst, who composed *The Planets* here after falling in love with the town on one of his walking tours. His legacy was revived in 1980, and the festival continues to attract the very best classical performers, as well as other genres, including some celebrated tribute bands. With concerts over four consecutive weekends, it's a wonderful way to spend a summer's evening. Refreshments are provided in the Festival Club, situated opposite the church in Clarence House.

When:	Evening concerts for four weekends, starting late June
Where:	Thaxted Church, Thaxted, Essex
Duration:	1 month
Tel:	01371 831421
Website:	www.thaxted.co.uk

Ipswich Arts Festival

Join in the fun

Ip-art aims to 'comfort, delight, excite and challenge in equal parts'. There's a dynamic, contemporary-focused programme of visual and performing arts, literature, film and music, from national and local artists. The festival extends beyond traditional venues, with exhibitions and performances, often free, taking place in public buildings and spaces around the town. There are a number of participatory events, including in previous years a Writers Café in Starbucks, community painting and an Indian Summer Mela in Christchurch Park.

When:	Last week of June–first week of July
Where:	Ipswich, Suffolk
Duration:	2 weeks
Tel:	01473 433100
Website:	www.ip-art.com

Wisbech Rose Fair

Blooming marvellous

Wisbech is the centre of one of the country's main flower-growing areas, and the annual Rose Fair, a four-decade old event, is one of the most spectacular flower festivals in the country. Displays of exotic blooms and traditional English favourites are set against the backdrop of St Peter and St Paul's Church, which dates back to the early twelfth century. Every year there's a different theme, which can be anything from 'The Magic of Musicals' to 'Heroes of Freedom'. Other churches in the town also have fine displays, and strawberry teas and concerts add to the festive atmosphere.

When:	First week of July
Where:	Wisbech, Cambs.
Duration:	5 days
Tel:	01945 582508
Website:	www.wisbech-rosefair.co.uk

King's Lynn Festival

Nothing but the best at this high-prestige music fest

Back in 1951, Lady Fermoy (Princess Diana's grandmother) put together an impressive festival to celebrate the restoration of the early fifteenth-century Guildhall of St George, one of the oldest theatres in Europe. Her aim for the festival was 'nothing but the best', and she achieved it with a line-up that included Benjamin Britten, John Betjeman, Kathleen Ferrier, Peggy Ashcroft and Peter Ustinov. King's Lynn has made a fine effort of keeping up to this standard ever since, and the Guildhall is one of several venues. Classical music, including performances from some of the world's leading artists and orchestras, remains at the heart of the festival, but there are also literary dinners, lectures and a 'Festival Umbrella' with a range of events featuring local artists, performers and community groups.

When:	July
Where:	King's Lynn, Norfolk
Duration:	2 weeks
Tel:	01553 767557
Website:	www.kingslynnfestival.org.uk

Festival Too

One of Europe's largest free festivals

This festival provides music of a more populist streak than the concurrent King's Lynn Festival, and has grown over the past couple of decades into one of the largest free festivals in Europe. Over two weekends in July, a mixture of local and big-name acts perform evening concerts in Tuesday Market Square: the likes of Deacon Blue, The Stranglers, Human League and Buzzcocks have headlined over the years. On the two Saturdays, there's free family entertainment (clowns, balloon modellers, street musicians) to get shoppers in the festival spirit.

When:	Early July
Where:	King's Lynn, Norfolk
Duration:	2 weekends
Tel:	01553 817358
Website:	www.festivaltoo.co.uk

Strawberry Fair

Friendly free fair on a summer Saturday

FREE

This Cambridge institution is run annually on the first Saturday in July (at the height of the strawberry season), and attracts hordes of local residents and disciples from across the country. Entry and entertainments, including theatre and a range of bands (excellent reggae) are free. There's a particular emphasis on kids' activities, with free rides and a dedicated children's entertainment area. Midsummer Common, on the banks of the river, provides a lovely setting and there's a tremendous atmosphere. Entry may be free, but beware of spending more than you meant to at the many enticingly eccentric trade stalls.

When:	First Saturday in July
Where:	Midsummer Common, Cambridge
Duration:	1 day
Website:	www.strawberry-fair.org.uk

Ely Folk Festival

Folk in the Fens

£ £ £

You can't miss Ely: the twin towers of its majestic cathedral can be seen for miles around, floating above the flat landscape of the Fens. It's a great venue for a folk festival, though most of the events (a few morris dancing displays apart) take place on a site 20 minutes' walk from town, with camping attached. The festival features performances from big names and emerging talent on the British folk scene, but the focus is on participation: bring your instruments to join in sessions and singarounds in the real ale bar, sign up to perform in the club tent or take part in a workshop. There's a friendly atmosphere and juggling, storytelling and other fun for kids. You can bring your dog too.

When:	Second weekend of July (Fri–Sun)
Where:	Ely Outdoor Centre, Ely, Cambs.
Duration:	3 days
Tel:	01353 614164
Website:	www.elyfolk.co.uk

East of England

39

John Clare Festival
'The Peasant Poet' celebrated in his home village

[FREE] [🏃]

John Clare, the nineteenth-century 'Northamptonshire Peasant Poet', was born in the village of Helpston, near Peterborough, and though he died in Northampton Lunatic Asylum, is buried in Helpston churchyard. The village celebrates his legacy with an annual festival around his birthday in July. Local children lay turfs studded with wildflowers on his grave, and there are talks, readings and walks inspired by Clare's nature poems, with live folk music performances in the evenings.

When:	Weekend closest to John Clare's birthday (13 July)
Where:	Helpston, Peterborough
Duration:	Weekend
Website:	www.johnclare.org.uk

Latitude
Music, theatre, poetry and a lake (and resident sheep)

[£££££] [🏃] [⛺]

Billed as a 'performing arts festival', Latitude offers more than just a top-notch musical line-up (previous headliners have included Arcade Fire, Jarvis Cocker and Wilco). While comedy, theatre and the like are mere sideshows at many music festivals, here they're a major attraction in themselves. The comedy arena hosts many of the best stand-ups on the circuit, the theatre tent shows specially commissioned performances from the likes of the Royal Court, the Bush Theatre and Paines Plough and there are even outdoor Shakespeare performances. Bookworms could happily spend the whole weekend in the Literature Tent, which plays host to the coolest book club imaginable. The children's area is a mini-festival in itself, with workshops, wildlife trails, circus skills training and a recording studio thrown into the mix of things going on. An idyllic lakeside setting and some surprise parties in the woods are the icing and Smarties on an already very appetising cake.

When:	Second or third weekend of July
Where:	Henham Park, Southwold, Suffolk
Duration:	4 days
Tel:	020 7792 9400
Website:	www.latitudefestival.co.uk

East of England Championship Dog Show

Who's a good boy then?

Over 9,000 top pooches from around the world are put through their paces at this three-day canine extravaganza. There are 130 breeds on show, with a different category each day: Hounds, Toys and Terriers, Gundogs and Utilities, Working and Pastoral. Wednesday includes the country's largest Festival of Hunting, with over 1,500 hounds from over a hundred packs on show. Dog lovers should note that apart from guide dogs only competing dogs are allowed.

When:	Third week of July (Tues–Thurs)
Where:	East of England Showground, Peterborough
Duration:	3 days
Tel:	01733 234451
Website:	www.eastofengland.org.uk

Secret Garden Party

Raid the dressing-up box for adventures in Wonderland

The best festivals make you feel like you've escaped into a different world; a more colourful, fantastical and friendlier place. You return to reality refreshed, your faith in humanity restored. That's the ethos of the Secret Garden Party. The vibrant music line-up and tranquil country setting are enticing enough, but it's that you can immerse yourself in the experience that makes this one so special. Inspired by the Burning Man Festival in Nevada, the organisers insist that everyone is a performer – so join in the alternative Olympics, rummage in the dressing-up boxes, strip down for nearly naked Twister, pretend to be your favourite superhero, or express yourself in whatever crazy way takes your fancy in this little patch of Wonderland. Check in with the Secret Garden Party team to find out what this year's theme is and how you can take part.

When:	A 'secret location' near Abbots Ripton, Huntingdonshire
Where:	Last weekend of July
Duration:	4 days
Website:	www.secretgardenparty.com

Cambridge Folk Festival

The cream of folk in an intimate atmosphere

£ £ £ £

One of the world's leading folk festivals, Cambridge Folk Festival has been going strong since 1964, when a young Paul Simon put in an appearance. All the leading lights of the genre have played here over the years, though the definition of 'folk' is broad enough to encompass the likes of Joe Strummer and Jimmy Cliff on the two main stages. There are plenty of music-makers among the audience as well – look out for impromptu, intimate performances from big names in the Club Tent. The Hub, in a funky Bedouin tent, is dedicated to 11- to 18-year-olds, with workshops, sessions and performances by young folk stars (send a demo in by May if you want to perform). There's also a crèche and supervised activities for children.

When: Last weekend of July
Where: Cherry Hinton Hall, Cambridge
Duration: 4 days
Website: www.cambridgefolkfestival.co.uk

Peterborough Beer Festival

The UK's second biggest beer festival

£

Held in massive marquees on the banks of the River Nene, the Peterborough CAMRA Beer Festival is second in scale only to the Great British Beer Festival in London. Take your pick from 350 draught beers, a great range of continental bottled beers, a hundred ciders and two dozen perries. There's also live music and a good selection of food, from sausages and a hog roast to an olive bar.

When: Late August
Where: The Embankment, Peterborough
Duration: 5 days
Website: www.beer-fest.org.uk

Lincoln International Chamber Music Festival

Chamber treats across the county

£?

Although a relative newcomer to the classical scene, this festival has quickly gained an impressive reputation. Its line-up boasts high-calibre performers, including the likes of violinist Sarah Chang. The music takes a different theme each year, which are as varied as the 'Romantic Experience' and 'Music from the Czech Republic'. Concerts take place over three consecutive weekends, and most are performed in at least two of the various venues across the county.

When:	End of August–beginning of September
Where:	Lincolnshire (various)
Duration:	3 weekends (Fri–Sun)
Website:	www.licmf.org.uk

English Wine Festival

Fine wines and fun for all the family

 £

The English wine industry isn't just a product of global warming. Wine came here with the Romans, and in the Middle Ages England had many vineyards, though it's only in recent years that quality English wines have been rediscovered by the connoisseur. New Hall Vineyards in Essex has run a summer wine festival since the early 1970s. As well as wine tastings (the first few included in the entry fee) there's a craft fair, Essex oysters and seafood, music and folk arts, plus a varied children's programme including a vineyard treasure hunt.

When:	First weekend of September (10.30 a.m.–5.30 p.m. each day)
Where:	New Hall Vineyards, Purleigh, nr Maldon, Essex
Duration:	2 days
Website:	www.newhallwines.co.uk

East of England

Burghley Horse Trials

'The equestrian social event of the year'

Two thousand bottles of champagne and 40,000 cups of tea and coffee are consumed by the thousands of spectators who come to enjoy four days of world-class three-day eventing in dressage, cross country and show jumping. Competitors must complete each section and rack up the points to have a chance of winning the hefty cash prize, and some impressive world records have been attained at the show over the years. Burghley House is one of the finest Elizabethan stately homes in the country, and over 600 stalls sell everything from country crafts to bespoke kitchens. The famous Food Walk offers gourmet local and luxury products. If you fancy a break from horsey pursuits, you can put the family pooch through its paces at the Pedigree Dog Agility trial.

When:	First weekend of September (Thurs–Sun)
Where:	Burghley House, Stamford, Lincs.
Duration:	4 days
Tel:	01780 752131
Website:	www.burghley-horse.co.uk

Lynn Poetry Festival

Poems and panel discussions in friendly surroundings

£?

King's Lynn's second literary festival of the year, founded by poet and novelist George MacBeth, is given over to poetry. There are recitals from leading contemporary poets and lively discussions, including a plenary session on Sunday afternoon where (almost) all the writers join in. Winners of the King's Lynn Poetry Award include Peter Porter (*A King's Lynn Suite*) and C. K. Stead (*King's Lynn and the Pacific*).

When:	Last complete weekend in September
Where:	Thoresby College, King's Lynn, Norfolk
Duration:	Long weekend
Tel:	01553 691661
Website:	www.lynnlitfests.com

Corby Glen Sheep Fair

Free entertainment with nobody out to fleece you

FREE

Britain's oldest sheep fair has been held in Corby Glen, Lincolnshire, every October since 1238, when Henry III granted a charter. Should you want to buy a sheep, the auction takes place on the first Monday after 3 October, but the scene is set the preceding weekend with a lively traditional village fete. Roads are closed to traffic all weekend as market stalls, brass bands, street entertainers, funfair rides and vintage vehicles take over the village. The focus is firmly on family fun and all the entertainment is free.

When:	First weekend of October
Where:	Corby Glen, Lincs.
Duration:	3 days
Tel:	0870 755 5088
Website:	www.sheepfair.co.uk

Lincoln Christmas Market

Get your shopping done at the biggest Christmas market in Europe

FREE

Here's a great advertisement for town twinning: just before Christmas in 1981, some Lincoln city councillors visited their German twin town of Neustad. They were taken to the town's traditional Christmas market, and decided to bring the idea home with them. The first Lincoln Christmas Market opened in 1982 with 14 stalls; 25 years later, it had over 320 stalls and was attracting 150,000 visitors, making it the largest Christmas market in Europe. Browse handmade gifts, sip potent mulled wine and munch on chestnuts as Lincoln Cathedral and Castle provide a fairytale festive backdrop.

When:	December
Where:	Lincoln Castle Square, Lincoln
Duration:	1 month
Tel:	01522 873503
Website:	www.lincoln.gov.uk/information

North East

Jorvik Viking Festival

Get face to face with Vikings

The Jorvik Viking Centre is well worth a visit at any time, but York's Norse roots are brought to life spectacularly during the Jorvik Viking Festival. Hundreds of Vikings descend on the city to rape and pillage – or at least, re-enact battles, demonstrate training routines, display replica boats and crafts and generally celebrate Anglo-Scandinavian heritage. Scandinavian sagas are told and tenth-century wares traded, and there are talks and tours of archaeological sites. A best Viking beard contest and the inevitable Abba tribute band add to the fun.

When:	Second week of February (Weds–Sun)
Where:	Jorvik, York
Duration:	5 days
Tel:	01904 543400
Website:	www.jorvik-viking-centre.co.uk

AV Festival

Europe's largest festival of electronic arts

The best of new media art comes to the north east for this biennial festival, which is held in various venues around Newcastle and Gateshead, Sunderland and Middlesbrough. It features some of the world's most innovative artists in visual art exhibitions and audio installations, concerts and films, and there are always high-profile commissions and world premieres. As well as performances in traditional arts venues, there are site-specific events in some surprising public places. There are also plenty of hands-on workshops, and eye-opening lectures and symposia.

When:	Early March
Where:	NewcastleGateshead, Sunderland, Middlesbrough
Duration:	10 days
Tel:	0191 232 8289, extension 112
Website:	www.avfestival.co.uk

South Tyneside International Magic Convention

Don't forget to wave the magic wand

Magic comes to South Shields for one of Europe's most popular magicians' conventions. Delegates gather to show off new tricks, pick up tips and try to work out each others' secrets. There are gala shows open to the public on Friday and Saturday evenings, featuring some of the finest illusionists in the business; there's also a midnight show, but this is open to magicians only. Amateur magic enthusiasts can also attend talks, close-up magic demonstrations and special children's shows.

When:	Third weekend of March (Fri–Sun)
Where:	Customs House Theatre, South Shields, Tyne and Wear
Duration:	3 days
Website:	www.southtyneside.info

Festival of Science and Technology

Eye-opening events for National Science Week

This festival aims to demonstrate the 'breadth, and often hidden depths, of science'. There's a mixture of learned but lively discussion on topical scientific issues ('The social and clinical implications of Stem Cell Research: what's possible, what's likely?') and opportunities for interactive discovery aimed at kids, teenagers and scientific illiterates. Anyone who ever wanted to be a train driver shouldn't miss the chance to explore some historic engine cabs and even have a go at driving one at the National Railway Museum.

When:	Mid-March
Where:	York
Duration:	10 days – coinciding with National Science Week
Tel:	01904 554533
Website:	www.sciencecityyork.org.uk

National Student Drama Festival

A refreshing programme of theatre from the pick of Britain's raw talent

£ £ £ £ £

Drama students are often unfairly derided for acting pretentious and pretending to be trees, but they also make some of the most vibrant and exciting theatre around. Ten of the very best student productions from around the country are selected for this festival where countless theatre professionals have made their debuts over the years: Simon Russell Beale, Pete Postlethwaite, Stephen Fry and Meera Syal, to name but a few. There's also a packed programme of workshops by some leading actors and theatre practitioners covering everything from acting, directing and writing to design and lighting. For anyone considering a career in the theatre, or just curious, it's an unmissable event.

When:	End of March
Where:	Stephen Joseph Theatre, Scarborough, North Yorks.
Duration:	6 days
Tel:	020 7354 8070
Website:	www.nsdf.org.uk

Pennine Spring Music Festival

Bring your voice or instrument for some marvellous music-making

£ £ £ £

Amateur musicians come from all over the country to the medieval hilltop village of Heptonstall in the Pennines for this week-long festival of music-making. A choir and orchestra are created by an experienced musical director and put on a series of concerts through the week in the parish church. There are also contributions and recitals from visiting professionals, such as soloists from Opera North. The rehearsal schedule is gruelling, but the atmosphere is friendly and fun, and there's the odd morning off to go and explore the wonderful countryside. Most participants stay all week, but are welcome for shorter stays too; instrumentalists are expected to be around Grade 6 standard.

When:	Spring Bank Holiday week
Where:	Heptonstall, Hebden Bridge, West Yorks.
Duration:	7 days
Website:	www.penninespringmusic.co.uk

Evolution Festival

The largest free music festival in the North East

Crowds of 50,000 line the banks of the Tyne for Evolution on Bank Holiday Monday, one of the biggest and best free music festivals in the UK. There are two outdoor stages in the Quayside area. Spillers Wharf in Newcastle has a mainly indie-rock feel, while the stage by the Gateshead Baltic is more dance-focused, though the line-up on both is fairly eclectic. Music runs from around midday till well into the evening, when there are a number of after-parties. Although it's a free event, they aim to raise money for WaterAid, so give generously. There's also a strong selection of paid-for concerts at various venues throughout the city in the same week.

When:	Spring Bank Holiday Monday (and preceding week)
Where:	NewcastleGateshead Quayside, Tyne and Wear
Duration:	1 week
Website:	www.evolutionfestival.co.uk

Morpeth Northumbrian Gathering

A celebration of Northumbrian nationalism

While some counties are little more than convenient administrative districts, others have their own proud identities, and none more so Northumberland, centre of the ancient kingdom of Northumbria. With its own tartan and bagpipes, it has more in common with lowland Scotland than southern England, while its distinctive dialects are much older than conventional English and have similarities with Scots, Dutch and Scandinavian languages. This gathering, first held in 1968, celebrates and keeps alive its history and folklore in more than 50 events over a long weekend. Northumbrian pipes (more mellifluous than their Scottish cousins) and tunes take centre stage in concerts, singarounds and barn dances, though traditional music from all parts of the UK is also welcome. The Border Cavalcade is a unique pageant commemorating the return of Lord Greystoke from the Battle of Otterburn in 1388, a reminder of the many battles seen in this frontier country. It's followed by a day of street performances, theatre, storytelling, stalls, crafts and other 'Northumbriana'.

When:	Weekend after Easter
Where:	Morpeth, Northumberland
Duration:	3 days
Tel:	01670 513308
Website:	www.northumbriana.org.uk

North East

Swaledale Festival

Chamber concerts in chapels and churches in the Yorkshire Dales

World-class music in intimate venues in one of the most beautiful corners of England – it's not hard to understand the appeal of the Swaledale Festival. Chamber music concerts are held in churches and chapels across Swaledale, Wensleydale and Arkengarthdale, including St Andrew's at Grinton – 'the Cathedral of the Dales'. Jazz, folk and world music also feature, and the festival commissions new works each year. Away from the music, there's theatre, comedy, dance, poetry and visual arts as well as talks, workshops and guided walks.

When:	End of May/early June
Where:	Swaledale, North Yorks.
Duration:	2 weeks
Tel:	01748 880018
Website:	www.swaledale-festival.org.uk

Northern Rocks

Not your usual rock festival

The North Pennines are one of the last wildernesses in England, an Area of Outstanding Natural Beauty and a UNESCO European and Global Geopark. This two-week geology festival gives visitors the chance to explore and understand the secrets of this breathtaking landscape. There are themed walks and talks, geological holidays and a host of other activities to educate and inspire. Climb some rocks, go abseiling, take a tour of an old lead-mine or help rebuild some drystone walls.

When:	End of May/early June
Where:	North Pennines, County Durham/Northumberland/Cumbria
Duration:	2 weeks
Tel:	01388 528801
Website:	www.northpennines.org.uk

Middlesbrough Music Live

Free music festival with an indie-rock vibe

[FREE] [👥]

You'd usually pay good money to hear the flavours of the month, future stars and local favourites that play at Middlesbrough Music Live. Thanks to the generosity of the city council and local promoters Ten Feet Tall, the lucky people of Middlesbrough have seen the likes of The Fratellis, Editors, Razorlight, Kaiser Chiefs, Kasabian and Bloc Party perform in the town centre – for free. As the aforementioned names suggest, the festival is slanted towards indie-rock, but there's a wealth of other talent on show across seven (count them!) stages, including a brilliant open-mic stage. The all-day event begins at 11 a.m. and you're free to come and go as you please, although each stage has a limited capacity, so there's sometimes one-in-one-out queuing to contend with.

When:	First Sunday of June
Where:	Middlesbrough town centre
Duration:	1 day
Tel:	01642 729138
Website:	www.middlesbroughmusiclive.co.uk

Whitley Bay Jazz Festival

Hot jazz line-ups in a luxurious venue

[£ £ £ £]

Whitley Bay calls itself 'the connoisseur's jazz festival', and with Humphrey Lyttleton as a patron, they have a point. The focus is on classic jazz in all its forms, from ragtime to swing. The festival is held in a single hotel, with four separate stages, and the music runs from noon till midnight, Friday to Sunday (the ticket price doesn't include accommodation, but there are special weekend rates available). There are dozens of performers from all over the world. In past years, the festival has opened on the Thursday night with a big-name concert at the Sage, Gateshead.

When:	Second weekend of June (Fri–Sun)
Where:	Menzies Silverlink Park Hotel, Newcastle upon Tyne
Duration:	3 days
Tel:	0191 200 7026 (box office)
Website:	www.whitleybayjazzfest.org

North East

Grassington Festival

Starry nights with the stars

[£?] [👥]

The large village of Grassington in beautiful Wharfedale is buzzing during this fortnight-long midsummer festival. There's a good variety of concerts, including classical recitals, folk and world music, as well as comedy, talks and a strong visual art element. The festival culminates with the Festival in the Field, four nights of big-name concerts held in a marquee with fine views over the dale and a firework display to end. The Yorkshire Dales National Park provides some wonderful accommodation for anyone thinking of making a holiday of it.

When:	Last two weeks of June
Where:	Grassington, Wharfedale, North Yorks.
Duration:	2 weeks
Tel:	01756 752691
Website:	www.grassington-festival.org.uk

Beverley Folk Festival

Friendly festival of first-rate folk

[£ £ £ £] [👥] [⛺]

Small enough to remain laid back and friendly but big enough to attract the big names, Beverley is well established in the premier league of British folk festivals. The music is diverse, and certainly not limited to trad-folk. The Festival Village is centred around the Beverley Leisure Complex, which has a large concert hall and smaller venues; camping and catering facilities are on site. Alongside concerts and dancing, there are workshops in music, song and dance, storytelling and special activities for children and young people, and there is no entry charge to the festival for children. Other events take place in the centre of the historic Minster town of Beverley, a short walk away. There are dance displays and street shows all weekend, and informal sessions in many pubs.

When:	Third weekend of June
Where:	Beverley, East Yorks.
Duration:	3 days
Tel:	01377 217569
Website:	www.beverleyfestival.com

Newcastle Hoppings

Europe's largest travelling funfair

'The Hoppings', which began life in 1882, claims to be the largest travelling funfair in Europe (although Nottingham Goose Fair and Hull Fair say the same thing). A mini-city of white-knuckle rides, carousels and fairground favourites, sideshows, stalls, fortune-telling booths and other attractions sprawls over 30 acres of the Town Moor, just north of the city centre. It attracts thousands of thrill-seekers and families over the course of the week, and the fairground lights at night are quite a sight.

When:	Last week of June
Where:	Town Moor, Newcastle
Duration:	1 week
Website:	www.newcastle-hoppings.co.uk

International Friendship Festival featuring The Kite Festival

Painting the sky with kites

For some people, kite flying is a hobby. For the international specialists who come to the free Sunderland Kite Festival, it's an art form. Thousands of handmade kites, wind sculptures, flying paintings and other creations fill the skies in stunning acrobatic, aesthetic and competitive displays (look out for the rokkaku fights, where fliers attempt to knock each others' kites out of the air). These include the Friendship Kite with its 130-metre long tail, flown every year since the festival's launch in 1986 to symbolise worldwide friendship through kite flying (hence the cloying if not unfitting official name of the festival). But it's not just about kites: there's also street theatre, children's activities, a large arts and craft fair and some great open-air world music.

When:	First weekend of July
Where:	Northern Area Playing Fields, Usworth, Washington, Sunderland
Duration:	2 days
Tel:	0191 553 2000 (Tourist Information)
Website:	www.sunderland-kites.co.uk

York Early Music Festival

Pre-Classical period music sounding fresher than ever

This festival is recognised as the premier event of its kind in the UK. Audiences come from all over to hear the world's finest interpreters of medieval, renaissance and baroque music performing in some wonderful settings, including the Minster and other medieval churches, guildhalls and historic houses. The late-night candlelit concerts are particularly magical. There are also lectures and educational workshops run by the award-winning National Centre for Early Music, situated in St Margaret's Church, York.

When:	Early July
Where:	St Margaret's Church, Walmgate, York
Duration:	10 days
Tel:	01904 658338
Website:	www.ncem.co.uk

> The NCEM also runs the Beverley Early Music Festival over the Spring Bank Holiday at the end of May and, just for variety, hosts the York Late Music Festival at the beginning of June, featuring an eclectic mix of post-1900 classical music, jazz, world and avant-garde.
> www.latemusicfestival.org.uk

Brass: Durham International Festival

Horns aplenty

The mining communities of County Durham have long been a stronghold of brass band music, and you'll hear many community bands at this unique event. There's far more to this festival than just traditional brass band music, though – it's a celebration of brass-based music from all over the world, with styles ranging from classical to funk, jazz to ska. Street bands perform in the town centre, while around 30 brass bands march through the streets for the Miners' Gala – an event that dates back to the nineteenth century and attracts tens of thousands of spectators.

When:	Early July
Where:	Durham and surrounds
Duration:	16 days
Tel:	0191 332 4041
Website:	www.brassfestival.co.uk

Selefest

Bands, boards, blades, BMX...

FREE

Selefest is unusual in being aimed at young people – specifically those aged 8–25 (although the 'young at heart' are welcome, and under 13s should be accompanied by an adult). It's held at a skate park in Hexham called the Sele, and includes acrobatic skateboard, rollerblade and BMX contests, displays and coaching, live bands, graffiti art, a climbing wall and plenty more. A steering group of young people help plan the festival, which is an alcohol-free zone.

When:	First Saturday in July
Where:	Hexham Parks, Hexham, Northumberland
Duration:	1 day
Tel:	01434 652121
Website:	www.tynedale.gov.uk

Cleckheaton Folk Festival

A small festival that packs a big punch

£ £ £

Cleckheaton's small festival attracts some big-name performers, along with folkies and morris teams from up and down the country. A festival parade, dance troupes and street entertainers take over the town centre on Saturday, while Sunday is a 'family fun day', filled with stilt walkers, Punch and Judy shows, balloon modellers and the like. There's a craft fair and a farmers' market all weekend, and workshops, sessions and singarounds in pubs and other venues throughout 'Cleck'. If you want a break from the music, the Pennine hills are right on the doorstep.

When:	First weekend of July (Fri–Sun)
Where:	Cleckheaton, Kirklees, West Yorks.
Duration:	3 days
Tel:	01924 404346
Website:	www.cleckheatonfolkfestival.org

North East

Bradford Mela

Something for all the senses

A mela – from a Sanskrit word meaning 'to meet' – is a gathering of people coming together in celebration. The Bradford Mela is one of the largest in Europe, attracting 140,000 people of all cultural backgrounds over two days. Stage performances come from leading Asian and global musicians, emerging British-Asian artists and community groups, with music ranging from Indian classical to urban beats. There's an endless international market – more than 200 stalls – and delectable global food. Activities include a huge funfair, a sports arena and workshops, and there's plenty for the kids to get stuck into in the innovative children's area. Street theatre, belly dancers, circus acts and buskers add to the sights and sounds.

When:	Second weekend of July
Where:	Peel Park, Bradford
Duration:	2 days
Website:	www.bradfordmela.org.uk

Rothbury Traditional Music Festival

Bring along your instruments and join in the fun

This small, friendly festival draws musicians from throughout the country and overseas to the beautiful Coquet Valley in the heart of Northumberland. There are open competitions on the Saturday for adults and juniors in categories such as fiddle, accordion, ceilidh band and original composition, as well as local disciplines (Northumbrian pipes, dialect poetry). The contests are only part of the fun, though, and informal music sessions go on throughout the weekend. Ceilidhs and concerts take place in the evenings, and there are outdoor dancing displays at the market cross, plus singing and piping workshops.

When:	Second weekend of July (Fri–Sun)
Where:	Rothbury, Northumberland
Duration:	3 days
Tel:	01669 620887
Website:	www.rothbury-traditional-music.co.uk

North East

Brinkburn Festival

Divine music in a 900-year-old priory

The fine twelfth-century Brinkburn Priory, on the banks of the River Coquet, is the venue for this classical music festival, held over two summer weekends. The priory provides an atmospheric setting and marvellous acoustics for a world-class classical line-up (Joanna MacGregor, the Gabrieli Consort and the King's Singers have all performed here). You can enjoy gourmet picnics and local Northumbrian produce in the festival marquee, and singers who are good at sight-reading are invited to join the Brinkburn Festival Choir, who perform at the festival after a series of rehearsals in June.

When:	Early July (two weekends)
Where:	Brinkburn Priory, Longframlington, Northumberland
Duration:	2 weekends
Tel:	0191 265 7777
Website:	www.brinkburnfestival.co.uk

Harrogate Crime Writing Festival

Your only crime would be to miss it!

£ £ £ £ £

Want to know how crime writers research the latest developments in forensics, understand psychopathology, cook up red herrings or work out whodunnit? You can find out at Europe's biggest crime writing festival, now an annual fixture in Harrogate. Readings, talks, interviews and panel discussions feature some of the biggest fiction writers in the business. The town is swarming with agents and publishers as well as authors, so this a good opportunity for wannabe authors to pitch their crime thrillers. The festival is held at the Crown Hotel, where accommodation is always booked up, but ticket holders can find special accommodation deals for a range of budgets.

When:	Third week of July (Thurs–Sun)
Where:	Crown Hotel, Harrogate, North Yorks.
Duration:	4 days
Tel:	01423 562303
Website:	www.harrogate-festival.org.uk/crime

Harrogate International Festival

A magnificent mix of musical maestros

£? | ♠

The Harrogate International Festival is a long-running three-week festival acclaimed by *The Times* as 'the North of England's leading arts festival'. There's an established programme of excellent orchestral and classical music which attracts leading international performers and orchestras as well as up-and-coming maestros in the Young Musicians series. The jazz and world music strand is strong, too, with Amy Winehouse, Van Morrison and Youssou N'Dour among past performers. Other events include theatre, a continental market, family concerts and visual art shows.

When:	End of July–beginning of August
Where:	Harrogate, North Yorks.
Duration:	15 days
Tel:	0845 130 8840
Website:	www.harrogate-festival.org.uk

Billingham International Folklore Festival

Brush up on your dance moves at this truly multicultural event

£? | ♠

Billingham was ahead of its time when it pedestrianised its town centre back in the early 1960s. When Phil Conroy, a teacher from Sunderland, brought his dance troupe to perform in the town square, he remarked that this would make it an ideal venue for the sort of folklore festival in which his group had performed on the continent. Councillors liked the idea, and in 1965 the first Billingham Festival was held, with performers from Austria, Estonia and Hungary. The festival is now the largest of its kind in the UK, and over the years performers from nearly a hundred countries have brought their traditional dances and costumes to Teeside. There are gala concerts and displays in the Forum Theatre and in the town centre as well as workshops for kids and adults alike.

When:	Last week of July
Where:	Billingham, Stockton-on-Tees
Duration:	8 days
Tel:	01642 553220
Website:	www.billinghamfestival.co.uk

North East

Ryedale Festival
Music over the moors

Having begun life as a small series of concerts in Helmsley, this festival has spread its wings to cover the wider region of Ryedale, with its market towns, remote villages, dales and moors. Internationally acclaimed artists perform alongside local performers, and there's an annual theme, often putting the spotlight on the music of a particular nationality. Concerts are held in Ampleforth Abbey and sometimes York Minster as well as other historic venues, while the great houses of Hovingham Hall and Settrington House stage opera. A series of coffee concerts in several beautiful village churches is particularly popular, and there's a programme of family performances.

When:	Mid–late July
Where:	Helmsley and Ryedale, various venues
Duration:	16 days
Tel:	01751 475777
Website:	www.ryedalefestival.co.uk

Stockton International Riverside Festival
The finest street arts in the North East

Stockton-on-Tees may seem like an unlikely host for one of Europe's finest performing arts festivals, but that's what's in store at this colourful and vibrant street art spectacular. Be prepared for terrifying acrobatics, mind-bending physical performances, surreal street theatre and circus acts, bizarre installations and electrifying pyrotechnics from groundbreaking international artists. There's a strong sense of community involvement in the carnival, which features some stunning artworks, and an entirely free fringe event featuring several top bands and comedians.

When:	First week of August
Where:	Stockton-on-Tees, Co. Durham
Duration:	5 days
Tel:	01642 525199 (box office)
Website:	www.sirf.co.uk

Alnwick International Music Festival

A celebration of music and dance overlooked by the majestic Alnwick Castle

[£?] [∦]

Since the first festival in 1976, Alnwick has gone from strength to strength. The town itself is part of the allure – dominated by Alnwick Castle, it's been voted the best place to live in Britain. Northumbrian musicians and dancers hold their own against visiting troupes from across Europe and worldwide, often resplendent in traditional costumes. A visiting Ukrainian group have even written a special Alnwick Festival song. There are daily performances in the market square and evening concerts in the Playhouse Theatre. Many of the groups run workshops for children, who get a chance to show off what they've learnt in a public performance in the market place.

When:	First week of August
Where:	Alnwick, Northumberland
Duration:	8 days
Website:	www.alnwickfestival.com

Stanley Blues Festival

Enjoy an afternoon of mellow blues in this small town with the big ideas

[FREE]

This laid-back festival showcases the best-quality blues music from the North East in a field behind the King's Head pub. What started as a small town get-together back in 1993 has now grown to a 12,000 strong event. Entry is free, though there's a small charge for parking, and it runs from noon to 6.30 p.m., which means you can party all afternoon and still make it home in time for tea. What's not to like?

When:	First Saturday in August
Where:	Kings Head Fields, Stanley, Co. Durham
Duration:	1 day
Tel:	01207 507310
Website:	www.stanleyblues.co.uk

Beached

Free party on the beach – all invited...

FREE 🚶

Scarborough's Beached began in 2001 with a simple thought: *'How cool would it be to see some bands on a beach?'* Things really took off when The Libertines played the following year, setting the tone for more top indie bands alongside local acts. It's now one of the biggest free festivals around, running over four days and including films and an orchestra night. There's no need for a ticket – just turn up on the beach (but place a donation in the collecting buckets – free festivals don't keep happening without a bit of help). Children are welcome and they can have their hair braided and faces painted down in the Beached Village – the organisers do warn that some of the acts later in the day may not be entirely suitable for younger ears, though. There's accommodation for all budgets in Scarborough but it gets busy around festival weekend – try www.discoveryorkshirecoast.com for more information.

When:	Second weekend of August
Where:	Scarborough Beach
Duration:	4 days
Website:	www.beached.net

Whitby Folk Week

Seven days of dancing in the streets and singing in the pubs, and a whole lot more

£ £ £ £ £ 🚶 ⛺

There's something about Britain's loveliest seaside resorts that attracts folk festivals. Whitby's is right up there with Sidmouth and Broadstairs – and has better fish and chips than either. Over 600 events are sandwiched into Folk Week, from concerts and dance displays to sessions, singarounds, ceilidhs and workshops. The emphasis is on traditional music, dance and crafts from the British Isles. You'll find musicians wherever you turn – someone strumming a banjo on a bench, a sing-song on some steps – and with thousands of people around, there's a festive feel wherever you go. There's a basic campsite for season ticket holders only – other accommodation and campsites around the town get booked up well in advance.

When:	Week before August Bank Holiday
Where:	Whitby, North Yorks.
Duration:	7 days
Tel:	01757 608600
Website:	www.whitbyfolk.co.uk

Whitby also hosts the Moor and Coast Festival, a good value folk festival held over the May Day weekend, with concerts, dance displays, workshops, ceilidhs and numerous pub sessions and singarounds.
www.moorandcoast.co.uk

Leeds Festival
The Reading of the North

£££££

Despite being one of the biggest in the country, Reading Festival could never meet the feverish demand for tickets – so in 1999 the organisers decided to open a sister festival 200 miles up the M1. This northern leg features the same heavyweight line-up over the same weekend (although there are a few differences, including a local unsigned bands stage that's unique to Leeds). The atmosphere has mellowed since Leeds Festival moved to historic Branham Park in 2003 (there's camping on site) and it's now firmly established as the leading rock festival in northern England. (For more on the Reading Festival, see South East section)

When: August Bank Holiday weekend
Where: Branham Park, Leeds
Duration: 1 weekend
Website: www.leedsfestival.com

Leeds West Indian Carnival
Europe's first Caribbean carnival

£?

Back in the summer of love of 1967, Arthur France, a Leeds University student from St Kitts, conceived the first specifically West Indian carnival in Europe. Over 40 years later it's still going strong, attracting crowds of 100,000 people. There's entertainment right across the long weekend, with the noisy main procession making its ways round Chapeltown on the afternoon of Bank Holiday Monday. Potternewton Park is the scene for a big party – BBC 1Xtra has provided coverage and a major sound system in recent years.

When: August Bank Holiday Monday
Where: Potternewton Park, Leeds
Duration: 1 day
Tel: 0113 307 0001
Website: www.leedscarnival.co.uk

Hull International Sea Shanty Festival

What shall we do with the drunken sailor?

Sea songs and splendid ships bring Hull's maritime history alive in this major maritime festival. Traditional barges and sailing ships fill the marina, hornpipes are danced and shanties sung. There's a craft marquee featuring nautical creativity like rope-making and ship-bottling, and all sorts of activities for kids, including street entertainers and tattoo painting.

When:	First weekend of September (Sat/Sun)
Where:	Boatshed, Hull Marina
Duration:	2 days
Website:	www.hullcc.gov.uk

Alnwick Food Festival

The flavour of the North

Northumberland has a distinctive culinary tradition, and the lovely medieval town of Alnwick is widely recognised as a 'gastro-hub'. You can taste for yourself at this lively food festival, the largest in the region. The market square overflows with stalls selling local produce and the Town Hall transforms into the Festival Bistro, offering snacks, drinks and Northumbrian delicacies. There's street entertainment, cookery displays and competitions, wine tastings and a beer festival running alongside.

When:	Third weekend of September
Where:	Alnwick, Northumberland
Duration:	2 days
Website:	www.alnwickfoodfestival.co.uk

Hexham Abbey Festival

A week of heavenly music and a magical candlelit concert

Historic Hexham Abbey – there has been a church on the site for more than 13 centuries – is an inspiring setting for this week-long music festival, which itself has been running for over half a century. World-class classical and choral concerts form the core programme, though the festival has branched out to cover jazz, folk and world music, as well as street theatre, film and exhibitions. The choral music is a particular treat as the abbey's acoustics are just right for it. The highlight remains the annual Candlelight Concert, where thousands of candles create a magical atmosphere.

When:	End of September–beginning of October
Where:	Hexham Abbey, Hexham, Northumberland
Duration:	10 days
Tel:	01434 652477
Website:	www.hexhamabbey.org.uk/festival

Hull Fair

One of the oldest and largest fairs in Europe

Hull Fair was granted a royal charter more than 700 years ago, and now vies with Nottingham Goose Fair and the Newcastle Hoppings for the title of the largest fair in Europe. Hull's reputation attracts some of the biggest rides around, and there are nearly a hundred attractions to choose from, as well as all manner of food stalls, sweets and candyfloss.

When:	Early October
Where:	Walton Street, Kingston-upon-Hull
Duration:	9 days
Tel:	0114 222 7231
Website:	www.hullfair.net

Houghton Feast

Line your stomach for winter with a traditional ox roast

Houghton-le-Spring has held a feast at Michaelmas since the 1100s. It was once a hugely popular fair, with an 1827 account describing how 'the town becomes crowded with strangers at an early hour'. Amusements include funfair rides, fireworks displays, a carnival parade, horticultural show and outdoor community hymn singing. The traditional ox roast is particularly popular, with hundreds of roast ox sandwiches selling out in a couple of hours.

When:	Early October
Where:	Houghton-le-Spring, Tyne and Wear
Duration:	10 days
Website:	www.houghtonfeast.co.uk

Ilkley Literature Festival

Get inspired at the biggest literature festival in the North

'Ilkley is the right size for a Festival town... large enough to provide various amenities and small enough to stroll around and run into everybody.' That was J. B. Priestley's view of the first Ilkley Literature Festival in 1971, and it holds true today, though the festival is now the biggest literature festival in the north. Literary heavyweights who have come to read and talk at the Yorkshire spa town over the years include W. H. Auden, Maya Angelou, Alan Bennett and Ted Hughes, along with opinion-formers such as Germaine Greer and Jeremy Paxman. There's also a fringe programme focusing on Yorkshire writers new and established, including exhibitions, theatre and activities for children, such as poetry workshops.

When:	Beginning of October
Where:	Ilkley, West Yorks.
Duration:	17 days
Tel:	01943 816714
Website:	www.ilkleyliteraturefestival.org.uk

Whitby Gothic Weekend

Plenty for Goths to smile about at this Goth-fest

£££

Whitby, the location for parts of Bram Stoker's *Dracula*, has a Dracula museum and attracts a constant trickle of vampire-nuts. So when Jo Hampshire, a lonely only-Goth-in-the-village, decided to organise a get-together of her *NME* pen pals, it seemed the ideal place. More than ten years later, the twice-yearly Whitby Gothic Weekend has grown into the UK's leading Gothic gathering. Headline bands in the past have included Goth giants like All About Eve, Inkubus Sukkubus and the Mission's Wayne Hussey and underground acts with fantastically Goth names like Clan of Xymox, Screaming Banshee Aircrew and Skeletal Family. The Bizarre Bazaar is full of stalls selling clothes, CDs and other gothic accessories. Various club nights and other fringe events go on over the course of the weekend. Contrary to stereotype, the Goths here can be witnessed smiling, having fun and building sandcastles on the beach. The locals are mostly unfazed, but you can contact the organisers for a list of 'Goth-friendly' accommodation.

When:	Last weekend of April/weekend closest to Hallowe'en (Fri–Sat)
Where:	Whitby, North Yorks.
Duration:	2 days
Website:	www.wgw.topmum.co.uk

York Roman Festival

When in York, do as the Romans do...

£?

Before the Vikings, York (or Eboracum) was full of Romans. The Imperial Court was even based there for three years at the end of the third century, and their cultural and military legacy is marked by this annual extravaganza. It's popular with historical re-enactors – the Romans v. Barbarians battles are always a high point – and there are chariot races, gladiators, marches, a living history camp, music, crafts and kids' battle drills. There are plenty of fascinating tours and talks about York's Roman heritage going on, and if you're feeling brave you could try a ghost tour of the city with the Lost Legion.

When:	Last weekend of October
Where:	York
Duration:	3 days
Website:	www.yorkromanfestival.com

NewcastleGateshead Winter Festival

Lighting up the winter nights in the country's arts capital

NewcastleGateshead hass been voted the UK's arts capital, and a number of cultural events at its excellent arts venues light up the darkest days of winter. Look out for light-based artworks and installations illuminating parks and public places as well as a range of festive markets and performances. Glorious 'Glowmobiles' – illuminated 'art cars' and other vehicles that do everything from breathe fire to set off fireworks – have lit up the streets in previous years. The festival culminates in a massive New Year's Eve firework display.

When:	November/December
Where:	NewcastleGateshead, various venues
Duration:	2 months
Tel:	0191 277 8000 (Tourist Information)
Website:	www.newcastlegateshead.com

Huddersfield Contemporary Music Festival

Pushing the boundaries of music

£ £ £ £ £

For the past three decades, Huddersfield has been the unlikely launch pad for an exploration of the furthest out-there reaches of contemporary music. Avant-garde orchestral works, innovative electronica and cutting-edge jazz collide with less conventional left-field leanings. A recent festival highlight was the Vienna Vegetable Orchestra, who perform on instruments made from fresh vegetables (which are whizzed up into soup at the end of the performance). More than 50 performances take place over the ten-day festival, including many world and UK premieres and a number of specially commissioned works, as well as installations, talks and an active outreach programme. Populist? Never. Pretentious? Sometimes. Interesting? Always.

When:	Late November
Where:	Huddersfield, Yorks.
Duration:	10 days
Tel:	01484 430528
Website:	www.hcmf.co.uk

Allendale Baal Bonfire

Blazing barrels to see in the New Year

FREE

The most striking English New Year's tradition happens close to the Scottish border in Allendale, Northumberland. In a ritual that dates back to Viking times, 30 men of the town parade in fancy dress through the streets balancing 15-kilo whisky barrels, filled with burning tar, on their heads. At midnight, they chuck them on to the unlit Baal Bonfire and a massive blaze erupts to the delight of the thousands of revellers squeezed into the town centre. Accommodation in Allendale gets booked up well in advance, but there are places to stay nearby in the beautiful North Pennines countryside.

When: 31 December
Where: Allendale, Northumberland
Duration: 1 day

North West

National Winter Ales Festival

None of your iced lager here…

£?

Winter beers like stouts and porters tend to be darker and heavier – and often stronger – than their summer equivalents. This CAMRA (Campaign for Real Ale) festival features over 200 from Britain, Belgium and beyond, along with a selection of ciders and perries. The festival plays host to the Champion Winter Beer of Britain Awards, and special third-pint measures ('nips' or 'gills') allow you to sample a good selection of the entrants while still retaining the ability to walk. There's live music in the evenings to help the beer go down.

When:	Mid-January
Where:	New Century Hall, Manchester (has also been held in Burton-on-Trent and Glasgow)
Duration:	4 days
Website:	www.winterales.uku.co.uk

Weekend Arts and Books Festival (Wordsworth Trust)

A weekend with Wordsworth

£ £ £ £ £

William Wordsworth called his adopted home of Grasmere 'the loveliest spot that man hath ever found', and he wasn't far wrong. The annual Arts and Books Festival is organised by the Wordsworth Trust, and is held just a hundred yards from his home, Dove Cottage. It's a residential event based at the Waterside Hotel, right on the shores of Grasmere, with talks, lectures, workshops and surgeries on various art- and book-related themes. Non-residents can also attend morning or evening sessions or individual lectures, but need to book in advance.

When:	End of January/end of July to beginning of August
Where:	Grasmere
Duration:	Jan: 6 days ; July/Aug: 9 days
Tel:	01539 435544
Website:	www.wordsworth.org.uk

> Grasmere is also the venue for Wordsworth conferences in summer and winter aimed at academics and enthusiasts alike. Enjoy al fresco lectures from some of the country's leading literary lights, readings and brisk walks on the fells: see www.wordsworthconferences.co.uk for details.

Chester Food and Drink Festival

Fine food and wine to get those taste buds tingling

This two-week gastronomic extravaganza culminates in the Taste Festival on Easter weekend at Chester's racecourse, with over 80 local and international produce stalls, tastings and cooking demonstrations from celebrity chefs. There's a glittering Gala Dinner on the closing night, where each course is created by a celebrity chef especially for the event. Many restaurants have special offers on during the festival, and there's an increasingly popular cheese rolling competition, where you can cheer on the Cheshire team against visitors from Lancashire and Stilton.

When:	Easter period
Where:	Chester
Duration:	12 days
Tel:	01244 663400 ext 339
Website:	www.chesterfoodanddrink.com

Burnley Blues Festival

From the Deep South to the North West

£ £ £ £

Burnley is bound to the blues by a cotton thread. As cotton pickers sang the blues in the American South in the early twentieth century, the cotton was spun thousands of miles away in this booming Lancashire textile town. The first festival was held in 1988, helping to kick-start the British blues revival. It's now acknowledged as an event of international significance: Chicago, which knows a thing or two about this sort of music, chose Burnley as its twin festival back in 2003. True blue concerts are held over Easter weekend at the Burnley Mechanics, the centre of Burnley's arts and entertainment since 1855, and there are fringe concerts around the town. Weekend and day tickets are available, but there's no festival accommodation.

When:	Easter weekend (Fri–Sun)
Where:	Burnley Mechanics, Manchester Road, Burnley, Lancs.
Duration:	3 days
Tel:	01282 664400
Website:	www.burnleymechanics.co.uk/blues

Futuresonic

Find out what the future looks and sounds like

£ £ £ £

For a glimpse of the music and artistic media of the future, Manchester's Futuresonic is the place to head. Billed as a festival of 'art, music and ideas', this annual event brings groundbreaking exhibitions, live events, workshops and talks to over 30 venues across the city. Unique one-off projects and collaborations, emerging technologies, digital and interactive media, and unlikely spaces figure prominently. The festival explores a different theme each year, and internationally important discussions on new social, technological and cultural trends take place. Alongside the main festival is EVNTS, a vibrant fringe – or 'wiki' festival, if you will. Delegate passes, weekend wristbands and individual event tickets are all available.

When:	Beginning of May
Where:	Manchester, various venues
Duration:	5 days
Tel:	0871 222 8223 (Visitor Information Centre)
Website:	www.futuresonic.com

Cockermouth Festival

Georgian joys by the Lakes

£?

The beautiful Georgian market town of Cockermouth, lying on the edge of the Lake District, was the childhood home of William Wordsworth. Its summer festival spans the summer with dozens of diverse events, ranging from an agricultural show and a wool festival to its own mini-rock festival (called – yes! – Cockrock). There are exhibitions, open days, concerts, films, plays, walks, storytelling and inevitable Wordsworth-related events. Early in the festival, at the beginning of May, the popular Georgian Fair celebrates Cockermouth's rise as a prosperous centre for the wool and weaving trade at that time. Wear Georgian costume, compete in sedan chair races, and try to speak in rhyming couplets.

When:	Summer (various dates May–early August)
Where:	Cockermouth, Cumbria
Duration:	Several months
Website:	www.cockermouth.org.uk

Southport Weekender

Possibly the only music festival where you don't need to bring your wellies

£ £ £ £ £

Enjoy the festival experience, but not too keen on camping, mud, bad toilets and the vagaries of the British weather? The Southport Weekender could be just what you're looking for. The setting is Pontin's holiday camp, which means comfy self-catering chalets to sleep in, swimming pools and all the other camp amenities at your disposal, with the beach only five minutes away. The music, in four purpose-built indoor arenas, is chilled and funky: soulful house, rare groove and R&B figure prominently. Any DJ who's anybody has played here over the past 20 years, along with a range of live acts. There's a 24-hour alcohol licence and the beats go on all night. Pontin's has never been so much fun.

When:	Twice yearly: early May and early November, Fri–Sun
Where:	Pontin's, Southport, Lancs.
Duration:	3 days
Tel:	0870 990 1987
Website:	www.southportweekender.co.uk

Queer Up North

World-class arts in Manchester's gay village

£?

Not only is Manchester one of the most creative cities in the country, but it also has one of the most dynamic gay scenes. Mix the two together, and you get this vibrant arts festival, presenting work from leading queer artists – theatre, cabaret, performance art, music, dance, film, exhibitions and other events of the very highest standard, and appealing to people of every persuasion. There's plenty of hedonistic fun to be had in the clubs of Manchester's canal-side gay village, too.

When:	May
Where:	Manchester, various venues
Duration:	17 days
Tel:	0161 234 2942
Website:	www.queerupnorth.com

Keswick Jazz Festival

Get jazzed up in this pretty market town

| £ £ £ £ |

This popular Lake District festival features the world's leading exponents of mainstream and traditional jazz (though you'll hear other genres as well). Around a hundred concerts take place in various venues around the town, including a number of outdoor events which add to the festive atmosphere. Five- and four-day stroller passes allow you to wander at will throughout the festival, and there are also day tickets available. There are plenty of B&Bs, guesthouses and self-catering cottages in Keswick and the surrounding Lakeland countryside, but do book well in advance.

When:	Second week of May
Where:	Keswick, Cumbria
Duration:	5 days
Tel:	01768 774411
Website:	www.keswickjazzfestival.co.uk

Preston City Caribbean Carnival

Carnival royalty and soca sounds

| FREE | 👤 |

West Indian immigrants in Preston started the carnival as a spontaneous celebration back in the 1970s. Since then it's grown into one of the largest events in the region, attracting tens of thousands of visitors and embracing other cultures while remaining true to its roots. Before the event, there's a hotly contested competition to find the talented young people who'll become the carnival king, queen, princes and princesses who lead the procession. At least 15 bands take part in the procession, with soca and calypso still the favoured sounds. There's also staged music during the day, but if you want to keep on dancing into the evening you'll need to keep an ear out for one of the after-parties organised by various carnival groups.

When:	Last Sunday in May
Where:	Preston, Lancs.
Duration:	1 day
Website:	www.prestoncarnival.org

Isle of Man TT

Manx motorcycle mania

£ £ £

For a fortnight every year for over a hundred years, the usual tranquillity of the Isle of Man is shattered as 12,000 motorcycles (and a fair few sidecars) roar onto the island. The TT (Tourist Trophy) is an awesome test of strength and courage, and for many the 37¾-mile Mountain Circuit is simply the greatest road race in the world. The races take place entirely on public highways, thanks to a 1904 law that allows them to be closed for racing, including some hair-raising mountain roads. With around 40,000 visitors coming to the island, TT fortnight has a carnival atmosphere, like a revved-up Tour de France, and the island's stunning scenery lends itself to race-side picnicking. Bear in mind, though, that since the roads are closed for the event, getting around can be tricky. Accommodation can be hard to come by, but many local families put people up or rent out their homes – look for homestays on the website forum.

When:	Last week of May (practice week)/first week of June (race week)
Where:	Isle of Man
Duration:	2 weeks
Website:	www.iomtt.com

Holker Festival

Feast your senses at this garden party extraordinaire

£ £ £

Set in the magnificent grounds of Holker Hall, near Morecambe Bay, this three-day garden festival is a feast for all the senses. Horticultural displays and exhibitions create a riot of colour and fragrances; the best real-food producers from Cumbria and around the country tickle the taste buds; there are hands-on arts and crafts displays, and music to keep your ears happy. A full programme of entertainment and activities means the kids won't be bored.

When:	Last weekend of May, Fri–Sun, 10 a.m.–5.30 p.m. daily
Where:	Holker Hall, Cark-in-Cartmel, nr Grange-over-Sands, Cumbria
Duration:	3 days
Tel:	01539 558328
Website:	www.holker-hall.co.uk

Whit Friday

Whit Friday walks, a brass band extravaganza and a sponsored pub crawl

FREE

You can tell a festival is important when local children are given the day off school and businesses close to let people take part. Whit Friday walks were once a common sight in the north east: 'a joyous scene, and a scene to do good,' according to Charlotte Brontë. Church congregations would turn out in their finery – children were usually given new clothes for the occasion – behind brass bands and banners. Although the tradition has died out in many places, it's still going strong in the villages around Saddleworth and the Western Pennines. As well as the walks, a series of open-air brass band contests have taken place since 1884, and now attract over a hundred bands from around the country. For a more profane perambulation, stay on to the Saturday and join in the Saddleworth Roundtable Beerwalk: 11 miles, ten pubs and over a thousand people raising money for charity.

When:	Whit Friday (eight weeks after Good Friday)
Where:	Saddleworth Villages, Oldham, Greater Manchester
Duration:	1–2 days
Website:	www.whitfriday.brassbands.saddleworth.org.uk
Website:	www.beerwalk.co.uk

Southport International Jazz Festival

Jazz with a Mersey beat

£?

Some of the biggest jazz performers from around the world come to Southport for this weekend festival. There are major concerts at the Southport Theatre and Arts Centre, and a whole host of other events in two dozen venues around the town. Apart from the headline concerts, the vast majority of the 60-plus other gigs are free, and the music ranges from trad to acid jazz. There's no festival camping, but seaside Southport has ample accommodation for all budgets.

When:	Last weekend of May (Thurs–Sun)
Where:	Southport Theatre/Arts Centre, Southport, Merseyside
Duration:	4 days
Website:	www.southportjazz.com

Ulverston International Music Festival

A real musical adventure

Founded in 2003 by pianist Anthony Hewitt, the Ulverston Music Festival brings classical music of the highest calibre to the Lake District. Hewitt was inspired by the world class performances he heard in his childhood at the Grizedale International Piano Festival, which sadly no longer exists. There's a mixture of established names and young performers, and the festival seeks to attract a younger audience, breaking down artificial barriers between genres.

When:	First week of June
Where:	Coronation Hall, Ulverston, Cumbria
Duration:	1 week
Website:	www.ulverstonmusicfestival.co.uk

Feast! Picnic by the Lake

Probably the most amazing picnic you'll ever go to

FREE

Going for a picnic by a lake with friends and family is a lovely way to spend a summer's evening. When thousands of other people are doing the same thing, and have brought along candles, lanterns, tree hangings and decorations, it becomes something special. When you add in performances, installations and strange happenings from innovative outdoor theatre companies and performance artists, strolling minstrels, puppets and torch-lit spectacles, it turns into a magical experience. Bizarre, beautiful, funny and friendly, Feast! is one of the highlights of the programme of festive events organised by Manchester International Arts. Friday and Saturday evenings feature performances by over 40 street art groups, while Sunday's programme includes some great world music, much of it performed by refugees living in Manchester. You don't have to bring a picnic, or a rug – food and tea and coffee are available, and there are plenty of chairs dotted around. Entry is free; the experience is priceless.

When:	First weekend of June
Where:	Platt Fields Park, Wilmslow Road, Manchester M14 6LA
Duration:	3 days
Tel:	0161 224 0020
Website:	www.streetsahead.org.uk

Manchester International Festival
New and original work takes centre stage in the world's first modern city

Manchester calls itself 'the world's first modern city', and here's a festival to prove it. Launched in 2007, this biennial event is the world's first festival dedicated exclusively to new, original work. A series of world premieres are commissioned from leading artists right across the popular cultural spectrum, with music particularly prominent: the inaugural event included Gorillaz' mind-bending, genre-busting musical *Monkey: Journey to the West*. Keep an eye on www.notmanchesterinternationalfestival.co.uk for fringe events.

When:	June/July, alternate years
Where:	Manchester, various venues
Duration:	2 weeks
Tel:	0161 238 7300
Website:	www.manchesterinternationalfestival.com

World Championship Viking Longboat Races
Dragon boats on the Isle of Man

Founded in 1963, this colourful spectacle draws large crowds as up to 70 teams race round Peel harbour in Viking longboats. Rowing the heavy boats takes strength and skill, but most teams are in fancy dress and are there for the fun of it. Most competitors raise money for charity, though the healthy cash prize will buy the winning crew a few drinks afterwards.

When:	Third Saturday in June
Where:	Peel, Isle of Man
Duration:	1 day
Website:	www.gov.im

Middlewich Folk and Boat Festival

Love folk music? Love boats?

Middlewich is on the junction of the Trent and Mersey and Shropshire Union canals. Its watery heritage is celebrated in this popular folk festival, founded by local Irish folk band the Middlewich Paddies. Come and enjoy big-name folk performers and informal sessions in a variety of canalside venues. There are various fringe events around the town, with every waterside pub holding concerts, sessions or morris dance displays, plus workshops and the like. A small armada of historic narrowboats moors up for the weekend; you can admire heritage boats, horse-drawn boat demonstrations and traditional canal crafts. Camping is available for those not lucky enough to be water-borne.

When:	Third weekend of June
Where:	Middlewich, Cheshire
Duration:	3 days
Website:	www.midfest.org.uk

Africa Oyé

Uplifting beats and mouth-watering foods fresh out of Africa

While the media tells a depressing tale of Africa – famine, Aids, war, poverty – Africa Oyé celebrates the continent's wonderful and uplifting music, dance and performance. Star names like Femi Kuti, Baaba Maal and Tinariwen have played in recent years. It's the largest African music event in the UK (although other world musicians also perform) and a major free festival, attracting crowds of 40,000 happy people. To give your dancing feet a break, explore The Village, where there's an incredible array of fair-trade arts, crafts and clothes from around the world and mouth-watering international cuisine. Hair-braiding, face-painting and henna tattoos add to the colourful atmosphere; if you want to relax even further, healing massage is on offer.

When:	Third weekend of June (Sat/Sun)
Where:	Sefton Park, Liverpool
Duration:	2 days
Website:	www.africaoye.com

Knowsley Hall Music Festival

Big names in beautiful surroundings

£££

Lakes, landscaped gardens and 2,500 acres of parkland provide a perfect setting for the largest music festival in the North West. Crowds of 80,000 descend on Knowsley Hall for two days of quality music. The likes of The Who and Keane have topped the bill on the main stage, and you'll find some of the best unsigned acts around on the MySpace stage. The music finishes at 11 p.m. each night, and there's no overnight camping. They're strict about you not bringing your own food and drink onto the site, but you will find plenty of eating and drinking options once you're there. You can park on site, but you're better off travelling on one of the many shuttle buses. These go several times an hour from Liverpool, Warrington and St Helen's, and there's also one daily from Manchester.

When:	Third weekend of June (Sat/Sun)
Where:	Knowsley Hall, Prescot, Merseyside
Duration:	2 days
Tel:	0151 707 1309
Website:	www.knowsleyhallmusicfestival.co.uk

Bawming of the Thorn

A celebration of the ancient English tradition of decorating trees

FREE

'Bawming' or decorating trees was once a widespread practice, but this ceremony is now unique to the Cumbrian village of Appleton Thorn, where the tradition was revived in the 1960s. On the Saturday closest to Midsummer's Day, the hawthorn tree from which the village takes its name is decorated with ribbons and garlands. Children dance around the tree, singing the traditional bawming song.

Games and sports follow. The hawthorn in Appleton was planted by Adam de Dutton, a twelfth-century crusader, and is said to be a cutting from the Holy Thorn at Glastonbury which, legend has it, sprang from the staff of Joseph of Arimathea.

When:	Saturday nearest Midsummer's Day
Where:	Appleton Thorn, Warrington
Duration:	1 day

North West

Chester Mystery Plays

Only performed twice a decade – don't miss them

The famous Chester Mystery Plays are only performed every five years, but are worth the wait. Performed on the Cathedral Green, they make up one of the country's largest community arts events, with hundreds of people involved. Mystery plays, witty vernacular retelling of Biblical tales, date back to medieval times. Scripts survive from only five towns – Chester's fourteenth-century set of 24 plays is the most complete cycle, all the way from the Creation to the Day of Judgement.

When:	June–July, every 5 years
Where:	Cathedral Green, Chester
Duration:	1 month
Website:	www.chestermysteryplays.com

Arley Garden Festival

Plants and Pimms

Historic Arley Hall forms the backdrop to one of the North West's largest horticultural events. There are floral displays in the halls and marquees, guided tours of the gardens and a huge range of plants and garden equipment on sale. Green-fingered experts will also be on hand to answer your gardening questions and Lord Ashbrook conducts tours of the Grove garden which he created. Pimms, champagne, ice cream and jazz add to the atmosphere, while kids can enjoy activities including donkey rides and pot painting.

When:	Last weekend of June
Where:	Arley Hall, Northwich, Cheshire
Duration:	2 days
Tel:	01565 777353
Website:	www.arleyhallandgardens.com

Gawsworth Hall Open Air Theatre Festival

Open-air Shakespeare at the home of the Dark Lady

The historic manor house Gawsworth Hall was home to Mary Fitton, one of the favourites for the true identity of the 'Dark Lady' of Shakespeare's sonnets. Today, you can watch Shakespeare and other plays performed in the stunning surroundings of the covered open-air theatre. The festival season runs from the end of June to mid-August, and there are performances from Wednesday to Sunday. Bring a blanket and a picnic to enjoy in the spectacular surrounding grounds, or indulge in a cream tea at the hall's quaint tea rooms.

When:	Late June–mid-August
Where:	Gawsworth Hall, Macclesfield, Cheshire
Duration:	End of July–Mid-August
Tel:	01260 223456
Website:	www.gawsworthhall.com

Coniston Water Festival

Celebrate village life down by the water

The village of Coniston sits in a peerless location at the heart of the Lake District on Coniston Water. The villagers celebrate their lucky lot in life during this week-long festival dating back to the mid-nineteenth century. Colourful boat dressing, a water parade and various boat races combine with art exhibitions, sporting events and folk nights.

When:	Second week of July
Where:	Coniston, Cumbria
Duration:	5 days
Website:	www.conistonwaterfestival.org.uk

Brampton Live

The largest folk and roots festival in the North

Begun in 1995 with no budget and an audience of 350, Brampton Live has grown into the largest folk and roots festival in the North. Headline artists come from all over the world – previous performers include Richard Thompson, Loudon Wainwright III and Suzanne Vega – and there are also some fine local performers. There are three stages plus plenty of food and drink stalls, workshops, free camping and stuff for kids.

When:	Third weekend of July
Where:	William Howard Centre, Brampton, Carlisle, Cumbria
Duration:	3 days
Tel:	01228 534664
Website:	www.bramptonlive.net

Yn Chruinnaght

The smallest Celtic kingdom welcomes its neighbours

Yn Chruinnaght (that's 'The Gathering' for anyone who doesn't speak Manx Gaelic) is a celebration of Manx culture and of the island's historic links with its Celtic relatives, Scotland, Wales, Ireland, Cornwall and Brittany, all of which are represented at the festival. Music, dance, arts and crafts keep traditional culture alive and bring it into the twenty-first century. Language and dialect play an important role, and there are also walks, lectures and more. The festival takes place in some beautiful venues, indoors and out, on the wild west coast of the island.

When:	Third week of July (Weds–Sun)
Where:	Centenary Centre, Peel, Isle of Man (and other venues)
Duration:	5 days
Website:	www.ynchruinnaght.com

Chester Summer Music Festival

Music galore in the festival city

[£?] [♪]

Chester calls itself a 'festival city', and this week of music-making is one of the highlights of its busy annual festival programme. The line-up caters to all tastes, and includes orchestral, choral and chamber concerts, world music, folk, jazz, pop and local acts. Venues range from the cathedral to the open air, and attractions include free community concerts and performances by talented young musicians from Cheshire.

When:	Third week of July
Where:	Chester, Cheshire
Duration:	1 week
Tel:	01244 304618
Website:	www.chestersummermusicfestival.co.uk

Saddleworth Folk Festival

Concerts and crafts in the Pennines

[£ £ £] [♪] [▲]

Saddleworth's folk festival has a busy programme of concerts and ceilidhs, dance displays, a parade, craft fair, workshops and plenty of informal sessions and singarounds. The venues are churches and halls around the villages, and most offer full disabled access. Camping is available in a picturesque location in the valley, with excellent facilities and catering provided on site.

When:	Third weekend of July
Where:	Saddleworth villages, Oldham, Greater Manchester
Duration:	3 days
Website:	www.safra.org.uk

Fleetwood Transport Festival

Vintage vehicles meet working trams

Fleetwood in Lancashire is unique for having the only original electric tramway in the British Isles still running along its main street after more than a hundred years. It's an appropriate venue for one of the largest free transport festivals in the country. Vintage vehicles of all sorts from omnibuses to traction engines are on display on 'Tram Sunday', along with street organs, sideshows, trade stalls, entertainers and musicians, miniature railways and fairground rides.

When:	Third Sunday in July
Where:	Fleetwood, Lancs.
Duration:	1 day
Tel:	01253 770601
Website:	www.fleetwoodtransportfestival.co.uk

Manchester International Jazz Festival

Jazz around the clock

One of the country's biggest and best jazz fests promises a week of music morning, noon and night. A non-profit organisation, the festival was set up to give a platform to talented musicians in the North West; today, you'll hear jazz styles from all over the world, although the local scene remains well represented. Jazz here is interpreted in its loosest sense: it might not all please the purists, but lovers of vibrant new music should find plenty to surprise and delight. There are good value concerts in the evenings and a variety of free gigs throughout the day, including outdoor events in St Ann's Square.

When:	Last week of June (Sat–Sat)
Where:	Manchester, various venues
Duration:	8 days
Tel:	0161 228 0662
Website:	www.manchesterjazz.com

Brouhaha International Street Festival

Bringing the international spirit of community and carnival to Merseyside

Brouhaha is a rather wonderful Merseyside arts charity that puts together community celebrations across the region. Every year, in collaboration with a diverse mix of local groups and international artists, they organise this vibrant festival. It centres around Liverpool but there are events in Merseyside and the Wirral, including Bootle, Southport and Wigan. Streets, parks, stages, schools, community centres and concert halls are brought to life with street theatre, acrobatics, dance, music and carnival arts. Community involvement is crucial, and artists collaborate with local people. Among the many highlights are The World in Princes Park, where musicians and performing arts companies from around the globe perform across four stages, the flamboyant multicultural Liverpool International Street Carnival, and the Liverpool International Mela celebrating South Asian arts.

When:	July–August
Where:	Liverpool and regionally
Duration:	3 weeks
Tel:	0151 709 3334
Website:	www.brouhaha.uk.com

24:7 Theatre Festival

Non-stop new theatre

Four venues, seven days, 21 plays, 105 performances... There's barely time to pause for breath during this explosion of new theatre. The plays are up to an hour long, so squeezing three into a day is manageable. None of the plays on show have had a mainstream theatre run, but the quality is always high, and the range wide, with drama, storytelling and comedy of all varieties. Anyone interested in entering a script needs to get it in by the end of January, and the festival organisers and companies involved are always on the look-out for actors, technicians and front-of-house volunteers.

When:	Last week of July
Where:	Midland Hotel, Manchester and Pure, The Printworks, Withy Grove
Duration:	1 week
Tel:	0845 408 4101
Website:	www.247theatrefestival.co.uk

Rebellion Festival

Punk's not dead

Old punks never die... They just wind up playing festivals in Blackpool. Rebellion (formerly known as Wasted and held in Morecombe) is the self-professed biggest and best punk festival in the world. There are hundreds of bands playing across four stages, including both big and obscure names from the first wave of punk, summoning up as much attitude as ever, despite the paunches and receding spikes. A treasure-trove of stalls sells obscure vinyl and T-shirts, plus any amount of other punk memorabilia. There's no festival camping, but you can find plenty of cheap accommodation in Blackpool if you book ahead.

When:	Second weekend of August (Thurs–Sun)
Where:	The Winter Gardens, Blackpool, Lancs.
Duration:	4 days
Tel:	02476 601678 (booking)
Website:	www.rebellionfestivals.com

Manx Grand Prix

More Manx motorcycle mania

While the Isle of Man TT attracts the world's leading professional riders, the Grand Prix, held over the last two weeks of August, is the amateur motorcyclists' Mecca. Three and a half thousand riders turn up for their chance to compete on the famous 'Mountain Circuit'. The 'Manx' is hugely popular with motor racing fans and the atmosphere is more laid back than for the TT, with a lot of live music around the island.

When:	Last 2 weeks of August
Where:	Manx, Isle of Man
Duration:	2 weeks
Tel:	01624 644649
Website:	www.iommgp.com

Saddleworth Rushcart

Follow the rushcart through the village and enjoy morris dancing and pubs en route

FREE

Back in the days before carpets or flagstones, rushes were spread on church floors. The bringing of freshly cut rushes on the back of a cart became a popular annual festival in many villages, especially in the North West, and the rushcarts became increasingly elaborate. The tradition had all but died out by the early twentieth century, but was revived in the Pennine parish of Saddleworth in 1975 by a group of local morris dancers. The 15-foot high Rushcart wends its way to St Chad's Church ridden by a 'jockey' and pulled along by around 150 men. It's become one of the biggest events in the morris dancing calendar – expect dancing displays, mummers' plays and music in the pubs.

When:	Second weekend after 12 August (Saddleworth Wakes Week)
Where:	Uppermill, Saddleworth, Oldham, Greater Manchester
Duration:	2 days
Tel:	01457 834871
Website:	www.morrismen.saddleworth.org.uk

Other rushbearing festivals
Rushbearing traditions live on in five Cumbrian churches.
St Oswald's Church, Grasmere: Saturday nearest St Oswald's day (5 August)
St Mary's Church, Ambleside: first Saturday in July
St Columba's Church, Warcop: 29 June (unless Sunday, then 28 June)
St Theobold's Church, Great Musgrave: first Saturday in July
St Mary and St Michael's Church, Urswick: Sunday nearest St Michael's day (29 September)
On the other side of the Pennines, Sowerby Bridge, near Halifax, holds a similar rushbearing festival on the first weekend of September. There's music, morris dancing and real ale trails: see www.rushbearing.co.uk for more.

Manchester Caribbean Carnival

Carnivals come together in a cosmopolitan community

FREE

The first West Indian carnival was held in Manchester in 1970, but recently the presence of two rival carnival organisations has rather marred the spirit of community celebration. They seem to have resolved their differences now, so expect this event to get bigger and better. Over 20 troupes participate in the parade on the Saturday, and there's live calypso, soca and reggae over two days in Alexandra Park.

When:	Third weekend of August (Sat/Sun)
Where:	Alexandra Park, Moss Side, Manchester
Duration:	2 days
Website:	http://ccom.awardspace.com

North West

Blackpool Illuminations

Lighting up the autumn sky with an array of glittering displays

FREE

Most seaside resorts start switching off at the end of August, but Blackpool does the opposite. The Illuminations, among the most spectacular festivals of lights in the world, run for 66 days from the end of August. Founded in 1879 – a year before Edison invented his light bulb – and, give or take a few war years, run every year since, the display now stretches six miles along the Promenade and uses over a million bulbs. Over the years, top celebrities including George Formby, Kermit the Frog and Geri Halliwell have flicked the 'on' switch at the Big Switch On (Friday after August Bank Holiday), an event which is now accompanied by performances from top pop acts. There are also brilliant (literally) art installations and spectacles running alongside the lights. And before you complain about the carbon footprint, the Illuminations run on green energy and are set to be carbon neutral by 2010.

When:	End of August–early November
Where:	Blackpool Promenade
Duration:	5 days
Tel:	01253 478222
Website:	www.visitblackpool.com

Manchester Pride

Round the clock partying down at The Village and a simply fabulous procession

FREE

Manchester Pride began in the early 1990s as a fundraiser for HIV charities, and has now grown into a ten-day LGBT (Lesbian, Gay, Bisexual, Transgender) festival with arts and entertainment, sporting events and debates. The festival culminates in The Big Weekend, where 24-hour-party people can enjoy entertainment from Friday evening to midnight on Bank Holiday Monday. The main stage has a glittery line-up of gay icons, the Sackville Park stage features cabaret, acoustic acts and orchestral music, and the pubs and clubs in The Village are all in party mode. There's also a Lifestyle Expo with LGBT organisations offering everything from legal advice to holistic therapy. The Manchester Pride Parade itself takes place on the Saturday; 250,000 onlookers are greeted with outrageous costumes and around 80 floats. A memorable recent entry was a military tank painted pink, blowing soap bubbles.

When:	10 days leading up to August Bank Holiday Weekend
Where:	Gay Village (around Canal Street), Manchester
Duration:	10 days
Tel:	0161 236 7474
Website:	www.manchesterpride.com

Solfest

Family-friendly fun on the Solway Firth

With the Solway Firth on one side and the Lakeland hills on the other, you already have the basic ingredients of a great camping holiday. Throw in some great live bands and DJs and the unique Drystone Stage, featuring some of the best musicians, comedians, poets and storytellers you've never heard of, and you have a very tasty recipe indeed. There are also workshops including t'ai chi, dream healing and didgeridoo. Check out the website for the mind-blowing variety of children's activities – far too many to list here, and new things added every year. Solfest is run as a social enterprise and has won awards for its family-friendliness. If you're worried about the Cumbrian weather, it's worth knowing the site is on well-drained sandy soil – no mud-baths here.

When:	August Bank Holiday weekend
Where:	Tarnside Farm, Tarns, Silloth, Cumbria
Duration:	3 days
Website:	www.solwayfestival.co.uk

Grasmere Sports and Show

A hands-on sporting event inspired by the Vikings

After a good session of sacking and pillaging, the Vikings used to work off their excess energy through wrestling and other sports. Their sporting events influenced the Grasmere Sports, which have been held in their present form since 1852 and are one of the most popular traditional events in the Lake District. Events include Cumberland and Westmorland wrestling, fell running, hound trials and mountain bike races. There are also stalls, tugs of war, fairground rides, craft displays and all the trappings of a proper country fair. You can enter any event on the day – just report to the Sports Ground Pavilion in good time.

When:	August Bank Holiday Sunday
Where:	Grasmere, Cumbria
Duration:	1 day
Website:	www.grasmeresportsandshow.co.uk

Creamfields

Dance till you drop at this party in the park

£ £

What happens when you transfer legendary Liverpool nightclub Cream to a field? Creamfields. One of the UK's leading dance music festivals, it features the *crème de la crème* of DJs and dance-friendly live acts and attracts a crowd of 50,000 happy hedonists. As a one-day event, it's all about dancing like a mad thing to house, electro, drum and bass, nu rave, techno, trance and probably several other genres that haven't yet been invented at the time of going to press – but if your legs need a break, there are also skateboard and BMX displays on Europe's tallest portable ramp and a gaming truck for PlayStation addicts. If you fancy somewhere a little more exotic than Runcorn, Cream also runs Creamfields festivals across the globe from Portugal to Peru; the biggest and best is in Buenos Aires.

When:	August Bank Holiday Saturday
Where:	Daresbury Estate, Halton, Cheshire
Duration:	1 day
Tel:	0151 707 1309
Website:	www.cream.co.uk

The Great British R&B Festival

Blues for blues' sake

£ £ £ £

That's R&B in the old-school rhythm and blues sense. This festival in Colne, Lancashire, is probably the biggest blues event in the country, with over a thousand artists appearing across the long weekend, including names like The Hamsters, Dr Feelgood and The Animals. The festival runs over four evenings, with concerts starting in the early afternoon and continuing until the early hours of the morning – the last band normally takes to the stage at midnight. There are three main stages – international, British and acoustic – and a number of smaller affiliated venues (pubs, hotels, rugby clubs) around the town. Weekend and day tickets are available, with wristbands allowing you to wander at will, and there's festival camping at nearby Holt House.

When:	August Bank Holiday weekend
Where:	Colne, Lancs.
Duration:	4 days
Tel:	01282 661234
Website:	www.bluesfestival.co.uk

Fylde Folk Festival

Songs and sea air on the Lancashire coast

Folky folk flock to the Fylde coast for this well-established annual festival, which takes place at the end of the summer in the old fishing port of Fleetwood. International stars mix with local artists and there are ceilidhs, morris dancing, juggling, workshops, crafts, informal pub sessions and bracing sea breezes aplenty.

When:	End of August/beginning of September
Where:	Fleetwood, Lancs.
Duration:	3 days
Tel:	01253 872317
Website:	www.fylde-folk-festival.com

Kirkby Lonsdale Victorian Fair

A nostalgic tribute to the splendour of the Victorian age

In an age of clone towns, visiting the ancient market town of Kirkby Lonsdale always feels like stepping back in time. The feeling is heightened during the two-day Victorian Fair, which attracts some 20,000 people – around ten times the town's population. The streets are closed to cars, shopkeepers dress their windows and stalls outside in Victorian garb and many people wear fancy dress. Victorian entertainments include Punch and Judy shows, fire eaters, stilt walkers and brass bands, and there are demonstrations of traditional crafts including coracle making and thatching.

When:	First weekend of September
Where:	Kirkby Lonsdale, Cumbria
Duration:	2 days
Tel:	01524 271437
Website:	www.kirkbylonsdale.co.uk

Hope Street Feast

An all-day street party

Liverpool's Hope Street is closed to cars for this one-day free festival, and instead welcomes a farmers' market (enjoy some free tastings), craft stalls, street art and thousands of people. Liverpool Philharmonic Hall – 'The Phil' – hosts a free open day with concerts and a chance to glimpse behind the scenes, and there are backstage tours at the Everyman Playhouse on the same day. Neighbouring restaurants and other businesses get into the spirit with concerts, exhibitions, performances and special menus.

When:	Second Sunday in September
Where:	Hope Street, Liverpool
Duration:	1 day
Website:	www.hopestreetfestival.com

Egremont Crab Fair

Can you face down the world's greatest gurners?

The Cumbrian market town of Egremont has a quirky claim to fame as the home of the World Gurning Championships. Gurning, for the uninitiated, is the art of pulling the ugliest face possible. The World Championships are the highlight of Egremont's venerable Crab Fair, held annually since 1267 – biting into a sour crab apple is excellent preparation for would-be gurners. Other events during the day include climbing a greasy pole, Cumberland and Westmorland wrestling, horn blowing, hound trails, an apple cart parade and joke-telling and sentimental song-singing contests. While still retaining a friendly community feel, the fair attracts national and international interest – there's a good chance of your gurning face being caught by a TV camera.

When:	Third Saturday in September
Where:	Egremont, Cumbria
Duration:	1 day
Tel:	01946 820564
Website:	www.egremontcrabfair.org.uk

Ulverston Lantern Procession

Lighting up the Lake District

FREE

Lanternhouse International, a pioneering theatre company specialising in large-scale participatory events and festivals, are the driving force behind this legendary Lantern Procession in September. Hundreds of local people take part, making giant lanterns from willow and tissue paper on a particular theme. The procession through the streets makes for a fantastic and uplifting spectacle, and culminates in a classy display of fire drawing and pyrotechnics.

When:	Third Saturday of September
Where:	Ulverston, Cumbria
Duration:	I day
Website:	www.ulverston.net

The market town of Ulverston calls itself a 'Festival Town', and enjoys an almost non-stop calendar of festivities, including (deep breath): the Flag Festival, Beer Festival, Charter Festival, Folklore Festival, Walking Festival, Literary Festival (Word Market), two Buddhist Festivals, Print Fest, Carnival Parade, Furness Festival of Tradition, Summer Music Festival, Festival of Fashion and lively Feast of St George. Ulverston is also the birthplace of Stan Laurel, which is a good excuse for a Comedy Festival. Not bad for a town with a population of around 12,000...

Liverpool Biennial

The UK's only International Festival of Contemporary Art

£?

Every two years, the European Capital of Culture 2008 hosts this huge and highly prestigious festival of contemporary art, which attracts up to half a million visitors from all over the world. The Biennial commissions around 40 ambitious and challenging artworks from some of the world's most exciting artists, which can be seen in galleries including Tate Liverpool and in public spaces around the city. Among the many exhibitions on show is the John Moores prize exhibition. Established half a century ago, it's the UK's leading open painting competition, with a £25,000 prize at stake. Alongside the main events, there's a buzzing independent programme of exhibitions, installations and performances around the city.

When:	September–November
Where:	Liverpool, various venues
Duration:	10 weeks
Tel:	0151 709 7444
Website:	www.biennial.com

Manchester Food and Drink Festival

'Britain's most engaged and creative urban food event' – The Observer

Manchester becomes foodie heaven at the beginning of October with one of the biggest and best food festivals in the country. Tens of thousands of visitors turn out to sample the festive fare. Discover local produce at the market in St Ann's Square, attend a cookery class, watch master mixologists at work in a cocktail competition or take a brewery tour. There are hundreds of events going on, and restaurants, cafes and other venues right across Greater Manchester pull out all the stops with special menus and meal deals.

When: Early October
Where: All over Greater Manchester
Duration: 11 days
Tel: 0161 839 4753
Website: www.foodanddrinkfestival.com

Manchester Literature Festival

Beyond words

The long-standing Manchester Poetry Festival has expanded to take in the written word in all its forms at this boundary-pushing event. The festival has three strands: 'Read' features leading national and international authors giving readings, performances and lectures or chatting, often in unusual and intimate surroundings; 'Independent' focuses on the best new talent from independent publishers in the region and beyond; the more experimental 'Freeplay' explores the blurry boundaries between new writing and technology, new media and performance. If you want to digest more than words, look out for food-themed events run in conjunction with the Manchester Food Festival, which is held around the same time.

When: Early October
Where: Manchester (various venues)
Duration: 11 days
Tel: 0161 236 5725
Website: www.manchesterliteraturefestival.co.uk

Chester Literature Festival

A whirlwind of words takes the city by storm

Words whirl around the historic city throughout October at the annual literary festival. Poet Laureate Andrew Motion is a patron and the festival attracts a stellar line-up of literary luminaries and celebrity guests, as well as many local writers and a good number of children's authors. There are readings, talks and workshops, with poetry particularly well represented. Bookworms can refresh their shelves by bringing along their old novels to the big Book Swap.

When:	October
Where:	Chester
Duration:	1 month
Tel:	01244 304618
Website:	www.chester-literature-festival.org.uk

Liverpool Irish Festival

Celebrating the city's Irish heritage

By the mid-nineteenth century, half a million Irish people had settled in Liverpool, helping to forge the city's unique identity. Liverpool celebrates its Irish heritage with one of the strongest showcases of Irish culture outside the Emerald Isle. Expect high profile concerts from Irish musicians, plays by Irish playwrights, stand-up from Irish comedians and readings from Irish authors. There are also traditional music sessions in pubs, exhibitions, talks and plenty of opportunities to drink Guinness.

When:	Late October
Where:	Liverpool (various venues)
Duration:	17 days
Website:	www.liverpoolirishfestival.com

Manchester Comedy Festival

A laugh a minute

Aching sides and laughs abound in Manchester as more than a hundred of the finest comedians on the circuit descend on the city. Performances are held in two dozen venues across Greater Manchester and range from A-list favourites familiar from TV shows to up-and-coming talents, including a handful of if.comedy (formerly Perrier) Award nominees fresh from the Edinburgh Fringe.

When:	Late October
Where:	Various venues, Manchester
Duration:	12 days
Website:	www.manchestercomedyfestival.co.uk

Homotopia

Liverpool's annual festival of queer culture

Liverpool's gay community comes out in force for this three-week cultural celebration. There's a strong programme of theatre, film, visual and performing arts, as well as talks, literary events and city tours exploring Liverpool's gay heritage. While visiting the festival, look out for the pansies: artist Paul Harfleet plants the flowers on sites where people have received homophobic abuse.

When:	November
Where:	Liverpool (various venues)
Duration:	3 weeks
Tel:	0151 233 6753
Website:	www.homotopia.net

North West

International Guitar Festival of Great Britain

A celebration of the guitar and its music

The guitar in its many incarnations – blues, jazz, rock, country, folk, flamenco, electric, acoustic, pedal steel, classical – is at the heart of so many forms of music. It gets the love it deserves at this unique celebration of things six-stringed. Some of the world's greatest guitarists of every imaginable stripe have come to the Wirral over the past couple of decades, from John Williams to Albert 'Mr Telecaster' Lee. Concerts are held in venues ranging from concert halls and theatres to pubs and ferry terminals, a medieval priory and even a double-decker bus.

> **When:** November
> **Where:** Birkenhead and the Wirral Peninsula, Merseyside
> **Duration:** 3 weeks
> **Website:** www.bestguitarfest.com

DaDaFest

Celebrating artistic ability

Nothing to do with the anarchic dada movement, this is the UK's leading festival of Deaf and Disability Arts. The month-long festival showcases outstanding work from leading international deaf and disabled artists alongside performers from the North West. Theatre, visual arts, poetry, dance and music all figure. All venues have disabled access, and performances are sign-interpreted and audio-described.

> **When:** November
> **Where:** Liverpool and Manchester (various venues)
> **Duration:** 1 month
> **Tel:** 0151 707 1733
> **Website:** www.nwdaf.com

Lancaster litfest

Lancashire's leading literary event

Lancaster's literature festival has been running annually since 1978. These days, litfest focuses its energy on a year-round programme of literary development in Lancashire and Cumbria, but the festival still features a strong line-up of poets and contemporary writers. Reading, talks and workshops aim to engage readers and audiences, develop writers and celebrate literary excellence. You can pick up books by litfest authors in the Book Shop and litfest event tickets will gain you a discount at selected eateries during the festival.

When:	Mid-October to Mid-November
Where:	The Dukes, Lancaster
Duration:	1 month
Tel:	0845 344 0642
Website:	www.litfest.org

Cornerstone Festival

'The best of more than a dozen city-based festivals' – Liverpool Echo

From modest beginnings in 2001, the Cornerstone Festival has grown into a nationally acclaimed arts event. There's a diverse programme of theatre, music, film, dancing, literature and visual arts, with a particular emphasis on new writing. The festival is held in the award-winning Cornerstone Building, part of Liverpool Hope University, and students take part alongside internationally renowned practitioners, ground-breaking young artists and people from the local community in Everton.

When:	November–December
Where:	The Cornerstone, Liverpool Hope University, Liverpool L3
Duration:	17 days
Tel:	0151 291 3578 (box office)
Website:	www.hope.ac.uk/cornerstonefestival

Ulverston Dickensian Christmas Festival

Get in the festive mood and pick up some great gifts

[FREE] [🚶]

Here's the perfect solution for anyone who can't face the idea of high street Christmas shopping: get into the Christmas spirit and browse around a great Christmas market and a treasure trove of old curiosity shops. In the traditional cobbled streets of Ulverston, it doesn't take too much imagination to be transported back to the 1850s. Fancy dress, Victorian entertainment on three stages, steam bus and donkey rides, processions and Christmas lights should kindle Christmas cheer in any Scrooge.

When:	Last weekend of November
Where:	Ulverston, Cumbria
Duration:	2 days
Tel:	01229 580640
Website:	www.dickensianfestival.co.uk

Arley Hall Christmas Floral Extravaganza

Deck the halls with boughs of holly, tra-la-la-la-la-la…

[£?] [🚶]

There's a magical atmosphere at Arley in the run up to Christmas as flowers and foliage fill the Hall. Candlelit and carol evenings add to the festive feel and there are celebrity floral demonstration evenings. Kids can meet Santa in his grotto, while carriage rides across the park and walks through the floodlit gardens as night falls transport you to a winter wonderland.

When:	Beginning of December
Where:	Arley Hall, Northwich, Cheshire
Duration:	10 days
Tel:	01565 777353
Website:	www.arleyhallandgardens.com

North West

Scotland

Up Helly Aa

Lerwick is set ablaze during this Viking fire festival

The Shetland Isles, Britain's most northerly outpost, may be dark for most of the winter, but they're set ablaze in January in what some claim is the world's largest fire festival. Up Helly Aa celebrates the Shetlands' Viking heritage, and grew out of riotous Yuletide fire rituals which often involved rival groups clashing over flaming tar barrels. The biggest Up Helly Aa event takes place in Lerwick, but similar ceremonies are held across the islands during the winter months. Squads of 'guizers' parade through towns and villages in themed costumes, led by a 'Jarl' dressed as a figure from Norse legend (becoming a Jarl is quite an honour: you need to have participated for at least 12 years before even being considered). After nightfall, they form a dramatic torchlit procession, dragging behind them a replica Viking longboat with the Jarl at the helm. At the culmination of the procession, the galley is ceremonially put to the torch (the Jarl is allowed to disembark first). In most places it is sent out to sea in true Viking tradition, but in Lerwick it's left to burn to the ground. The guizers then set off for a serious all-nighter, calling in and performing skits and songs at private parties held in halls and houses throughout the town. The next day is, out of necessity, a holiday.

When:	Last Tuesday in January (for Lerwick – other events vary)
Where:	Lerwick, Shetland
Duration:	1 day
Website:	www.uphellyaa.org

Celtic Connections

The best of Celtic music in the depths of winter

There's no festive lull for Glasgow between Hogmanay and Burns Night as the hugely popular Celtic Connections festival lights up the city. The line-up features leading contemporary and traditional Scottish musicians alongside top performers from all corners of the globe. Gaelic language acts – enjoying something of a renaissance at the moment – are well represented, while Scottish pipe bands and solo pipers are joined by their counterparts from British Columbia, Brittany and the Balkans. There are free open stage concerts every evening at the Concert Hall, ceilidhs, and cracking jam sessions in the Festival Club till the wee hours of the morning.

When:	January–February
Where:	Glasgow, various venues
Duration:	3 weeks
Website:	www.celticconnections.com

Aye Write

Celebrating Scottish writing

The Glasgow literary scene is among the most dynamic in the UK, and this festival reflects its energy and excellence. It's packed with talks, readings, workshops, discussions, lectures, poetry, storytelling, book launches and more besides, with leading writers from Scotland and around the world. Over 200 authors take part in the festival, which attracts an audience of 25,000. There's also a children's festival held the same week, with more than 70 free events.

When:	Early March
Where:	Mitchell Library, Glasgow
Duration:	9 days
Tel:	0844 847 1683
Website:	www.ayewrite.com

Glasgow International Comedy Festival

Who'll have the last laugh?

The laughs come thick and fast in Glasgow in March. Some of the biggest names in comedy perform rare live shows, cult heroes show off their latest material and up-and-comers try to win over notoriously belligerent Glasgow audiences. More than 250 shows are held, including stand-up, sketches, films and plays. You can take in 'A Play, a Pie and a Pint' at lunchtime, sample a selection of festival highlights at the Bumper Value Comedy showcases, stay up for The Late Show, followed each night by a DJ set, and, if your liver can handle it, brave Stand Up Drink Up – the Merchant City Comedy Crawl. There are also stand-up comedy workshops and special shows, films and workshops for kids.

When:	March
Where:	Glasgow, various
Duration:	18 days
Tel:	0141 352 4917
Website:	www.glasgowcomedyfestival.com

Niel Gow Fiddle Festival

The legacy of Scotland's best-loved fiddler lives on

£?

The great seventeenth-century fiddle player Niel Gow was famous throughout Scotland, and his tunes, from strathspeys to slow airs, still figure prominently in the traditional repertoire. He is buried in the churchyard in Dunkeld, on the banks of the River Tay, where his legacy lives on in this festival of fiddle music. Scotland's pre-eminent fiddle players give concerts and recitals, solo and with bands, and many lead workshops. Sunday night culminates in a ceilidh dance.

When:	Third weekend of March
Where:	Taybank Hotel and other venues, Dunkeld, Perthshire
Duration:	3 days
Tel:	01350 728920
Website:	www.niel-gow.co.uk

Edinburgh International Science Festival

Open your mind to the exciting world of science

£?

In 1989, not content with holding the world's leading arts festival, Edinburgh decided the sciences deserved their turn. Its programme of educational but fun events for children (or anyone interested in looking at the world with inquiring wonder), interactive exhibits, talks and discussions struck a chord with the public, and has since been emulated all over the world. The festival's aim is to take science out of the lab and to the all-too-often uninformed public; it achieves it brilliantly. Around 150 events take place during the festival, attracting tens of thousands of visitors. In the past, curious kids have dug up dinosaurs, built robots from Lego and unwrapped Egyptian mummies. Adults find their minds equally blown by 'Big Ideas' talks from leading figures on the hot scientific topics of the day. Past topics have included 'The Last Generation: How Nature Will Take Her Revenge for Climate Change', 'Why Intelligent Design Is Stupid' and 'The Neurobiology of Love and Beauty'.

When:	Easter school holidays – March/April
Where:	National Museum of Scotland and other venues, Edinburgh
Duration:	12 days
Tel:	0131 524 9830 (box office)
Website:	www.sciencefestival.co.uk

Glasgow International

Biennial festival of contemporary visual arts

Now held every two years, Glasgow International curates and commissions exhibitions and large-scale works from leading international artists and emerging talents from Glasgow's own thriving contemporary arts scene. Exhibitions, seminars, talks and specially developed events, installations and interventions are held in galleries and other places across the city, including some unconventional temporary venues and found spaces.

When:	April
Where:	Glasgow, various venues
Duration:	17 days
Website:	www.glasgowinternational.org

Triptych

Three cities, five days, countless great musicians

Held simultaneously in venues across Aberdeen, Edinburgh and Glasgow, Triptych presents an enviable, inspirational line-up of exceptional music. It's wonderfully diverse, with legendary innovators lining up alongside underground sensations. From Cat Power to CSS, Hot Chip to Herbie Hancock, Aphex Twin to Arab Strap, you can't be sure what you'll be getting – but can rest assured it will be worth hearing. Sadly, you won't get to everything, as events are individually ticketed and there's simply far too much going on.

When:	End of April
Where:	Aberdeen, Edinburgh and Glasgow
Duration:	5 days
Website:	www.triptychfestival.com

Highlands and Islands Music and Dance Festival

The best of Highland music, from harps to hornpipes

£? 🚶

Over the past two decades and more, this festival has done much to promote traditional Scottish music and dance. People of all ages compete in 125 classes, including piping, fiddle, clarsach (harp), Scottish country dancing and Highland dancing. The 'Fiddle Masters' is a particular highlight as violin virtuosos show off their jigs, reels, strathspeys, airs and hornpipes. Events are held at a variety of venues, including the Oban Distillery. Concerts are open to the public, but capacity is often limited and tickets should be booked in advance.

When: First weekend of May (Thurs–Sun)
Where: Oban, Argyll
Duration: 4 days
Tel: 01631 710787
Website: www.obanfestival.org

Knockengorroch World Ceilidh

Bringing the music back to the hills

£ £ £ £ 🚶 ⛺

A natural amphitheatre in Scotland's Southern Uplands provides a spectacular setting for this hidden gem of a festival. The music is a vibrant fusion of roots artists and beats from Scotland and around the world, kicking off on Thursday night and running through to the early hours of Monday morning. You can also look forward to street theatre, wind- and solar-powered cinema, showers and sauna, a Celtic fire spectacular and Eastern healing. It's a family-friendly event, and there's a Kids' Marquee with a packed programme of activities. Beautiful riverside camping is included. Parking is limited at the remote site – take the special Knock Bus from Glasgow or Edinburgh. The same not-for-profit organisation runs the Hairth Festival in September, which shares a similar feel, and you can buy good value combined tickets.

When: Spring Bank Holiday weekend (Thurs–Sun)
Where: Knockengorroch farm, Carsphairn, Kirkubrightshire
Duration: 4 days
Tel: 01644 460662
Website: www.knockengorroch.org.uk

Isle of Skye Music Festival

The music festival with the best view in Britain

£ £ £ £

Perhaps the most imposing vista in the British Isles, the Cuillin mountain range on the Isle of Skye forms a spectacular backdrop to this 'Fan Friendly Festival' (UK Festival Awards 2006). With the sea close by on the other side, the setting alone is enough reason to pack your tent, but the music's good too – a mix of contemporary indie and dance (look out for local boy Mylo) and more traditional Celtic styles at the brilliantly named Shipping Forecast Stage. Don't plan on getting an early night – the music goes on till 4 a.m., so you get your money's worth out of two days.

When:	Spring Bank Holiday weekend (Fri/Sat)
Where:	Ashaig Airstrip, Broadford, Isle of Skye
Duration:	2 days
Tel:	0141 204 7970
Website:	www.skyemusicfestival.co.uk

Dumfries and Galloway Arts Festival

The international arts scene comes to beautiful rural Scotland

£?

The scattered rural communities of Dumfries and Galloway don't get many opportunities to enjoy music, theatre, dance, literature and other cultural events of the highest international quality – which makes this festival all the more special. Performances include classical and opera, world music, jazz and folk, stand-up comedy and plays, and there are exhibitions, literary evenings and children's events. Venues range from the Theatre Royal in Dumfries to tiny rural halls.

When:	End of May
Where:	Various locations in Dumfries and Galloway
Duration:	9 days
Tel:	01387 260447
Website:	www.dgartsfestival.org.uk

Perth Festival

Big-name classical singers at this festival with music at its heart

Over the past four decades, the Perth Festival has firmly established itself as one of Scotland's leading arts festivals. Music is at the heart of the festival, with the newly built Perth Concert Hall providing the main venue. The festival has a history of attracting the very best classical singers, including Bryn Terfel, Kiri Te Kanawa, Emma Kirkby and Lesley Garrett. Elsewhere, the music has covered everything from the Royal Philharmonic Orchestra to Courtney Pine, The Magic Numbers and Jonathan Ross' house band, 4 Poofs and a Piano. Touring opera and ballet companies also appear.

When:	End of May
Where:	Perth, Perthshire
Duration:	10 days
Tel:	0845 612 6330
Website:	www.perthfestival.co.uk

Common Ridings

Back in the Middle Ages, when lawlessness was rife in the badlands of the Borders, townsfolk would regularly ride round the boundaries of their common land, checking that all was well. Over the centuries, these 'Common Ridings' developed into a magnificent series of festivals, during which a colourful cavalcade of hundreds of horses sets out at dawn to ride the boundaries of the burgh. The riders follow behind their flag, borne by a young unmarried man of the town. Many riders carry banners and old songs are sung. Feasting, dancing, music, sporting contests and other celebrations ensue, often lasting several days.

The largest and best-known event is held in Hawick, in the first week of June. Festivities continue from Thursday to Saturday, but Common-Riding Day proper is Friday – and you need plenty of energy to participate to the full. The town is woken up at 6 a.m. by the town Drum and Fife Band, and presently a large crowd gathers to try and grab a pinch of snuff in the mêlée of the Snuffin' ceremony, then heads off for rum and milk (yes, it's going to be that sort of day…). After breakfast, the riders set off on the traditional tour of the burgh, with various chases, races, rituals, refreshments and songs along the way. The evening culminates in the Common-Riding Ball. As dawn breaks, the flag-bearer leads the partygoers to the top of Moat Hill to watch the sunrise. There's one last reel, then it's time for a couple of hours' kip before the Drum and Fife Band rouses everyone again at 9.30 a.m.

Selkirk's Common Riding (second Sunday in June) attracts as many as 500 riders – it's been called the largest equestrian gathering in Europe. A notable part of the festival is the 'casting of the colours', commemorating the Battle of Flodden in 1513. Only one man of Selkirk returned from the battle alive, bearing a blood-stained English flag, an event which is re-enacted in a solemn and moving ceremony.

Other notable Common Ridings include Jedburgh, Lauder and Langholm, but there are similar festivals throughout the Borders from June to August.

Imaginate Festival

Theatrical treats for stage-struck youngsters

There's far more to children's theatre than annual trips to the panto. This is the UK's largest and most successful performing arts festival aimed specifically at children and young people, and features performers from several different countries. There are events for different age groups, from babies and toddlers to 11 upwards, and the standard of performance and creativity on show is enough to keep imaginative accompanying adults entertained too.

When:	End of May/beginning of June
Where:	Edinburgh
Duration:	1 week
Tel:	0131 225 8050
Website:	www.imaginate.org.uk

Dundee Jazz Festival

The Apex of cutting-edge jazz

One of the longest-running jazz festivals in the UK, the Dundee Jazz Festival presents a host of leading international jazz names and top Scottish talent. The focus is on contemporary jazz in the broadest sense – previous headliners have included crossover star Courtney Pine and mad Edinburgh-based Klezmer merchants Moishe's Bagel. There's plenty to please the traditionalists, though, and an increased focus on young talent. The festival has recently moved to a new home at the chic Apex hotel in the regenerated City Quay area, where Jazz Dundee puts on concerts throughout the year.

When:	First weekend of June (Fri–Sun)
Where:	Apex City Quay Hotel and Spa, Dundee
Duration:	3 days
Tel:	0131 553 4000
Website:	www.jazzdundee.co.uk

West End Festival

Glasgow's answer to the Edinburgh Fringe and the Notting Hill Carnival

This event has been growing rapidly since its inception as a local event in Byres Road in 1996. The centrepiece of the festival is the Mardi Gras carnival parade with its extrovert floats and live dance bands, which attracts more than 100,000 people. There are half a dozen stages with live music in the streets around Byres Road and in Kelvingrove Park, as well as street cafes, magicians, craft stalls and face painting. More than 350 events have sprung up over the festival fortnight, including comedy, street theatre, drama, children's events, street markets and live music of all varieties (a free outdoor concert by Glaswegian cult darlings Belle and Sebastian in the Botanical Gardens in 2004 was recently voted one of the top 20 gigs of all time by *The Scotsman*).

When:	June
Where:	Glasgow West End
Duration:	17 days
Tel:	0141 341 0844
Website:	www.westendfestival.co.uk

Rock Ness

The only festival with its own monster

Festival sites don't come much more spectacular than the banks of Loch Ness, and the fact that darkness barely falls up here in early June means the party doesn't pause for breath. Despite the name, this is more of a dance do than a rock one, but then bad puns are a feature of the weekend, as few acts can resist referencing Nessie as they unleash another, ahem, monster anthem. On top of that, there's the wonderful Nesstival Arena, where the creative geniuses behind the Isle of Wight's Bestival (see South East section) lay on chilled-out beats, a Bollywood bar and other delights.

When:	First full weekend of June (Fri–Sun)
Where:	Clune Farm, Dores, Inverness
Duration:	3 days
Website:	www.rockness.co.uk

St Magnus Festival

A midsummer celebration of the arts

Orkney resident Sir Peter Maxwell Davies, currently Master of the Queen's Music, founded Britain's northernmost arts festival in 1977. Since then, it's grown into a highly regarded and adventurous festival that attracts top-drawer musicians including the likes of Vladimir Ashkenazy, André Previn and Evelyn Glennie, as well as some of the world's finest ensembles. It has a history of commissioning new work from leading contemporary composers – James Macmillan, Richard Rodney Bennett, Thea Musgrave – and premiering major new pieces by Sir Peter Maxwell Davies himself. Drama, dance, literature and visual arts also have a strong presence, and community participation (particularly involving young people) plays an important role. Orkney is a wonderful place to visit in the never-ending days of midsummer, and many festival-goers make the trip year after year.

When:	Mid-June
Where:	Orkney
Duration:	6 days
Tel:	01856 871445
Website:	www.stmagnusfestival.com

Scottish Traditional Beer Festival

Sample the Champion Beer of Scotland

Scotland has a vibrant brewing industry, and over a hundred Caledonian concoctions are gathered under one roof at this festival, held in the elegant music hall in Edinburgh's Assembly Rooms. Look out for past and future winners of the Champion Beer of Scotland Awards, which take place during the festival.

When:	Mid-June
Where:	Assembly Rooms, George Street, Edinburgh
Duration:	3 days
Website:	www.edinburghcamra.org.uk

Outsider Festival

Escape into the majestic Cairngorms

First held in 2007 but already beloved by many, the Outsider Festival is a boutique beauty. It's held on the historic Rothiemurchus Estate, amidst the majestic Cairngorms, surrounded by lochs and forests. There's a strong line-up of live music and DJs, with a Scottish bias (never a bad thing – Idlewild, KT Tunstall and Eddie Reader), comedy and plenty of fair-trade and eco-friendly stuff to eat, drink and buy. What sets the Outsider Festival apart, though, is the range of outdoor activities on offer. With all that breathtaking National Park scenery around, it would be a shame not to explore: you can go on mountain bike rides, runs (including the organised 12-km and entirely appropriately named Most Beautiful Run), guided nature walks, gorge walks, or go rock climbing or rafting. For a truly memorable experience, book onto the guided 'midsummer bivvy and sunrise' walk: set off up the mountain in the evening, bivouac down on the mountainside, watch the sunrise and get back to the site the next morning.

When: Third weekend of June (Fri–Sun)
Where: Rothiemurchus Estate, Aviemore, Badenoch and Strathspey, Highlands
Duration: 3 days
Website: www.outsiderfestival.co.uk

Edinburgh International Film Festival

Roll out the red carpet for the world's longest-running film festival

The Edinburgh International Film Festival, founded in 1947, is the longest continually running film festival in the world. It used to run as part of the Edinburgh Festival in August, but has now moved to a separate slot in June to give it the breathing space it deserves. It may not match the glamour of Cannes or Venice, or the hype of Sundance – although becoming 'the Sundance of Europe' is the festival's stated aim – but it's undoubtedly on the festival A-list. There's no shortage of glitzy red carpets and gala shows, but the festival also has a strong reputation for showcasing challenging films and emerging talent.

When: End of June
Where: Edinburgh – various cinemas
Duration: 10 days
Tel: 0131 228 4051
Website: www.edfilmfest.org.uk

Glasgow International Jazz Festival

Eclectic sounds beside the Clyde

With a strong mix of Scottish and international performers, major stars and up-and-coming players, Glasgow has established itself as one of the country's leading jazz festivals. The line-up is eclectic, with DJs and crossover acts along with more traditional styles. As well as the big-name concerts, there's a packed programme of fringe events – mostly free – in bars, cafes and hotels around the city. Don't miss the free Late Night Jazz Club at the City Cafe (open into the wee hours), where top musicians get together for one of the best jam sessions you're ever likely to hear. Another popular event is the Riverboat Shuffle, a jazz cruise along the Clyde on Britain's oldest ocean-going paddle steamer, the *PS Waverley*.

When:	End of June
Where:	Glasgow – various venues
Duration:	9 days
Tel:	0141 552 3552
Website:	www.jazzfest.co.uk

Mendelssohn on Mull

The classical stars of tomorrow follow in Felix's footsteps

The 20-year-old Felix Mendelssohn visited the Isle of Mull in 1829, and composed his 'Hebrides Overture' after a choppy boat ride to see Fingal's Cave, a sea cave on the uninhabited island of Staffa. The island landscapes continue to provide inspiration to young musicians today in this unique summer festival. Under the direction of violinist Levon Chilingirian, some of the country's most promising music students and recent graduates are put through their paces by a team of experienced mentors. They play free concerts in some glorious venues, including Iona Abbey, Torosay Castle and Oban Cathedral. Members of the public are also welcome to sit in on rehearsals in Aros Hall, Tobermory.

When:	End of June/beginning of July
Where:	Mull, Inner Hebrides
Duration:	1 week
Tel:	01688 301108
Website:	www.mullfest.org.uk

Newcastleton Traditional Music Festival

Friendly folky competition in the Borders

The picturesque Borders village of Newcastleton hosts what claims to be 'probably the longest continuously running music festival in Scotland'. Traditional musicians perform in a series of contests – the 'Grand Winners Concert' on Saturday night is always a highlight. There are plenty of non-combatants joining ad-hoc sessions, with singarounds in every conceivable space around the village, and organised ceilidhs and dances in the evenings. Ample camping is available, but B&Bs and other accommodation in the area gets booked up well in advance.

When:	First weekend of July (Fri–Sun)
Where:	Newcastleton, Borders
Duration:	3 days
Tel:	01387 376254
Website:	www.newcastleton.com

T in the Park

Not your average tea party...

Since its launch in 1994, Scotland's T in the Park has grown into one of the UK's top festivals, with a line-up that more than holds its own against Glastonbury and Reading. Bands are the main attraction, but there's also a dance area, a ceilidh tent, a post-curfew Silent Disco (don some headphones and get into a celebrity DJ set – or just watch the dance floor writhing to music only they can hear), a funfair and plenty of stalls, including a 'healthy T' area with cookery demonstrations from celebrity chefs. The capacity continues to expand, but still can't keep pace with the demand for tickets, which sell out within an hour or two. Despite its growth and the uninspiring airfield setting, T (from Tennent's, the main sponsor since its inception) retains a great atmosphere – the punters' sense of humour seems to endure despite the often awful weather.

When:	Second weekend of July
Where:	Balado Airfield, Kinross
Duration:	3 days
Website:	www.tinthepark.com

Stonehaven Folk Festival

A light-hearted folk fest with a quirky side

Whether it's swooning to the voices of Eddi Reader or Kate Rusby, or joining in an impromptu jam session down by the harbour, Stonehaven is full of delights for music lovers over this long weekend in July. There are concerts and ceilidhs in the town hall and around the town, featuring folk acts contemporary and traditional, local and international. Other events include workshops, late-night blues, a Kiddie's Concert and an acoustic stage for teenagers. The festival has a winning light-heartedness: don't miss the unique Aqua Ceilidh in the Art Deco open air swimming pool on Sunday morning, or the World Paper 'n' Comb Championships. There's a basic festival campsite at Mineralwell Park, about ten minutes' walk from the town centre – it's run by the Sea Cadets, who do a brilliant breakfast.

When:	Second weekend of July (Thurs–Sun)
Where:	Stonehaven, Aberdeenshire
Duration:	4 days
Tel:	01569 766211
Website:	www.stonehavenfolkfestival.co.uk

Indian Summer

Outdoors but intimate

£ £ £ £

Victoria Park, Glasgow's prettiest park hidden away in the West End, is a lovely, leafy setting for this weekender of quality live music. The main stage features off-beat alternative acts (Flaming Lips, Clap Your Hands Say Yeah), there are underground discoveries to be made at the BBC 6 Music Hub Stage, acoustic acts at the Beanscene coffee house stage and a festival-within-a-festival at the Optimo (Espacio) club area. Away from the music are cafes, record stalls and a friendly indie vibe.

When:	Second weekend of July
Where:	Victoria Park, Glasgow
Duration:	2 days
Website:	www.indiansummerglasgow.com

Fèis an Eilein – Skye Festival

The biggest small festival in Scotland

Serene Sleat in the south of Skye is the scene for 'the biggest small festival in Scotland'. Fèis an Eilein is based around the Gaelic college Sabhal Mòr Ostaig, and Gaelic artists feature prominently (if you've ever wanted to hear Bob Dylan songs sung in Gaelic, this is the place), but there's also theatre, traditional music, world music, dance, films, visual arts and comedy. There's also a series of literary events at the Aos Dana book festival. Other attractions include workshops, exercise classes, rambles and a family cafe – herring and tattie supper, anyone? The college includes an outdoor amphitheatre with breathtaking views across to the mainland, and performances are also held in nearby Armadale Castle.

When:	Last fortnight of July
Where:	Sabhal Mòr Ostaig, Armadale, Skye
Duration:	14 days
Tel:	01471 844207
Website:	www.feisaneilein.com

Hebridean Celtic Festival

Lots to do on Lewis

You don't really need an excuse to visit the Isle of Lewis in the Outer Hebrides, but here's a great one anyway. The Hebridean Celtic Festival presents the cream of Celtic music, traditional and modern. Free concerts take place in the stunning surroundings of Lewis Castle, Stornoway, while other concerts, ceilidhs and community events are organised across Lewis and the adjoining Isle of Harris. Look out for sailing trips, street theatre, Gaelic storytelling and island tours. It all adds up to a wonderful and welcoming festive atmosphere. Book your accommodation well in advance.

When:	Third weekend of July (Thurs–Sun)
Where:	Isle of Lewis
Duration:	4 days
Tel:	01851 621234
Website:	www.hebceltfest.com

The Wickerman Festival

Fiery frolics

Every festival should culminate in the burning of a 30-foot high wicker effigy on Saturday night. Even without that spectacular climax, though, there's plenty of reason to visit Wickerman, which boasts impressively eclectic music, esoteric attractions and friendly freakishness. There are few small festivals that would find room for evergreen punks Sham 69, folk heart-throb Damien Dempsey, the Hacienda Tour featuring DJ sets from Bez and Peter Hook, and the Kazoo Funk Orchestra on the same bill. Edward Woodward fans can rest assured that, despite the remote location, there's nothing sinister here – it's a welcoming, family-friendly atmosphere. 'Wickerman debutantes' are told to 'expect sporadic mirth and frivolity alongside sustained barrages of contentment'.

When:	Third weekend of July
Where:	East Kirkcarswell, near Dundrennan, Galloway
Duration:	2 days
Tel:	01382 836816
Website:	www.thewickermanfestival.co.uk

Glasgow River Festival

Family fun on water and shore

The world's first commercial steamship was launched on the River Clyde in 1812, and for 150 years the river provided the city's industrial artery. The days of great shipyards and huge cargo ships on the Clyde may be gone, but with waterfront regeneration and a major clean up, the river is looking healthier than it has for many years. Over 85,000 visitors come along to enjoy the weekend's free entertainment, which includes events on the water – tall ship tours, Zapcat racing, powerboat rides, dinghy sailing – and on land, with marching displays by the HM Royal Marines of Scotland band, multicultural music and dance events, ceilidhs, street theatre and comedy, and a festival market. There's also stuff on for the kids at the Glasgow Science Museum, with everything from live science shows to circus workshops to keep them amused.

When:	Third weekend of July (Sat–Sun)
Where:	River Clyde (around Scottish Exhibition Conference Centre and the Science Museum)
Duration:	2 days
Tel:	0141 339 4998
Website:	www.glasgowriverfestival.co.uk

Aberdeen International Youth Festival

The world's largest participatory festival for young people

Over a thousand talented young people from some of the world's finest youth orchestras and ensembles, dance companies and academies flock to Aberdeen to take part in orchestral and choral concerts, classical and modern dance, world music, jazz and theatre. The Opera Garden project is a particular highlight, as young singers from around the world come together to put on a full-scale opera production in just three weeks. All events are open to the public, while a series of gala shows give a good taster of the best of what's on offer. There's also a series of free community events and workshops.

When:	End of July/beginning of August
Where:	Aberdeen
Duration:	10 days
Tel:	01224 213800
Website:	www.aiyf.org

The Edinburgh Festivals

For three weeks in August, the cultural axis shifts, and the world revolves around Edinburgh. The lofty aim of the first Edinburgh International Festival, held in 1947, was to 'provide a platform for the flowering of the human spirit'. That same year, a handful of theatre companies gatecrashed the party by holding their own alternative festival, which became known as the Edinburgh Festival Fringe. As the International Festival and its bastard offshoot grew, other events like the Edinburgh Book Festival and Edinburgh Jazz and Blues Festival grew up around them. For information about the August festivals and events in Edinburgh, go to www.edinburghfestivals.co.uk.

Edinburgh Jazz and Blues Festival

...and all that jazz

Edinburgh's jazz festival, begun in the late 1960s, is Britain's oldest, and one of the most diverse. No room for factionalism here: Chicago styles of the 1920s mix with cutting-edge contemporary sounds from around the world. You can buy batches of tickets to cover different shows, and also enjoy a number of free events, including a New Orleans-style Mardi Gras at the Grassmarket and relaxing 'Jazz on a Summer's Day' in Princes Street Gardens. Instrumental and singing workshops and residential courses are also held during the festival.

When:	Last Friday in July/beginning of August
Where:	Edinburgh
Duration:	10 days
Tel:	0131 225 2202
Website:	www.edinburghjazzfestival.co.uk

The Edinburgh Festival Fringe

The largest arts festival in the world

Despite being one of the world's major arts festivals, the 'official' festival has become almost a sideshow: for tens of thousands of visitors each year, Edinburgh is all about The Fringe. Around 1.5 million tickets are sold for 30,000 performances of 2,000 shows in 250 venues. Theatre, usually of the alternative variety, and comedy are the main strands, but there's also dance and physical theatre, music, children's shows and a fair few events that defy any form of classification. Venues range from 'super venues' like the Pleasance and The Assembly, which house several shows a day in a number of different spaces, to – well, anything at all, including taxis and public toilets.

As well as giving its name to a whole genre – fringe theatre – the Fringe has launched countless careers. Shows that have premiered here include *Rosencrantz and Guildenstern Are Dead* and *Jerry Springer: The Opera*, while comedians who got their big break at the festival include most of the Monty Python team, Fry and Laurie, Steve Coogan and the League of Gentleman. Comedy is one of the Fringe's strongest suits, and you can see new shows from many of the country's leading stand-ups. The if.comedy award (sponsored for many years by Perrier) is the most prestigious comedy award in the UK, and a guaranteed career boost for the winner and runners-up.

But there's far more to the Fringe than big names. It's an 'unjuried' event, meaning anyone can put a show on, regardless of quality – and there are some heroically awful offerings. These shouldn't necessarily be avoided: watching a devised show depicting the life story of Emily Brontë through the medium of physical theatre performed by a cast of earnest drama students that outnumbers the audience is an archetypal Fringe experience. There are areas of the city centre where it's hard to move for actors performing extracts from shows and thrusting flyers into the hands of unsuspecting passers-by. 'Fringe Sunday' (the first Sunday of the festival) provides a good opportunity to sample what's on offer as dozens of companies perform free shows on The Meadows. Look out for two-for-one preview offers on shows during the opening weekend.

The Scotsman, which runs the Fringe First awards, is a good source of reviews for theatre productions, and a number of other publications and websites provide extensive coverage. Word-of-mouth, though, remains the best source of information on what's worth catching. With shows running from breakfast till the early hours of the morning, your choice of viewing is limited only by your budget and your need for sleep.

When:	Mid-August
Where:	Edinburgh
Duration:	3 weeks
Tel:	0131 226 0026
Website:	www.edfringe.com

Scotland

Edinburgh Art Festival

Sights for sore eyes

Edinburgh in August is not just about performing arts: the visual arts more than hold their end up in this sprawling festival of painting, photography, sculpture, installations, video and much more besides. Leading galleries have high-profile exhibitions of old masters and contemporary commissions, while provocative young artists push the boundaries at a host of other spaces around the city. Look out for public artworks in the streets, and meditative pieces hidden away from the hustle and bustle. The festival also programmes illuminating walks and talks exploring common themes, and throws a few memorable parties too. Many events are free, but check in advance for the price of workshops.

When:	August
Where:	Edinburgh
Duration:	1 month
Website:	www.edinburghartfestival.com

Edinburgh Military Tattoo

Military might put to good use

The Tattoo is seen by more than 200,000 visitors annually and watched by a worldwide TV audience of 100 million. It's a spectacular performance of military bands, regiments and display groups that takes place on the esplanade in front of the floodlit castle. Scottish regiments and massed pipe bands are the highlight for many, but the Tattoo also includes military regiments from all over the world – over 40 countries have been represented to date, including African tribes. The evening ends with a lone piper playing a lament on the castle ramparts and a heartfelt rendition of 'Auld Lang Syne'. There are nightly performances from Monday to Friday, and two on Saturday, with a fireworks display after the late performance. Tickets sell out months in advance, although it may be possible to pick up returns.

When:	First three weeks of August
Where:	Edinburgh Castle, Edinburgh
Duration:	3 weeks
Tel:	0131 225 1188 (box office)
Website:	www.edintattoo.co.uk

The word 'tattoo' comes from the closing-time cry in the inns when British regiments were stationed in Flanders in seventeenth and eighteenth centuries: 'Doe den tap toe' ('Turn the taps off').

Edinburgh International Festival

One of the world's most prestigious arts events

The International Festival focuses on classical music, opera, dance and theatre. The programme aims for innovation and excellence, and hosts numerous world and UK premieres. Performers and companies appear at the invitation of the festival director, with the most prestigious international artists awaiting the call. Events take place at several of Edinburgh's largest venues, including the Festival Theatre and the festival's permanent home, The Hub, close to Edinburgh Castle. There are also more intimate chamber concerts, talks and visual arts events. The festival closes with a spectacular free fireworks concert in Princes Street Gardens. You can turn up on the night to watch the show from Princes Street, but places in the seated area in front of the Scottish Chamber Orchestra in the gardens are strictly limited: people camp out at dawn at The Hub on release date to secure their tickets.

When:	August
Where:	Edinburgh
Duration:	3 weeks
Tel:	0131 473 2015 (The Hub, booking office and information centre)
Website:	www.eif.co.uk

The Edinburgh International Book Festival

Get booked up in Charlotte Square Gardens

Back in 1983, the first Edinburgh Book Festival consisted of 30 'meet the author' sessions. Fast-forward a quarter of a century, and you'll find over 650 events, making it one of the biggest and busiest book festivals on the planet, attracting 220,000 visitors. There are still plenty of top authors to meet, while high-profile debates and discussions on topical issues make the Edinburgh Book Festival an important forum for thoughts and ideas. Alongside the main festival is a brilliant children's programme – the world's leading literary event for young people – with workshops, storytelling and discussions. Charlotte Square Gardens, in Edinburgh's historic heart, is transformed into a tented village for the course of the festival – there's great food and a superb bookshop (and a separate children's bookshop and activity area) on site.

When:	August
Where:	Charlotte Square Gardens, Edinburgh
Duration:	17 days
Tel:	0845 373 5888
Website:	www.edbookfest.co.uk

Belladrum Tartan Heart Festival

Home-grown heaven in the Highlands

£ £ £ £

Forget huge crowds and fields full of strangers: Bella is a welcoming festival on a human scale, in a lovely setting, where you're sure to make some new friends. Things kick off with a Thursday night ceilidh and finish off with the Invenetian Masked Ball after the music ends on Saturday night: wear your most fanciful fancy dress. In between, there's non-stop quality music (sample acts: James, Martha Wainwright, The Hoosiers) across several stages, and plenty more besides. Get your teeth into some poetry, comedy and debate at the Verb Garden, sample some weird and wonderful performance at the Venus Flytrap Palais, boogie down to Madame Fifi's dance parlour or enhance your karma at the Buddhist temple. It's great for kids too, with storytellers, puppet shows, workshops and games. There's on-site camping – head for the communal campfire to get into the spirit – and you can bring your own food and drink, though you'll find everything you need on site too.

When:	Second weekend of August
Where:	Belladrum Estate, by Beauly, Invernesshire
Duration:	3 days
Tel:	01463 741366
Website:	www.tartanheartfestival.co.uk

Kilsyth International Carnival

All the world comes to Lanarkshire

£? 👤

A great big multicultural party, Kilsyth's carnival parade sees pipe bands marching along with Cuban salsa, Chinese dragons and Ghanaian drummers, cheerleaders and flamenco dancers. The all-day event in Colzium Country Park costs next to nothing, and features four stages with contemporary, world, folk and dance acts. There's plenty for kids, with an adventure playground, a funfair and rides on the miniature steam railway. An arts and craft fair, a beer tent and a vast array of food options add to the shiny happy fun.

When:	Second/third Sunday of August
Where:	Colzium Country Park, Kilsyth, North Lanarkshire
Duration:	1 day
Website:	www.kic.me.uk

World Pipe Band Championships

The pipes, the pipes are calling

If bagpipes aren't your thing, you'd be advised to stay well away from Glasgow Green. More than 200 pipe bands, comprising over 8,000 pipers and drummers from across the globe, come to Glasgow hoping to be crowned World Champions. Along with the piping competitions, there's Highland dancing and Highland games 'heavy events' including caber-tossing and stone lifting. There's a traditional craft fair, acres of tartan and events for children. The day culminates with the massed ranks of pipers and drummers marching past and playing together – quite a sight, and quite a noise too.

When:	Third Saturday of August
Where:	Glasgow Green, Glasgow
Duration:	1 day
Website:	www.rspba.org

Innerleithen Music Festival

Bringing the stars of Celtic music to the Scottish Borders

Ally Bain, Martin and Eliza Carthy, and the Incredible String Band are some of the stars of Celtic and English folk music to have played in the Borders town of Innerleithen on the River Tweed. Along with the main concerts, there are workshops on anything from guitar finger-picking techniques to Appalachian clog dancing, and other music and events going on around the town. The Festival Club in the Union Club on the High Street is a great place for a drink and a song, and there are late-night singarounds and open sessions in local pubs and beer gardens.

When:	Third weekend of August (Fri–Sun)
Where:	Innerleithen, Borders
Duration:	3 days
Tel:	01721 729949
Website:	www.innerleithenmusicfestival.org

Connect

Spoil yourself at this up-market festival in a serene setting

£££££

An up-market offering from the organisers of T in the Park, Connect is held in the beautiful grounds of Inveraray Castle, family seat of the Duke of Argyll. You can sample champagne and oysters, salmon and mussels fresh from the loch and a range of malt whiskies. Still, the focus is on top-quality bands against the beautiful backdrop of Loch Fyne and high hills. Take in the thrills of the Unknown Pleasures tent, party after hours in your headphones at the Silent Disco or get pampered in the spa area. The view from the campsite is spectacular, and if you don't fancy lugging a tent along, book into Tangerine Fields and stay in a ready pitched tent or tipi. Word to the wise: it's the West of Scotland, it's late summer – make sure you pack your insect repellent.

When:	Last weekend of August/first of September
Where:	Inveraray, Argyll
Duration:	3 days
Website:	www.connectmusicfestival.com

Edinburgh Mela

From South Asia to Scotland

FREE

Edinburgh doesn't pretend to hold a traditional South Asian mela: instead, the traditions of the Indian subcontinent and other world cultures fuse with their modern Scottish setting to create something new and unique. You might hear flamenco and Japanese drumming alongside the bhangra and Bollywood. Bazaars offer crafts, fabrics and jewellery, there are colourful costumes and spicy smells from the food stalls; acrobats, astrologers, puppets, dancers, theatre, comedians, or just the chance to chat and chill with a cup of chai. There's a friendly atmosphere that welcomes people of all ages and backgrounds, and it's all free.

When:	First weekend of September
Where:	Pilrig Park, Edinburgh
Duration:	2 days
Website:	www.edinburghfestivals.co.uk/mela

Scotland

Inverness Highland Games

Gathering at the gateway to the Highlands

The capital of the Highlands hosts one of the most popular Highland games, with heavy events, solo and ensemble piping contests and Highland dancing. The 'Great Putt of the Inverness Stone' is a particular highlight – the stone weighs around 10 kilos, and is a cumbersome size and shape. Saturday features open heavy events for men and women; Sunday is for 'masters'. There's also a 'Mini Highland Games' for kids, with foam cabers and shots. Plenty of other attractions take place, including a funfair and a Highland craft fair.

When:	Third weekend of July (Sat–Sun)
Where:	Bught Park Arena, Inverness
Duration:	2 days
Website:	www.invernesshighlandgames.com

Highland gatherings and Highland games

In medieval times, Scottish clans would gather to demonstrate their warrior prowess through trials of skill, speed and strength, and celebrate their culture in song and dance. Such gatherings were often banned by the ruling classes, and all but died out with the Highland clearances, but were revived in the Victorian era and have remained a popular fixture throughout Scotland during the summer months.

The gatherings vary in size – some attracting thousands of visitors and a high standard of competition, others small community events – but most follow a similar format. In some of the larger gatherings, competitors come from worldwide (the USA, in particular, has its own large Highland games). There are a number of athletic events, including running races (often a hill race), tugs of war and the all-important 'heavy events': hammer-throwing, stone-putting and, most famously, caber-tossing.

Highland dancing is another vital ingredient. It's a highly athletic and technical solo pursuit, and at most games dancers perform their Highland Flings and other dances in front of a panel of judges, who assess them for timing, technique and artistic interpretation. It shouldn't be confused with Scottish country dancing: this is also a common feature, though the emphasis is on everyone joining in.

Also, inevitably, there are bagpipes. Most gatherings will include a piping competition, and the largest attract dozens of pipe bands. They come together at the end to form a massed pipe band with hundreds of players. Hearing this is undoubtedly a memorable experience (though whether it's a pleasurable one is a matter of personal taste).

If you're in Scotland in the summer, it's well worth seeking out a Highland gathering. The games are always fun to watch, the atmosphere is special and the surroundings are usually breathtaking. We've listed three of the best known.

Cowall Highland Gathering

The largest Highland gathering

The Cowall Games, held in Dunoon, Argyll, are the largest and arguably the most spectacular of all Highland gatherings, attracting crowds of up to 20,000 – twice the town's population. Events run over three days, though the highlight of the gathering is the final Saturday. Over 3,500 competitors take part, including expats from as far away as Canada, South Africa and New Zealand. The Cowall Championships are one of the most prestigious piping competitions, with around 150 bands participating. They all come together for the closing ceremony, as some 3,000 pipers and drummers make the mountains shake.

When:	Last week of August (Thurs–Sat)
Where:	Dunoon, Argyll
Duration:	3 days
Tel:	01369 703206
Website:	www.cowalgathering.com

Braemar Gathering

Highland games smiled on by royalty

Gatherings have been held among the beautiful heather-clad hills at Braemar since the days of King Malcolm III in the eleventh century: legend has it that the king organised a hill race to the summit of nearby Craig Choinnich, with the fastest runner becoming his royal messenger. Queen Victoria began taking an interest while staying at nearby Balmoral in 1848, and became the Games' patron; since then reigning monarchs have regularly paid a visit. The programme includes traditional track and field events – tossing the caber, throwing the hammer, putting the stone – as well as a tug of war and a children's sack race. Other entertainments include piping – there's always a huge massed pipe band – and Highland dancing.

When:	First Saturday in September
Where:	Braemar, Aberdeenshire
Duration:	1 day
Tel:	01339 755377
Website:	www.braemargathering.org

Retrofest

It was acceptable in the eighties…

Do you go to festivals wanting to hear the latest in cutting-edge contemporary music? No? Then you've come to the right place. Scotland's Retrofest, as the name suggests, is in love with the past – more particularly, the music of the 1980s. The inaugural line-up featured Bananarama, ABC, Human League, Howard Jones and other acts it's now OK to enjoy without irony. Dig out your puffball skirts and your stonewashed denim, and don't forget to backcomb your hair. Culzean Castle, meanwhile, is a timelessly breathtaking location.

When:	First weekend of September (Sat/Sun)
Where:	Culzean Castle, Ayrshire
Duration:	2 days
Website:	www.retrofest.co.uk

Merchant City Festival

Music and markets in the Glasgow streets

The Merchant City area of Glasgow explodes with energy and creativity over this long weekend in September. The festival promises over 250 events, including live music (classical to cutting-edge dance), theatre, comedy, dance, visual arts, film, fashion, street arts and installations. There are plenty of free events, including four outdoor music stages in the streets. The whole place is buzzing, with markets filling the streets and the bars and cafes overflowing. From 9 p.m., the Festival Club opens its doors at the Carnival Arts Centre, and live music and DJs keep the party going till 2 a.m.

When:	Third weekend of September (Thurs–Sun)
Where:	Merchant City district, Glasgow
Duration:	4 days
Tel:	0141 552 6027
Website:	www.merchantcityfestival.com

The Hairth Festival

Uplifting music in the uplands

££££ ⛹ ⛺

Following on from the Knockengorroch World Ceilidh in the spring, this late-summer (if you're lucky – early-autumn if you're not) weekend features a similar mix of Celtic roots, world and dance music. Away from big-name headliners and sound systems, you'll find an acoustic village, open-mic sessions, storytelling, t'ai chi workshops, fire spectaculars and a solar-powered cinema. There's a children's marquee and procession, global craft and food stalls and real Scottish ales. The on-site camping in this unspoilt upland area is a real treat.

When: Autumn Equinox – usually third weekend of September (Fri–Mon)
Where: Knockengorroch Farm, Carsphairn, Kirkubrightshire
Duration: 4 days
Website: www.knockengorroch.org.uk

The Royal National Mod

Scotland's premier festival of the Gaelic language, arts and culture

£? ⛹

The second-largest festival in Scotland, and the world's biggest Gaelic-language event, the Mod celebrates Gaelic culture through music and dance, drama, arts and literature. Like the Welsh Eisteddfod, it's a competition-based event, with classes ranging from original clàrsach compositions to telling of ancient folk tales. There are hornpipes and Highland dancing, choral singing and massed pipe bands. Visitors and competitors come from as far away as Canada, the USA and Australia, and the royal family often put in an appearance (the Queen is a patron). The festival was first held in Oban in 1892, and now takes place in a different part of Scotland each year.

When: Mid-October
Where: Held in a different part of Scotland annually
Duration: 9 days
Tel: 01463 709705
Website: www.the-mod.co.uk

Scottish International Storytelling Festival

Once upon a time...

Scotland's rich oral history has enjoyed something of a revival in the past couple of decades, thanks in part to this popular storytelling festival. Based around the Scottish Storytelling Centre on Edinburgh's Royal Mile, the festival includes around 150 events, and over 20,000 adults and children take part. Oral tales are at the heart of the festival, but it also embraces music, drama, multimedia, film and arts and crafts, as well as workshops for children and adults. Although the focus is on Scottish stories, the festival explores a variety of themes and connections with other cultures.

When:	Around October half-term
Where:	Scottish Storytelling Centre, 43–45 High Street, Edinburgh
Duration:	10 days
Tel:	0131 556 9579
Website:	www.scottishstorytellingcentre.co.uk

Glasgay!

Forget the straight and narrow...

As the name perhaps indicates, Glasgay! is a Lesbian, Gay, Bisexual and Transgender (LGBT) festival held in Glasgow. Since its launch in 1993, it's grown into a loud and proud month-long festival featuring leading artists from the Scottish gay scene and beyond. There's music (from hip-hop to classical), theatre (big shows and experimental studio pieces), dance (ballroom to contemporary), comedy, cabaret, literature and visual arts, as well as a hedonistic mix of parties and club nights. With 25,000 visitors attending each year, the appeal is certainly not limited to LGBT audiences.

When:	Mid-October/mid-November
Where:	Glasgow
Duration:	30 days
Tel:	0141 552 7575/8
Website:	www.glasgay.com

Edinburgh's Hogmanay

A wee party to see in the New Year…

£?

A four-day winter festival attracting 100,000 revellers, Hogmanay in Edinburgh has become as iconic as Mardi Gras in New Orleans or the Rio Carnival. Things kick off on 29 December with the Torchlight Procession. Some 20,000 people, many carrying flaming torches, form a river of fire snaking through the Old Town. Up on Calton Hill, wicker effigies are ceremonially burnt. The 30th is the Night Afore Fiesta, a free, family-oriented event. George Street is transformed into the world's biggest ceilidh: Highland flings are flung (join in the world's largest Strip the Willow), and street theatre, storytellers, giant puppets and many pipers piping add to the carnival atmosphere.

On New Year's Eve itself, big-name bands perform in Princes Street Gardens, at the Concert in the Gardens and there's Scottish dancing at the Ceilidh in the Gardens. Entrance to both is by (expensive) ticket only. DJs and live bands also perform on three stages on Princes Street – again, you need a ticket, but these are considerably cheaper. Wherever you go, you'll find a carnival atmosphere – just make sure your fancy dress costume is a warm one. The midnight fireworks display that lights up the sky above the castle is a truly breathtaking one, using around eight tonnes of explosives. The organised outdoor events finish at 1 a.m., but the partying continues till dawn in many pubs and clubs.

When:	29 December–1 Jan
Where:	Edinburgh city centre
Duration:	4 days
Website:	www.edinburghshogmanay.org

Hogmanay

Since the days of the Norsemen, the New Year has always been celebrated more extravagantly in Scotland than elsewhere in the UK. The Presbyterians didn't really approve of the Hogmanay (New Year's Eve) and Ne'er (New Year) festivities, but most of their energy was focused on banning Christmas instead. The twenty-fifth of December didn't become a public holiday north of the border till 1958, and Hogmanay was the main seasonal celebration. There are huge street parties with big-name Scottish bands in Glasgow, Stirling and Aberdeen (all ticketed, though Aberdeen's is still free), but you'll find live music, torchlit processions, bonfires and fireworks wherever you go.

The Stonehaven Fireballs

Goodness, gracious, great balls of fire…

FREE

The fishing village of Stonehaven, 16 miles south of Aberdeen, sees in the New Year in unique fashion. Some fifty strapping locals march along the High Street, swinging great balls of fire round their heads. The fireballs are wire cages up to three feet in diameter filled with paraffin-soaked materials and attached to strong, five-foot-long ropes. When the swingers reach the harbour, the balls are thrown into the sea. The extraordinary spectacle – which derives from a nineteenth-century fishermen's festival, but has echoes of distant pagan fire rituals – attracts around 12,000 visitors, equal to the town's population.

When: 31 December
Where: Stonehaven
Duration: 1 day
Website: www.stonehavenfireballs.co.uk

First Footing

If a tall, dark stranger appears at your door on the stroke of midnight on New Year's Eve with a lump of coal, don't call the police: it's good luck to let him in. First-footing is an essential part of Hogmanay celebrations. Traditionally, the first-foot brings a lump of coal (for warmth), some salt (for wealth) and cake (for food). In return, he'll expect a 'het pint' – a cocktail of ale, nutmeg and whisky – and a kiss from all the women of the house. Woe betide, though, if the first person to set foot over your threshold is blond (and therefore possibly a marauding Viking), a doctor, a gravedigger, a minister or a woman: bad luck is sure to follow.

South East

London International Mime Festival

Actions speak louder than words

If you think mime means somebody in a clown suit pretending to be stuck in a box, think again. Since 1977, the London International Mime Festival has showcased the best in contemporary visual theatre from Britain and around the world. Performances range from cabaret to dance to children's shows – there are workshops and lectures too. Expect unforgettable images, incredible physical performances, humour, pathos and theatrical magic.

When:	January
Where:	Southbank Centre, Barbican, ICA and other venues, London
Duration:	1 month
Tel:	020 7637 5661
Website:	www.mimefest.co.uk

Chinese New Year

The West End goes Oriental

Chinese New Year celebrations are among the most colourful spectacles on the planet. It's celebrated by the Chinese diaspora throughout the UK; the London event is the biggest outside China, and regularly attracts half a million visitors. The parade, which sets off from The Strand at 11 a.m., is a sight to behold. It's followed by an afternoon of staged entertainment, traditional and contemporary, in Trafalgar Square, featuring artists from China and London. Dragon and lion dances are always popular, and other displays are themed around the animal of the coming year. There are fireworks and Chinese firecrackers in Leicester Square and events, stalls and fantastic food (including special Dim Sum menus) throughout the lantern-festooned streets of Chinatown.

When:	January/February (Chinese New Year is based on the lunar calendar, so the date varies from year to year)
Where:	Chinatown, London W1
Duration:	1 day
Tel:	020 7851 6686
Website:	www.chinatownchinese.co.uk

Olney Pancake Race

Don't forget the Jif lemon...

FREE

In the Buckinghamshire market town of Olney they go in for pancakes in a big way. The town has hosted a pancake race on Shrove Tuesday since 1445, and is open to 'housewives or young ladies of the town' aged 18 and above. They wear a traditional housewife's costume (apron, skirt and head covering) and carry a pancake in a frying pan, which is tossed on crossing the finishing line. The 415-yard course runs from the Market Place to the Church, and the winner is rewarded with a kiss from the verger. The race attracts interest from around the world, and since 1950 the womenfolk of Olney have competed against those of Liberal, Kansas.

When:	Shrove Tuesday
Where:	Olney, Bucks.
Duration:	1 day
Tel:	01234 711679
Website:	www.olneytowncouncil.co.uk

Guildford International Music Festival/Spring Music Festival

The best musicians from around the world

 £ £

You're guaranteed some fine music in Guildford in March, but what you get depends on what year it is. The Guildford International Music Festival takes place in odd-numbered years and focuses on classical music, though jazz, world, folk and popular genres are also represented. It alternates with the Guildford Spring Music Festival, a week of concerts, workshops and masterclasses from musicians who have strong connections with the area.

When:	March, odd-numbered years
Where:	Various venues, Guildford
Duration:	2 weeks
Tel:	01483 444334 (box office)
Website:	www.surrey.ac.uk/Music/Festival

When:	March, even-numbered years
Where:	Various venues, Guildford
Duration:	1 week
Tel:	01483 531426
Website:	www.gsmf.co.uk

South East

Gosport and Fareham Easter Festival

For folkies who prefer a roof over their head

£ £ £ £

In contrast to most folk festivals, the concerts at this Easter festival take place indoors, and only hardy campers brave the weather this early in the year (there are plenty of hotels and B&Bs around). Despite this, there's a strong festival feel: season tickets are available, and there's a full range of workshops and dance displays. Along with some of the biggest stars of Celtic and English traditional music, unsigned acts appear in Showcase Concerts every teatime and there are informal sessions in a number of bars. (Although Gosport takes top billing, all the events actually now take place in Fareham.)

When: Easter weekend (Thurs–Mon)
Where: Ferneham Hall/Lysses House Hotel, Fareham, Hants.
Duration: 5 days
Tel: 02392 524551
Website: www.gosportfestival.co.uk

Wycombe Arts Festival

Culture in the Chilterns

£?

This well-established mixed arts festival is held around High Wycombe, Marlow and the surrounding countryside on the edge of the Chiltern Hills. The various venues include Hughenden Manor, former home of Victorian prime minister Benjamin Disraeli. Classical concerts include free lunchtime recitals and a regular appearance from the City of London Sinfonia; there's also folk music and cabaret-style jazz in the town hall. Spoken-word events and street theatre also figure.

When: End of April–beginning of June
Where: Various venues, High Wycombe, Bucks.
Duration: About 5 weeks
Tel: 01494 512000
Website: www.wycombeartsfestival.org

Hastings Jack in the Green

May Day morris mischief

The Jack in the Green was once a recurring character in May Day festivals; covered from head to toe in foliage, he's associated with the primeval Green Man and mischievous folk characters like Puck and Robin Hood. He's now the focus of this popular May Day weekend festival, where there's a programme of live music, dances and morris dancing in the streets from Friday to Sunday before the 'Release of the Jack' on Monday morning. Jack is attended by drummers called 'Bogies' and troupes of morris dancers for a boisterous procession round Hastings Old Town, lasting till mid-afternoon when he is ceremonially slain, releasing the spirit of summer.

When: May Day Bank Holiday weekend
Where: Old Town, Hastings, East Sussex
Duration: 4 days
Website: www.hastingsjack.co.uk

Brighton Festival and Brighton Festival Fringe

England's answer to Edinburgh

The Brighton Festival is the largest mixed arts festival south of the border, with over 200 events attracting half a million visitors over three weeks in May. A vibrant, creative city at any time, Brighton and Hove really comes to life during the festival. Theatre, dance, music and literature are well represented, with top international names. Outdoor spectaculars and street theatre also figure prominently, particularly over the Bank Holiday weekends. Brighton pioneered the Artists Open House concept: dozens of homes across the city turn into art galleries for the duration of the festival. The independent Fringe Festival is now England's largest open-access festival (and the third biggest in the world after Edinburgh and Adelaide), presenting well over 500 events and growing every year. As well as more established venues, any spare church hall or pub function room gets pressed into service. Look out for Fringe City in Jubilee Square on the opening weekend of the festival, where you can watch a selection of shows for free across several stages. Accommodation in Brighton gets booked up (and expensive) over the festival. In recent years, special late trains have been laid on to take Londoners back home in an hour. If you can find somewhere to stay, though, it's well worth making a holiday by the seaside of it.

When: May
Where: Brighton, various venues
Duration: 3 weeks
Tel: 01273 709709 (Ticket office)
Websites: www.brightonfestival.org, www.brightonfestivalfringe.org.uk

South East

Newbury Spring Festival

Marvellous music in Berkshire

This well-regarded music festival, which celebrated its 30th anniversary in 2008, features world-class classical concerts as well as jazz and world music. There are around three concerts a day in various venues in Newbury and the surrounding villages, including churches and country houses, plus talks, poetry, open artists' studios and a strong programme of workshops and concerts for children and young people.

When:	Second and third weeks of May
Where:	Newbury and surrounding villages, Berks.
Duration:	2 weeks
Tel:	01635 528766
Website:	www.newburyspringfestival.org.uk

Winchester Mayfest

Medieval meets modern in England's ancient capital

Medieval Winchester comes to life with this celebration of traditional and contemporary music, song and dance. Roots, blues and jazz are all well represented, and there are dance displays (in front of the cathedral), ceilidhs, workshops and children's events. The cathedral close is a wonderful setting for the Saturday festival market.

When:	Mid-May
Where:	Winchester, Hants.
Duration:	4 days
Website:	www.winmayfest.co.uk

Chelsea Flower Show

Experience the greatest flower show in the world

For five days every May, the grounds of the Royal Hospital, Chelsea burst into bloom for the world's most famous flower show. Garden designers, plant breeders and green-fingered folk everywhere flock to the horticultural event of the year, which has been organised by the Royal Horticultural Society since 1852, and in Chelsea since 1913. There are 20 or so large show gardens, plus many smaller gardens in a number of categories – chic, courtyard, roof and city. Over a hundred stunning floral displays in the grand pavilion create hallucinatory colours and aromas. Nurseries and growers from around the world display new and unusual plants, new garden products are launched and the latest trends and styles, from flower arranging to landscaping, are eagerly picked over. It's a glamorous event, too: look out for royalty and TV gardening experts. Tickets need to be bought in advance – none are available on the gate – and the first two days are for RHS members only.

When:	Third week of May (Tues–Sat)
Where:	Royal Hospital, Chelsea, London
Duration:	5 days
Tel:	020 7649 1885
Website:	www.rhs.org.uk

Wendover Canal Festival

Grand goings-on by the Union Canal

Held in aid of the restoration of the Wendover Arm of the Grand Union Canal at Tring, this is a community-oriented festival run by volunteers. It attracts around 10,000 people and 100 canal boats moor up for the duration of the weekend. A varied programme of entertainment includes everything from crafts to classic cars to clowns. A ride on a canal boat is essential.

When:	Bank Holiday weekend
Where:	Wendover Canal, Tring, Bucks.
Duration:	2 days
Website:	www.tringcanalfestival.org.uk

Black Horse Music Festival

The biggest little festival in Britain

Every Spring Bank Holiday weekend, thousands of people descend on the tiny Sussex village of Telham for the 'Biggest Little Festival in Britain'. Bands perform in a marquee in a field at the back of the Black Horse pub – but this is rather different from your average pub gig. The line-up in the past has embraced rock, folk, blues, jazz, reggae, ska, bhangra, punk, Cajun, country, dance, soul, indie, Latin and just about any other genre you care to mention, as well as occasional bouts of comedy and even performance poetry. Some bands are local, but they've also come from places as exotic as Cuba, Congo and Mauritania. Fairport Convention and Waterson Carthy are among the big names to have played in the marquee. The festival grew out of a folk club that met at the pub, and Saturday remains folk day. Sunday specialises in world music, while Monday turns into a popular party night; single day tickets are available. There's no on-site camping, but a couple of campsites are nearby, and a free bus is laid on from Battle train station.

When:	Spring Bank Holiday (Fri–Mon)
Where:	The Black Horse, Telham, Battle, East Sussex
Duration:	4 days
Website:	www.blackhorsemusicfestival.org.uk

Luton Carnival

An undeniably great reason to come to Luton

Vibrant colours, uplifting music and swarms of joyful people make Luton one of the most exciting places in the country. Not a sentence you'll often read, but true for one day a year, when one of the finest carnivals outside Notting Hill rolls into town. Over a thousand people join in the glittering parade from Wardown Park to the town centre. From noon till dusk the streets shake to non-stop live music and sound systems pounding out soca, samba and more. Stalls selling sugar cane and jerk chicken add tropical flavour, and 150,000 have broad smiles on their faces.

When:	Spring Bank Holiday, 12 p.m.–7 p.m.
Where:	Luton, Beds.
Duration:	1 day
Tel:	01582 582727
Website:	www.lutoncarnival.com

Tilford Bach Festival

Baroque music in the beautiful English countryside

Tilford is the sort of picturesque English village that Sunday-night TV drama producers dream about. For more than half a century, it's been home to an exquisite festival of baroque music. There are three concerts in Tilford Church and one in the Great Hall of Farnham Castle, featuring music by J. S. Bach and his contemporaries. The festival offers the opportunity to hear musicians of international standing including the heavenly soprano Emma Kirkby in intimate surroundings, while also offering a platform for up-and-coming soloists and ensembles.

When:	Last weekend of May and first weekend of June (Fri, Sat)
Where:	Tilford Parish Church, Farnham, Surrey
Duration:	2 days
Tel:	01428 713338
Website:	www.tilford-bach.org.uk

Charleston Festival

Intellectual and artistic pursuits with the Bloomsbury set

Charleston was the country home of the Bloomsbury Group. The farmhouse is uniquely decorated by artists Vanessa Bell and Duncan Grant, in a style inspired by Italian fresco painting and the Post-Impressionists. For half a century, Charleston was a home from home for many of the greatest writers, artists and thinkers of the day, including Virginia Woolf, E. M. Forster, Maynard Keynes and Lytton Strachey. The Charleston Festival celebrates this intellectual legacy as writers, performers, poets, film-makers and thinkers read, perform, talk, argue, entertain, share ideas and tell stories. The events take place in a large marquee in the garden, and the programme always includes several items connected to Bloomsbury Group members.

When:	End of May
Where:	Charleston, Firle, Lewes, East Sussex
Duration:	10 days
Tel:	01323 811265
Website:	www.charleston.org.uk

Glyndebourne Opera Festival

Exquisite entertainment for the elite

£££££

Taking in an opera in the pastoral surroundings of Glyndebourne, a country house just outside Lewes, has been a mainstay of the English 'social season' since the 1930s. Performances are held in the afternoon, finishing in time to catch the last train back to London Victoria. The long interval (over an hour) gives the audience the chance to enjoy picnics on the lawn – patrons are advised to bring their own furniture, since sitting on the grass doesn't suit the customary black-tie/evening dress – or a meal in a choice of restaurants in the grounds. Glyndebourne is not just about the social occasion, though. The London Philharmonic is the house orchestra, and productions are of the highest calibre; Mozart is a particular speciality. Many performances are preceded by talks from leading music academics.

When:	End of May–August
Where:	Glyndebourne, Lewes, East Sussex
Duration:	3 months
Tel:	01273 812321
Website:	www.glyndebourne.com

South of England Show

Everything from cows to saunas

££

The South of England Agricultural Society's annual flagship event attracts over 90,000 people from across Europe – not just farmers, then. The show celebrates all aspects of agriculture, equestrianism, horticulture, food and drink, country crafts, sports and entertainment; the daily cattle and livestock parade is a particular highlight. Over 1,500 trade stands sell everything from strawberries to saunas, and there are local meats, cheeses, wines and other produce on sale. It's a good day out for kids, who have the chance to handle all sorts of animals in the 'fur and feather' area.

When:	First weekend of June (Thurs–Sat)
Where:	South of England Centre, Ardingly, Haywards Heath, West Sussex
Duration:	4 days
Tel:	01444 892700
Website:	www.seas.org.uk

The South of England Agricultural Society holds a Spring Garden and Leisure Show over the May Day Bank Holiday, the Autumn Show and Game Fair at the beginning of October and a Festive Food and Drink Fayre in December.

Basingstoke Kite Festival

Come on, let's paint the sky with colour

Local, national and international kite flyers fill the skies over Basingstoke during this colourful weekend. Competitive events include Rokkaku fights using traditional Japanese fighter kites and an altitude contest, and people taking part are invited to design their own kite around an annual theme. There are kite making and flying workshops, kite retail stalls, trampolines and bouncy castles.

When:	First weekend of June (Sat/Sun, 10 a.m.–5 p.m.)
Where:	Down Grange Sports Complex, Pack Lane, Basingstoke, Hants.
Duration:	2 days
Website:	www.basingstokekitefestival.org.uk

Camden Green Fair

London's most popular free green event

Having begun life as a small community event, Camden Green Fair has grown into the biggest free environmental event in the UK. Its aim is to showcase the huge and rapidly growing number of sustainable companies and products, campaigns, movements and ethical lifestyle choices available to us – and inspire Londoners towards a greener, more sustainable future. If that all sounds a bit earnest, don't worry – along with the stalls and workshops, there's some great live music from around the world, a solar-powered cinema and a whole host of fun activities, from junk drumming to willow sculpture, in the Green Families Zone. The festival also incorporates Bike Fest, one of the largest urban cycling events, and the place to park your bike for the day.

When:	First Sunday in June, 12 p.m.–7 p.m.
Where:	Regent's Park, London
Duration:	1 day
Website:	www.camdengreenfair.org.uk

Spitalfields Festival

Community creativity in the East End

Spitalfields is home to a high concentration of creative people and a heady mix of cultures, so it should come as no surprise that its festival has such a buzz about it. Two festivals, in fact – there's a three-week summer programme and a ten-day winter festival as well as year-round programme of education and community work. A hugely diverse mix of high-quality music reflects the history and contemporary culture of the area, from Western classical music to bhangra, experimental jazz to samba. Venues range from splendid Christ Church and the atmospheric restored Wilton's Music Hall to Spitalfields Market. Concerts often feature specially commissioned premieres, and artists work energetically with community groups, young people and local performers. For once, Arts Council platitudes about cultural regeneration and diversity ring resoundingly true.

When:	June and mid-December
Where:	Spitalfields, East London (various venues)
Duration:	June 3 weeks, mid-December 10 days
Tel:	020 7377 0287
Website:	www.spitalfieldsfestival.org.uk

The Hampton Court Palace Festival

Spoil yourself in Henry VIII's palace

The open-air courtyard at Hampton Court Palace provides an elegant yet intimate setting for this series of concerts, perfect for an English summer's evening (though preferably not a wet English summer's evening). The diverse programme includes huge stars, from opera divas to rock legends, in front of an audience of 2,500. The Palace Gardens are a wonderful setting for al fresco dining beforehand (luxury hampers available), or you could blag your way onto a corporate hospitality package: meals are cooked by top chefs – Gordon Ramsay has been chef in residence – and served within the palace's state apartments.

When:	First three weeks of June
Where:	Hampton Court Palace, London
Duration:	3 weeks
Website:	www.hamptoncourtfestival.com

The Old Fair of Abinger

A medieval event: all pilgrims are welcome

FREE | 🧍

In the Middle Ages, the Church of St James on Abinger Common was a popular stopping-off point for pilgrims travelling the North Downs way to Canterbury or heading further afield to the tomb of St James in Santiago de Compostela. The villages would entertain the pilgrims with music, mumming and merriment, which developed into an annual fair to celebrate the feast of St James that continued into the 1930s. The fair was revived in 1956 to raise funds for the restoration of the church, hit by a stray bomb during the war. It's been going strong ever since, and though the strict medieval dress code has been relaxed a little in recent years, the emphasis is still on traditional entertainment. Attractions include Maypole dancing, horse shoes, 'Tossing the Sheaf', archery, falconry displays and a tug of war. Participants still go to great lengths to make or procure a suitable costume, and there are craft stalls, sweet meats and other more or less authentic food and drink.

When:	Second Saturday of June
Where:	St James' Church, Abinger Common, Surrey
Duration:	1 day
Website:	www.abingerfair.com

Charleston Manor Festival

A weekend of music-making in the idyllic South Downs

£?

Cellist Robert Cohen first played at Charleston Manor in 1986, aged 26, and fell in love with the idyllic setting. Three years later he returned as artistic director of his own festival and now every summer invites an outstanding selection of friends and colleagues to join him for a weekend of music-making in the South Downs. There are three nights of concerts in the atmospheric sixteenth-century tithe barn, featuring favourite classics and little-known masterpieces. The barn, which seats 300, has wonderful acoustics and provides an intimate and informal setting for chamber music. Afterwards, concert-goers can take a candlelit dinner in the Coach House or picnic on the Italianate lawn. This Charleston, by the way, is not connected with the festival held at the Bloomsbury Group's Charleston farmhouse a few miles away.

When:	Second weekend of June (Fri–Sun)
Where:	Charleston Manor, Seaford, East Sussex
Duration:	3 days
Website:	www.charlestonmanorfestival.com

South East

O2 Wireless Festival

'The coolest festival in the heart of the city'

£££

Some festivals have their origins shrouded in the mists of time. Others are joyful assertions of the collective identity of a community. Many are labours of love. And some are dreamt up by clever marketing departments. No prizes for guessing which category Wireless falls into. Authentic it's not, but the corporate muscle guarantees a strong musical line-up, and for the urban festival-goer who wants to keep their designer shoes clean and sleep in their own bed at the end of the night, it works very well. There's a special arena where O2 customers only can enjoy massages, deluxe toilets and other VIP treatment – this may go against the community spirit festivals ought to create, but hey, it's pretty cool if you're one of the chosen.

When:	Mid-June
Where:	Hyde Park, London/Harewood House, Leeds
Duration:	3–4 days
Website:	www.wirelessfestival.co.uk

Petworth Festival

Affordable classics and picnics in Petworth Park

£?

For three decades the world's finest classical musicians have travelled to the handsome West Sussex market town of Petworth to perform at this well-regarded festival. Despite the elite musicians on show, the festival has an inclusive, non-elitist ethos, and ticket prices are surprisingly reasonable. The festival now encompasses far more than just classical music, with jazz, roots and world music, literature, visual arts, open-air theatre and children's events. There's a family day in Petworth Park, a fine National Trust property with landscaped gardens designed by Capability Brown, including a lovely kite festival. Petworth Park also hosts open-air concerts featuring big names in various popular genres (Simply Red, Jools Holland, Il Divo) – picnics beforehand, fireworks after.

When:	Second and third weeks of June
Where:	Petworth, West Sussex
Duration:	2 weeks
Tel:	01798 343055
Website:	www.petworthfestival.org.uk

Stokefest

A green and friendly day out in the city centre

FREE | [👤]

Continuing the legacy of the Stoke Newington Midsummer Festival, Stokefest is a big happy summer Sunday afternoon in Clissold Park, Hackney. Kicking off at noon with a carnival procession down Stoke Newington High Street, it's green, community focused and all free. Over 300 artists perform across six stages (the meeting of local reggae sound systems is a particular highlight), there's a market with a hundred local charity, craft and organic food stalls, and plenty of workshops and interactive events to keep the whole family entertained. Around 30,000 people attend what must be one of the friendliest days in London.

When: Second Sunday in June, 12 p.m.–8 p.m.
Where: Clissold Park, Hackney, London N16
Duration: 1 day
Website: www.stokefest.co.uk

Hever Lakeside Theatre

Plays and picnics by Hever Castle

£?

The lakeside theatre in the grounds of Hever Castle is a sumptuous setting for a summer season of plays, opera, concerts and comedy. The auditorium is covered so the show will go on despite the rain, but you'll want to choose a nice evening to enjoy a picnic and the atmosphere. Suppers and drinks are available in the Pavilion Restaurant, and early booking is advised.

When: Mid-June–August
Where: Hever Castle, Edenbridge, Kent
Duration: 2 months
Tel: 01732 866114
Website: www.heverlakeside.co.uk

Isle of Wight Festival

They don't make 'em like they used to...

£ £ £ £ £ [A]

The first Isle of Wight Festival in 1968 was an intimate affair, but in 1969 Bob Dylan put the Isle of Wight firmly on the musical map when he made his first appearance since his pivotal motorbike crash, in front of a 150,000-strong crowd. The 1970 Isle of Wight Festival attracted a crowd of 600,000 – still the biggest concert audience the UK has ever seen, and all the more phenomenal when you consider the island's regular population is only 100,000. The 1970 line-up reads like a who's who of rock 'n' roll legends: Jimi Hendrix (in his last performance, a month before his death), The Who, The Doors, Miles Davis, Joni Mitchell, Joan Baez, Sly and the Family Stone, Free, Donovan, Leonard Cohen, Hawkwind...

But it wasn't the 1960s anymore, and the Isle of Wight Festival wasn't all peace and love. A double fence gave the site the appearance of a 'psychedelic concentration camp', logistics were a nightmare, and there was antagonism between those who'd paid for tickets and the many more who hadn't, particularly since the latter enjoyed a better view from the slopes of Afton Down. It was all too much for promoter Ron Foulk. 'This is the last festival,' he stated in the aftermath. 'It began as a beautiful dream but it has got out of control and it is a monster.' Parliament made sure of it, with the Isle of Wight Act banning any gathering of more than 5,000 people on the island for the next 30 years.

In 2002, though, 8,000 people came to see The Charlatans and Robert Plant at 'Rock Island', and the revived Isle of Wight Festival has grown steadily since. Dave Roe's classic psychedelic artwork on the posters is the only connection with its former incarnation, though the Isle of Wight Festival has commissioned a life-size statue of Hendrix. It now attracts crowds of 65,000 and the biggest bands on the planet queue up to play once again. Tickets sell out within hours of going on sale, and there's no point turning up without one these days. Proper 1960s hippies would be flabbergasted by the commercialism, the excellent organisation and the improved sound quality, and appalled to find that 'Strawberry Fields' is home to champagne and cocktail bars. The campsite includes a quiet area – ask for directions to 'Sleepy Hollow' – and there's a kids' zone.

When:	Second or third weekend of June
Where:	Seaclose Park, Newport, Isle of Wight
Duration:	3 days
Website:	www.isleofwightfestival.com

City of London Festival

Shaking up the Square Mile

There can be few places in the world as full of history as the Square Mile of the City of London. This summer festival, which has been going since 1962, brings the City to life. Many iconic buildings – including Mansion House, Stationers' Hall, Merchant Taylors' Hall and St Paul's Cathedral – become concert venues. Squares, gardens and other public spaces, as well as landmarks like Tower Bridge and the Monument, are also pressed into service. As well as a world-class high-brow classical programme, there's world music and jazz, literature, visual arts, films, architecture walks and talks. Just in case anyone working in the City can't afford a ticket, many events are free.

When:	City of London (various venues)
Where:	Mid-June–mid-July
Duration:	1 month
Tel:	020 7796 4949
Website:	www.colf.org

Meltdown

Hand-picked quality on the South Bank

Curated by a different artist each year, the Royal Festival Hall's Meltdown festival gives a fascinating insight into the influences and tastes of some of our finest musicians. Who'd have thought Scott Walker was into Asian Dub Foundation, or that Morrissey was a fan of Alan Bennett? (All right, so the latter isn't so surprising.) The musicians often use their connections to pull off a coup or two – Patti Smith coaxed fellow punk poets Television and Richard Hell out of retirement. Meltdown isn't limited to concerts – the guest curators have the run of the place, and programme films, talks, exhibitions, DJ sets and whatever else takes their fancy.

When:	Third week of June
Where:	Royal Festival Hall, Southbank Centre, London
Duration:	1 week
Website:	www.southbankcentre.co.uk/meltdown

Royal Ascot

First, choose your hat...

Royal Ascot is the world's leading festival of competitive hat-wearing, and an unmissable event for anyone who enjoys the sport of aristocracy-watching. Some rather prestigious flat racing also goes on, but this is an incidental attraction for most of the 300,000 visitors who make this the biggest racing event in Europe. It's also the world's oldest racing meet: Queen Anne first decided Ascot would be a good spot for a racecourse back in 1711. The Royal Family still pop by from nearby Windsor Castle, arriving in a horse-drawn carriage around 2 p.m. (racing starts at 2.30 p.m.), and the Queen has owned several winning horses over the years. Smart dress (shirt and tie/posh frock and hat) is required in the main arena (top hats and waistcoats/no bare midriffs or shoulders should you be invited into the Royal Enclosure) though there's no dress code in the Silver Ring. Ascot-goers down 185,000 bottles of champagne, munch 100,000 scones and nibble their way through 11,000 lobsters each year. At about 6 p.m., after the last race, there's a traditional communal sing-song (songbooks provided) around the bandstand, accompanied by a military band.

When:	Third week of June (Tues–Sat)
Where:	Ascot, Windsor, Berks.
Duration:	5 days
Tel:	0870 727 1234 (Ticket booking)
Website:	www.ascot.co.uk

Greenwich and Docklands International Festival

Better value than the Millennium Dome

Over four spectacular days, Greenwich and the Docklands area are treated to work from some of the best international circus and carnival artists, outdoor theatre companies, acrobats and street artists. Whether it's mechanical animals, unexpected apparitions, death-defying aerobatics, whirling dervishes or pyrotechnic extravaganzas, you're guaranteed some extraordinary experiences. Most events take place outdoors, while the old Millennium Dome, whatever anyone might say about it, makes a great venue for the free preview show.

When:	Third weekend of June (Thurs–Sun)
Where:	Various venues in the Greenwich and Docklands area
Duration:	4 days
Tel:	020 8305 1818
Website:	www.festival.org

Broadstairs Dickens Week

Dickens celebrated in his favourite 'watering place'

Charles Dickens loved Broadstairs, visiting 'our English watering place' regularly for his summer holidays from 1837 to 1859. He wrote much of *David Copperfield* in Bleak House, overlooking the harbour, and based the character of Betsey Trotwood on one Miss Mary Pearson Strong, whose house is now the Dickens House Museum. Broadstairs has celebrated the association since 1937 with a Dickens Festival, featuring costumed parades, music hall performances, melodramas, dramatic adaptations of Dickens' novels, talks and a Victorian cricket match. Be sure to wear Victorian dress.

When:	Third weekend of June (Thurs–Sun)
Where:	Broadstairs, Kent
Duration:	4 days
Tel:	01843 861827
Website:	www.broadstairsdickensfestival.co.uk

Chichester Festivities

Music and more in the cathedral city

With 170 events over 17 days in almost 30 venues in and around Chichester, there's something for most tastes during the Chichester Festivities. There's a wide range of classical, jazz and blues, world and folk music, talks from high-profile speakers and numerous outdoor and free events. Highlights include classical concerts in the cathedral, a fireworks spectacular at Goodwood Racecourse and outdoor theatre in West Dean Gardens. The festival is also an ideal time to take in a production at the acclaimed Chichester Festival Theatre, whose season runs from the end of May to early September.

When:	Late June–July
Where:	Chichester, West Sussex
Duration:	17 days
Tel:	01243 785718
Website:	www.chifest.org.uk

South East

Chichester Real Ale and Jazz Festival

Real ale and real music in a giant marquee

[£ £ £]

This festival started out in a small tent in 1981 and has grown to include a 25,000 square foot marquee, a 70-foot real ale bar, a wine bar, food stalls and capacity for 2,500 on each of the event's four nights. There's not much jazz these days, but there have been some impressive headliners over the years, including James Brown and Blondie. The picturesque setting of Priory Park, nestling in the city walls of historic Chichester, make it the perfect place to spend a lazy summer evening.

When:	First week of July, Weds–Sat
Where:	Priory Park, Chichester
Duration:	4 days
Tel:	0870 950 9669 (Tickets Only)
Website:	www.chichester-rajf.co.uk

Goodwood Festival of Speed

'The Greatest Show on Earth' – Daily Telegraph

[£ £ £ £] [🚶] [▲]

In 1993 the Earl of March, a motoring nut, decided to indulge his passion by holding a motorsport festival in the grounds of his ancestral home – which already had a distinguished history of motoring events. Some 25,000 people turned up to watch, and the Festival of Speed has now grown into the biggest and most diverse classic motorsport event in the world. Crowds of 150,000 come to see classic sports cars and the latest feats of high performance engineering put through their paces. The course runs through the incongruously peaceful parkland of Goodwood on the South Downs, and includes an infamous hill climb. Legendary racing drivers like Stirling Moss and Emerson Fittipaldi rub hubcaps with the Lewis Hamiltons and Fernando Alonsos of today. As well as being one of the highlights of the motoring calendar, the Festival of Speed is also a social occasion par excellence – The Times has described it as 'the garden party of the gods'. Away from the cars, there are spectacular aerial displays, over 200 stalls selling motoring paraphernalia, live bands, BMX and skateboarding acrobatics and special racing events for children. The 35 classic cars from around the world on display at the 2007 festival had a combined worth of over £40 million.

When:	Late June/early July (Fri–Sun) N.B. dates vary and are usually announced in early January
Where:	Goodwood, Chichester, West Sussex
Duration:	3 days
Website:	www.goodwood.co.uk/fos

Pride London

A loud, proud party for people of all persuasions

FREE

Rewind to 1972, to a society where homosexuality was seen as a sordid secret: the few hundred people who marched down Oxford Street in the first UK Gay Pride Rally were confronted with bemusement, suspicion, horror and outright hostility. Fast forward three decades, and Pride has grown into one of the UK's most popular and celebratory carnivals, attracting more than half a million people of every gender and sexual persuasion.

The centrepiece of Pride London is a huge parade through London's West End. Floats, music, outrageous costumes and a vast rainbow flag make for a joyous spectacle. Around 15,000 people join the parade (you need to arrive at the start promptly at 12 noon if you want to take part), with thousands more watching from the sidelines. It's followed by an afternoon of speeches, music and other entertainment on the main stage in Trafalgar Square or, if this is insufficiently camp, a Cabaret Stage in Leicester Square – 'Drag Idol' has been a popular feature in recent years. Romilly Street hosts a women's stage with exclusively female bands, comedy and DJs. The street entertainment ends in the early evening, but there's no shortage of parties afterwards.

Pride Day is the culmination of a fortnight's festivities, with over 300 events of an LGBT, er, bent, including exhibitions, film screenings, sporting events, concerts, theatre, comedy and cabaret. There are also plenty of parties and club nights, well attended by the many gay tourists who come to London from all over the world for Pride.

When:	Last Saturday of June/first of July
Where:	London West End
Duration:	1 day
Tel:	0844 884 2439
Website:	www.pridelondon.org

Guildford Summer Festival

From fairs in the high street to Shakespeare in the castle

Guildford has a festive feel throughout July. GuilFest (see below) is the best-known event of the Guildford Summer Festival, but is only one of many things going on. There's a wide-ranging programme of music and theatre from local and visiting artists, a craft fair and farmers' market on the High Street, sporting events, walks, riverboat gatherings and the obligatory 'much more'. Other highlights include the opening carnival, outdoor Shakespeare performances in the castle grounds and an al fresco Last Night of the Proms concert. If you're in the area in July, look out for the Great Gardening Show (www.greatgardeningshow.co.uk) at Loseley House with its famous walled gardens. There are show gardens, specialist nurseries and everything from garden statues to gourmet foods.

When:	July
Where:	Guildford, Surrey
Duration:	6 weeks
Website:	www.guildfordsummerfestival.co.uk

Bognor Birdman

Those magnificent men in their flying machines...

Latter-day Icaruses take to the skies – or at least, a few feet off the end of Bognor Regis pier – in this internationally contested flying competition, which attracts crowds of 30,000. Serious competitors in elaborate flying machines regularly achieve distances of over 50 m – a £25,000 prize is on offer for the first person to pass 100 m. Others don't so much fly as, well, fall, but they do raise money for charity and their costumes add to the spectacle. Mary Poppins, the Pope, a skateboarding cow, Ninja Turtles, a Tardis and a Summersdale book are just a few who have taken a dive over the years. At the time of writing, local lad Dave Bradshaw holds the record for an 89.2-m flight in 1992.

When:	Saturday/Sunday, early July
Where:	Bognor Regis pier, Bognor Regis, West Sussex
Duration:	2 days
Tel:	01243 825535
Website:	www.birdman.org.uk

Blissfields
Laid-back vibes and friendly fun

£ £ £ £ 👤 🔺

Winner of 'Best Small Festival' at the 2007 UK Festival Awards, this relaxed rural do has now outgrown its original village setting to move to the natural amphitheatre of Matterley Bowl near Winchester (formerly home to the now sadly defunct dance gathering Homelands). There's music across four stages, including some nationally known indie names as well as great up-and-coming bands and local acts, plus late-night dance music. The atmosphere is laid back and inclusive, and camping is a joy – the campsite includes a 24-hour cafe with a small acoustic stage and a recreational open space (bring your Frisbee).

When:	First weekend of July
Where:	Matterley Bowl, Winchester, Hants.
Duration:	3 days
Website:	www.blissfields.co.uk

Henley Royal Regatta and Festival
Toff spotting, and a spot of rowing

£?

Some people come to Henley Royal Regatta to watch the rowing. It is, after all, the largest regatta in the world, and Olympic champions take to the river along with amateur rowing clubs. For many, though, the more interesting spectator sport is observing the English upper classes. First held in 1839, and enjoying royal patronage since 1851, 'the Royal' is one of the essential events of the social season. Unless you have friends in very high places, you're unlikely to be admitted to the exclusive Stewards' Enclosure on the Berkshire bank, but wherever you are, blazers, flannels and straw boaters (gents) and posh frocks (ladies) are de rigueur; women's hats, for obscure reasons, are more controversial. Pimms, G&T and champagne are the drinks of choice – often in Olympian quantities. Henley-on-Thames is a quintessentially English old town, the banks of the river are the perfect place for a picnic and strawberries (and cream) are in season. There's no better place to play at being part of the English aristocracy.

When:	First/second week of July (Weds–Sun)
Where:	Henley, Oxon.
Duration:	5 days
Tel:	01491 843404 (box office)
Website:	www.hrr.co.uk

> Don't be alarmed if somebody offers you 'duck poo' – unless you object to drinking a cheaper brand of champagne, Canard Duchêne. Canard is French for duck, poo is short for shampoo, from champagne.

South East

Henley Festival

Exquisite evenings on the Thames

Each of these five evenings of concerts has highly diverse bill, which might feature a classical recital or two, some jazz, a top comedian and some surprising world music to usher in the climactic fireworks display. You might expect this approach to lead to lowest-common-denominator line-ups, but it seldom does – the organisers have good taste, and trust their audience to appreciate the quality. The main stage floats upon the Thames and while most of the audience take their seats in the grandstand, many listen from rowing boats on the river, bringing candles and champagne with them. Henley is full of corporate entertainment packages, and an evening's entertainment doesn't come cheap – certainly not if you include an à la carte meal from Albert Roux in the Riverside restaurant. Black tie is appropriate, and smart dress is essential. A marquee and other venues host more intimate performances, while artists and strolling performers add to the magic around the festival enclosure. Various other arts events take place around the town during the week.

When:	Second week of July (Weds–Sun)
Where:	Henley, Oxon.
Duration:	5 days
Tel:	01491 843404 (box office)
Website:	www.henley-festival.co.uk

GuilFest

Big names, friendly feel

GuilFest used to be the Guildford Festival of Folk and Blues, but now covers a much wider range of musical styles across several stages (though nothing that's likely to frighten listeners of official sponsor Radio 2). In fact, it has pretty much everything you'd want from a medium-sized music festival, while retaining a friendly – and family-friendly – atmosphere. Past headliners have included A-Ha, The Pogues and Supergrass, and the music continues till 1 a.m. on the acoustic and theatre stages. Campers in particular should take advantage of the outdoor swimming lido next to the festival site.

When:	Mid-July, Fri–Sun
Where:	Stoke Park, Guildford, Surrey
Duration:	3 days
Tel:	01483 454159
Website:	www.guilfest.co.uk

Bishop's Waltham Festival

Entertainment among the palace ruins

The ruins of the twelfth-century Bishop's Waltham Palace provide a fine setting for this week-long festival, which provides a good mix of professional and community-led events. The opening Sunday is Festival Day, a family fun day including entertainment from local schools. The following Saturday is a Folk Day with a strong musical line-up, and there's an afternoon's jazz to round things off.

When:	Second week of July
Where:	Bishop's Waltham Palace, Bishop's Waltham, Hants.
Duration:	1 week
Tel:	01962 840440 (Theatre box office)
Website:	www.bishopswalthamfestival.com

Ambient Picnic

Family-friendly, eco-friendly and wallet-friendly

Lecturing people about living a greener lifestyle can be counter-productive. Putting on a lovely day of music and arts events that happens to be informative, fun and kind to the environment is a much better strategy. The four music stages at the Ambient Picnic, which range from dance to acoustic, are powered by solar, wind and alternative brown fuel generators, and all contributors and traders at the event need to pass an environmental audit. There are workshops and demonstrations of environmental innovations, a natural healing zone, a family arts area, some great craft and food stalls and local real ale from the Hogsback Brewery. The whole friendly day out, which began in 1994 as a protest against the Criminal Justice Act, is deliberately priced to be friendly on the wallet too. The site is out in the sticks – if travelling by car goes against the grain, contact the organisers to try and set up a lift-share.

When:	Second Sunday in July (12 p.m.–9 p.m.)
Where:	Hook Road Arena, Epsom, Surrey
Duration:	1 day
Tel:	01372 742555 (Booking Office)
Website:	www.ambientpicnic.co.uk

South East

Glade Festival

'12 Stages. 3 Days. Open Air. Belter.'

£ £ £ £ £

In the same way that the most popular sitcom characters sometimes spawn their own spin-off series, Glastonbury's outdoor tree-lined dance stage The Glade now has its own multi-genre, 12-stage, three-day festival. Expect cutting-edge electronic music (psytrance, gabber techno, breakcore... and a few less populist genres) from the UK and around the world, an underground spirit, total sensory stimulation and good vibes. There's on-site camping, though don't plan on getting any sleep till morning.

When:	Mid-July
Where:	Wasing Estate, Aldermaston, Newbury, Berks.
Duration:	3 days
Website:	www.gladefestival.com

Winchester Festival

Cathedral city culture

£?

No cathedral city is complete without its own mixed arts festival, and Winchester duly obliges with a summer event that mixes music (mainly classical and jazz) with literature and other events. Along with professional artists, a lot of local young musicians are involved. The concerts in the glorious cathedral are always impressive.

When:	Mid-July
Where:	Winchester, Hants.
Duration:	10–12 days
Website:	www.winchesterfestival.co.uk

South East

Rathayatra

Hare Krishna!

Dating back more than 2,000 years, Rathayatra is a festival dedicated to the Hindu deity Krishna. The Lord Krishna in his most merciful form, Jagannatha, is pulled along in a giant wooden chariot, flanked by attendant deities in two other chariots. Ecstatic crowds sing, dance, play cymbals and drums and chant *Hare Krishna* as they follow the procession from Hyde Park to Trafalgar Square. Music, a stage show and a free vegetarian feast follow. In Orissa in India, the festival attracts pilgrims by the million. The UK version is smaller, but is still a joyful spectacle. After London it visits other UK cities including Leicester, Cardiff and Birmingham, as well as overseas.

When:	Third Saturday in July
Where:	Trafalgar Square, London
Duration:	1 day
Website:	www.rathayatra.co.uk

Lovebox Weekender

Join the Groove Armada

Lovebox began life in the early noughties as a Groove Armada club residency in London. Since then, the duo have taken their party around the country, and this two-day open-air event is its celebratory climax. There's a far wider range of musical styles in evidence than you might expect from a dance music event – Flaming Lips, the B-52s, Gogol Bordello and the Super Furry Animals have all played in the past. A Lovebox Weekender now runs concurrently in Dublin, and plans for world domination are coming along nicely.

When:	Third weekend of July (Sat/Sun)
Where:	Victoria Park, London
Duration:	2 days
Website:	www.loveboxweekender.com

Whitstable Oyster Festival

Oysters, arts and a blessing from St James

Long before it was 'discovered' by second-home-owning London foodies, Whitstable was famous for its oysters. The origins of the Oyster Festival go back at least a thousand years. An annual festival of thanksgiving would be held on 25 July – the feast day of St James of Compostela, patron saint of oysters – and the catch, the fishing fleet and the whole town would receive a blessing. The landing and blessing of the catch remains a central part of this nine-day summer festival; the oysters are delivered by horse-drawn cart to some of Whitstable's excellent restaurants, and there are many opportunities to sample them. Oysters apart, there's a strong programme of cultural and community events outdoors at the excellent Horsebridge Arts Centre, the Whitstable Playhouse and other venues around the town.

When:	Late July (starting the weekend nearest to St James' Day/25 July)
Where:	Whitstable, Kent
Duration:	9 days
Tel:	01227 862267
Website:	www.whitstableoysterfestival.co.uk

New Malden Korean Festival

Korea opportunities

Around 40,000 Korean people live in Britain – half of them in the London suburb of New Malden. The Korean Residents Society organises this annual free festival, the best display of Korean culture you're likely to find anywhere in Europe. Attractions include traditional music and dance with colourful costumes and fans, as well as more modern styles, tae kwon do bouts and a traditional Korean wedding pageant. There's also a mouth-watering array of food stalls cooking up Korean cuisine.

When:	Last Saturday of July
Where:	Fairfield Recreation Ground, Kingston-upon-Thames, London
Duration:	1 day
Tel:	020 8547 5757
Website:	www.kingston.gov.uk

Sundae on the Common

Live music, fairground attractions and all the ice cream you can eat

[£?] [👤]

Loveable multimillionaire hippie ice cream magnates Ben and Jerry lay on this two-day event on Clapham Common promising Peace, Love and Ice Cream. Tickets are a virtual giveaway given the strength of the musical line-up, and there's plenty of free ice cream as well as fairground attractions and live farm animals. And all the proceeds go to charity. And did we mention the free ice cream?

When:	Last weekend of July (Sat/Sun)
Where:	Clapham Common, London
Duration:	2 days
Tel:	01753 834034
Website:	www.benjerry.co.uk/sundae

Glorious Goodwood

The social set's South Downs garden party

[£?]

Edward VII described Glorious Goodwood as 'a garden party with racing tacked on', and a hundred years later the description holds true. The hilltop racecourse with stunning views across the South Downs and, on a clear day, over to the Isle of Wight is arguably the most picturesque in the world. The flat racing is fast and hard-fought, but most people come for the garden party side of things. Glorious Goodwood is one of the essential highlights of the English social season, but you don't have to belong to high society to enjoy it – just pretend you do. To blend in, it's linen suits and panama hats for gentlemen, pretty frocks and not-overly-ostentatious hats for the ladies (this isn't Ascot, darling). Blow your winnings on champagne to complete the effect.

When:	Goodwood, Chichester, West Sussex
Where:	End of July–beginning of August (Tues–Sat)
Duration:	5 days
Tel:	01243 755000
Website:	www.goodwood.co.uk/horseracing

Wickham Festival

Safe, friendly, pretty, folky, wonderful Wickham

£ £ £ £   👤   ⛺

The beautiful village of Wickham in the Hampshire downs provides an idyllic setting for this weekend folk festival. Gigs take place on farmland on the village outskirts, with some big folk-rock names (the likes of The Saw Doctors, Levellers and Show of Hands), an acoustic stage and chill-out zone, as well as craft stalls, real ale bars and an international food fair. Dancing and street entertainment (including children's entertainers) also spill into the streets and Georgian market square of Wickham, which is well stocked with excellent restaurants and bistros, tea rooms and country pubs. There's camping next to the main festival site, and B&Bs and other accommodation in the area.

When: First weekend of August (Thurs–Sun)
Where: Wickham, Fareham, Hants.
Duration: 4 days
Website: www.wickhamfestival.co.uk

Pride in Brighton and Hove

Proud to be Britain's gay capital

FREE

Brighton revels in the title of Britain's gay capital, and its huge, free August Pride festival is exactly the sort of camp, kitsch, colourful, creative, crazy carnival you'd hope for. It's not just enjoyed by Brighton's 40,000-strong LGBT community and gay people from across the country, either – tens of thousands of straight local people dress up and join in the fun. The Saturday parade is the highlight of ten days of festivities. It sets off from Madeira Drive on the seafront at 11 a.m., reaching Preston Park about an hour later – there are usually around 40 floats, designed around an annual theme (musicals, heroes and heroines, Carry On). Professional carnival arts company Same Sky runs workshops from groups who want to get involved, providing advice, ideas and access to materials and equipment. Stalls, funfair rides and other entertainment continue in Preston Park till 8 p.m., after which there's no shortage of party possibilities in Kemp Town and across the city. Accommodation gets booked up well ahead, but the council runs a basic campsite in East Brighton Park over the weekend of the parade.

When: First Saturday of August (parade)
Where: Preston Park, Brighton, East Sussex
Duration: 10 days
Tel: 01273 775939
Website: www.brightonpride.org

Cowes Week

High society messing around on boats

The oldest sailing regatta in the world, first held in 1826, Cowes Week is also one of the UK's biggest sporting and social events. As part of the 'social season', it's traditionally held between the end of Glorious Goodwood and the beginning of the grouse shooting season. There are 1,000-odd boats and 8,500 competitors taking part, ranging from Olympic medallists to weekend sailors, and 100,000 onlookers pack the shore or get up close to the action on spectator boats. As well as the racing, there are opportunities for beginners to try sailing, street entertainment, live music and much partying, including the renowned Yacht Club Balls. The atmosphere, on and off the water, is unique.

When: First week of August
Where: Cowes, Isle of Wight
Duration: 1 week
Website: www.skandiacowesweek.co.uk

Great British Beer Festival

'The biggest pub in the world'

For the ale enthusiast, this annual CAMRA (Campaign for Real Ale) shindig is heaven come to Earl's Court. There are over 700 British and foreign beers, ciders and perries to choose from, and some 66,000 visitors quaff 350,000 pints over the course of the week. Beer at the festival is competitively priced, and you can sample a wider selection by drinking 'nips' (third-pint measures). The opening Tuesday afternoon, for trade and press only, is when the Champion Beer of Britain awards take place. As well as the prestigious gold, silver and bronze medals, there are awards for different styles of beers, like bitters, milds and golden ales.

When: First week of August
Where: Earl's Court, London
Duration: 5 days
Website: www.camra.org.uk

Rewind to the 1970s, and British beer was in a parlous state. All too often, drinkers faced a Hobson's choice of identikit gassy lagers or bland keg bitters mass produced in factory breweries. The formation of CAMRA – the Campaign for Real Ale – in 1971 helped to revitalise British brewing traditions, and in 1977 they organised the first Great British Beer Festival at Alexandra Palace. Since then, beer festivals have multiplied – as have artisan microbreweries producing authentic real ales of genuine character. Britain now boasts more than 500 microbreweries, from Scilly to Shetland. You can sample their beers at the numerous festivals put on by local branches of CAMRA, pubs, student unions, rugby clubs and many other organisations.

Balloons over Basingstoke

Airborne and arena spectacles

The Hampshire skies come alive for this popular hot air balloon festival, the biggest event in Basingstoke's calendar. Over 50,000 come along to watch the mass balloon launches in the early mornings and evenings and the Night Glow (a spectacular balloon light show) on the Friday night. There are numerous daytime arena events, ranging from sky diving to dog displays.

When:	First weekend of August
Where:	War Memorial Park, Basingstoke, Hants.
Duration:	3 days
Tel:	01256 844844

Carnaval del Pueblo

London goes Latin

Can't make it to Rio? You'll find the next best thing in Southwark, which is now home to the biggest Latin American event in Europe. This free carnival is the highpoint of the year for Latino London, and attracts around 130,000 people of all backgrounds. The carnival procession, featuring floats and performers from 19 Latin American countries, sets out from London City Hall at noon and passes through London Bridge and Elephant and Castle before reaching Burgess Park around three hours later. Entertainment in the park goes on well into the evening. There's live music across four stations from some of Latin America's biggest stars as well as many London and Europe-based bands, and an open salsa dancing championships. A children's zone includes workshops, bouncy castles and funfair rides, and there are dozens of stalls selling food and drink and arts and crafts from Latin America and the Caribbean.

When:	First Sunday in August
Where:	Burgess Park, Southwark, London
Duration:	1 day
Tel:	020 7686 1633
Website:	www.carnavaldelpueblo.co.uk

Electric Gardens

Mount Ephraim's rock 'n' roll garden party

£ £ £ £ [A]

The garden of England gets its own garden festival at Mount Ephraim, a privately owned stately home seven miles from Canterbury (are stately homes the new rock 'n' roll?) Enjoy 800 acres of landscaped-gardens, orchards, woodland and fields – a great country setting for a discerning rock-indie-dance line-up. Numbers are limited to 10,000 a day (camp if you can – it's a great place for it) and the local food and drink is a treat.

> **When:** First weekend of August
> **Where:** Mount Ephraim, Faversham, Kent
> **Duration:** 2 days
> **Website:** www.electricgardensfestival.com

Broadstairs Folk Week

Bring guitar, dancing shoes, bucket and spade

£ £ £ £ £ [†] [A]

Broadstairs, with its horseshoe bay, sandy beaches, steep streets, cafe culture and slightly faded Victorian grandeur, bandstands and pavilions, is pretty much the perfect English seaside resort. For August's Folk Week, the whole place reverberates with music and dancing feet, as almost every pub, restaurant, church or cafe hosts concerts, sessions or singarounds. There are headline acts in the 500-seat marquee in Pierremont Park (with beer tent attached), ceilidhs, Cajun, zydeco and salsa till 1 a.m. in the Pavilion on the Sands which overlooks the harbour, while Hobby Horses and Clarence the Dragon take over the Bandstand. There's a large craft fair, plenty of traditional dancing and workshops for all ages. Season ticket holders can stay in the lively campsite, ten minutes' walk from the town centre.

> **When:** Second week of July
> **Where:** Broadstairs, Kent
> **Duration:** 1 week
> **Tel:** 01843 604080
> **Website:** www.broadstairsfolkweek.org.uk

Herne Bay Festival

Join the East Kent giants and brush up on your sandcastle building

This community festival begins with an impressive opening procession: the March of the Giants. The East Kent Giants, enormous puppets created by local people working with community arts company Strange Cargo, include Harry from Hawkinge, Flora from Singleton and John Drury from Sandwich as well as Herne Bay's own Lily. Herne Bay Rocks showcases the buzzing local music scene, and there's plenty of traditional seaside fun down on the beach, including Punch and Judy and sandcastle competitions. There are many free events, others are individually priced.

When:	Mid-August
Where:	Herne Bay, Kent
Duration:	10 days
Tel:	01227 862201
Website:	www.hernebayfestival.co.uk

Hythe Venetian Fete

Venice comes to England

Every two years, the Royal Military Canal in the historic Cinque Ports town of Hythe is transformed into Venice's Grand Canal at carnival time. OK, not exactly, but the Venetian Fete, held intermittently since 1869, is a fine spectacle, as a parade of impressive tableaux floats past – once in the daylight, and once, illuminated, after dark. There are various other entertainments, including magicians, music from concert bands and a fireworks display. The best seats are on the North Bank; the sea side is cheaper.

When:	Third Wednesday in August, alternate (odd) years
Where:	Royal Military Canal, Hythe, Kent
Duration:	1 day
Tel:	01303 269633
Website:	www.venetian-fete.com

In the even years, between Venetian Fetes, Hythe hosts a festival in the first week of July, with concerts, sporting events, talks, walks, exhibitions and other events, mostly organised by the local community. Most events are free: see www.hythe-festival.com.

Isle of Wight Garlic Festival

Not suitable for vampires, and not recommended for first dates either

Fancy trying garlic ice cream, garlic fudge or garlic beer? No? Well, fair enough, but even for the less gastronomically adventurous, the Isle of Wight Garlic Festival is a fun, family-friendly weekend. As well as all sorts of garlic-infused local food, there's live music (Noddy Holder even wrote a song especially for the festival), falconry and general country-fair fun. Farmer Colin Boswell first grew garlic commercially on the island in the 1970s, and it's now a highly prized export, even used in the restaurants of Paris.

When:	Third weekend of August
Where:	Newchurch, Isle of Wight
Duration:	2 days
Tel:	01983 863566
Website:	www.garlic-festival.co.uk

V Festival

Corporate but quality

The 'V' stands for Richard Branson's Virgin group, and this is as slick and commercial as festivals come, well stocked with mobile phone charge points and unlikely to cause many spiritual epiphanies. That's not altogether a bad thing, though – it's a well-organised affair, with a clean, non-threatening feel. It was also the first festival to be held simultaneously in two locations, Chelmsford and Staffordshire, with the same bands, give or take, playing on alternate days. It always attracts a decent line-up, with a sprinkling of poppier headliners (Girls Aloud, McFly) to spice up the usual indie suspects on the two main stages, along with the edgier third stage and a new bands tent.

When:	Penultimate weekend of August
Where:	Hylands Park, Chelmsford, Essex; Weston Park, Staffs.
Duration:	2 days
Website:	www.vfestival.com

South East

167

Arundel Festival

Concerts under castle walls

A proper castle, a cathedral, a river, fine houses on a hill and a hive of antiques shops and tea rooms make the Sussex town of Arundel an irresistible setting for this late-summer festival. Open-air concerts (look out for *X Factor* contestants, Classic FM favourites and bands who were big in the 1980s) and opera in the castle grounds are a highlight (bring a posh picnic). The concurrent fringe features a popular 'open house' Gallery Trail and the Theatre Trail, with ten short plays performed in various venues around the town every hour.

When:	Last week of August/August Bank Holiday
Where:	Arundel, various venues
Duration:	5 days
Tel:	0871 472 0414 (Booking line)
Websites:	www.arundelfestival.co.uk
Fringe:	www.arundelfestival.org.uk

Ryde Carnival

Cosmopolitan carnival on the Isle of Wight

More than 20 villages across the Isle of Wight stage carnivals over the summer, but the biggest and best is undoubtedly the Ryde Carnival. First held for Queen Victoria's Golden Jubilee in 1887, it's kept itself fresh by taking on influences from around the world – Rio, Trinidad, Notting Hill, New Orleans and Venice all feed into the original English masquerade. Thursday is the main procession, Friday is children's carnival and there's an illuminated procession on Saturday evening. Over 2,000 performers take part, and around 45,000 visitors come to watch.

When:	Last weekend of August (Thurs–Sat)
Where:	Ryde, Isle of Wight
Duration:	3 days
Website:	www.rydecarnival.co.uk

Reading Festival
Get ready to mosh in indie-rock heaven

£ £ £ £ £ ▲

If your idea of festival heaven is getting tanked up on Carling and moshing to the biggest names in alternative rock in a muddy field – and if you're 18, it probably is – then Reading is hard to beat. There's plenty here for the more discerning festival-goer too, though. Although Reading has a heavy-rock history, for years now it's catered more to the indie scene. The musical line-up is always first class, and with four main stages you certainly won't be short of options. There's also a comedy tent, a cinema and plenty of smaller cafes and tents with music and DJs. Choose your campsite carefully: the Village in the Purple Campsite is the place to keep on partying, with cafes, juice bars and shops open 23 hours (although the Silent Disco doesn't make much noise). Alternatively, there's the Quiet Campsite, with a free shuttle boat service. Since 1999, the Reading Festival has been successfully cloned in Leeds.

When:	August Bank Holiday weekend
Where:	Richfield Avenue, Reading, Berks.
Duration:	3 days
Website:	www.readingfestival.com

Reading crowds have a charming tradition of throwing bottles, often with unsavoury contents, at unpopular performers: a fate that's befallen the likes of Meatloaf, Daphne and Celeste, 50 Cent and My Chemical Romance over the years.

Twinwood Festival
It don't mean a thing if it ain't got that swing

£?

Twinwood Airfield is home to the Glenn Miller museum, and this festival is heaven for Glenn Miller fans: three days of easy listening orchestras, big bands, 1940s songs, jive, bebop, boogie-woogie, early rock 'n' roll... It attracts some of the best in the business, and there's a dance marquee, aircraft hangar dances, a 1940s/50s hair and beauty salon, exhibitions and a jazz bar to add to the atmosphere.

When:	August Bank Holiday weekend
Where:	Twinwood Arena and Airfield, Clapham, nr Bedford, Beds.
Duration:	3 days
Tel:	01923 282725
Website:	www.glennmillerfestival.com

Notting Hill Carnival

Europe's biggest street party

FREE

Not so long ago, the Notting Hill Carnival was seen by much of white Britain as a cradle of vice, drugs and crime. Several times in the 1970s it descended into rioting between hyped-up revellers and a heavy-handed police force riddled with institutional racism. The fact that it's now widely regarded as a British icon, a key date in the cultural calendar and a truly multicultural event is in itself cause for celebration.

The Carnival began life as an indoor event in 1959 as a community response to the UK's first race riots, which had broken out in Notting Hill the previous summer. By the 1970s it was attracting crowds of around 150,000. It was – as it still is – strongly influenced by the incredible Trinidad Carnival. Even before being brought to Britain, the Trinidadian carnival tradition was the heady product of a cultural melting pot, blending the pre-Lenten carnival of Catholic European colonisers with the rituals, rhythms, dancing and feathered headdresses of the African slaves.

Notting Hill Carnival today is the largest event of its kind in Europe, with as many as two million revellers taking to the streets. It features an incredible parade of spectacular floats, which winds for three miles through the streets of Ladbroke Grove. Countless people 'play mas' (masquerade) in extravagant costumes (even if you're not going to wear full-on carnival dress, you should at least buy a silly hat and a whistle). Steel-pan bands, calypso and soca music, the traditional Trinidadian soundtrack, remain an essential part of the experience. These days, though, there's a variety of other live music, while more than 40 static sound systems pump out reggae, dub, hip-hop, R&B, funk, samba and all manner of other rhythms, each one creating a distinctive party-within-the-party. Stalls line the streets, rum punch and Red Stripe flow freely, and wafts of jerk chicken, fried plantain and rice and peas set the taste buds tingling.

The Carnival wouldn't be what it is without the all-pervasive aroma of ganja wafting through the air, but despite (or possibly because of) this, crime and aggravation are low for a gathering of more than a million people. Families or people who can't stand crowds might be better off visiting on Children's Day (Sunday), which still boasts a spectacular procession but is less crowded (only around half a million people) and more overtly family-friendly.

When:	August Bank Holiday Monday
Where:	Notting Hill, London W11
Duration:	1 day
Website:	www.londoncarnival.co.uk

Rhythm Festival

Boutique festival in a natural amphitheatre

£ £ £ £ [figure] [figure]

The venue's a good start: a grassy, tree-lined amphitheatre. Events take place all year round at the Twinwood Arena, so facilities are excellent (Flush toilets! Showers!). Add two stages with quality music, plus comedy and folk stages, healing fields offering massage and all sorts of holistic stuff, a great kids' play area and a solar-powered cinema showing classic comedies, and it's not hard to see why the discerning crowd, limited to 5,000, rates the Rhythm Festival so highly.

When:	Twinwood Arena, Clapham, Bucks.
Where:	Last weekend of August
Duration:	3 days
Website:	www.rhythmfestival.net

Weyfest

As rural as rural gets

£ £ £ £ [figure] [figure]

This is a friendly and relaxed little weekender deep in the heart of rural Surrey – so rural, in fact, that it's actually held in a Rural Life Centre that features reconstructed historical buildings and over 40,000 rural artefacts from the past two centuries. It's a lovely venue, and you may even get a chance to ride the Old Kiln Light Railway. In between the museum browsing you can enjoy music across two outdoor stages and an indoor acoustic one. The music aims to offer something for everyone – all generations frequent the festival. Artists range from quality are-they-really-still-going? bands from the 1960s (Jethro Tull, Nashville Teens) to unsigned singer-songwriters. There's a Sunday afternoon car boot sale, plenty of food and craft stalls, children's entertainment (a travelling fairy grotto!) and on-site camping.

When:	First weekend of September
Where:	The Rural Life Centre, Tilford, Farnham, Surrey
Duration:	2 days
Website:	www.weyfest.co.uk

Rye Arts Festival

Discover why artists love Rye

The medieval port of Rye, with its balmy microclimate and gorgeous light, has long been a haven for artists and writers. Henry James wrote here, and the Flemish painter Van Dyck was a regular visitor. Its arts festival has established itself as one of the best small festivals on the calendar. There's a diverse mix of music, from classical to folk and blues, a stellar literary line-up and comedy and theatre, including events at the Barn Theatre at Smallhythe Place, once home to Ellen Terry. Rye's many art galleries host special exhibitions over the course of the festival, and there's also a fringe programme including free concerts, craft shows and outdoor family events.

When:	Beginning of September
Where:	Rye and surrounds, East Sussex
Duration:	2 weeks
Tel:	01797 224442 (Booking office)
Website:	www.ryefestival.co.uk

Bestival

A parallel universe on the other side of the Solent

Some people think the Isle of Wight is stuck in a 1950s time warp. If Bestival is anything to go by, however, it exists in some parallel future. It's not just the finger-on-the-pulse musical line-up put together by Radio 1 DJ Rob Da Bank – the whole experience is magically mad. Fancy dress is de rigueur – 2005 set the world record for the Biggest Fancy Dress Party, with 10,000 Cowboys and Indians – check this year's theme before you go. Other attractions include Club Dada, the Bollywood Bar, a beard and moustache championship and various punning areas (Breastival for new mothers, Restival to relax and recharge with hammocks, lanterns, chai, cake and poetry). Don't miss the famous Hidden Disco – top DJs in a tiny tent, but you'll have to find it for yourself. Robin Hill Country Park isn't just a pretty woodland setting, either – kids of all ages can enjoy rides, mazes, tunnels, miniature villages and other attractions which take on a surreal feel in a festival context. For a little luxury, you can hire a Bohemian Bivouac, Tipi, Yurt, Beach Hut, BusBed or PodPad at the boutique campsite. No surprise really that festival-goers have voted Bestival the Best Medium Sized Festival at the UK Festival Awards for three years running.

When:	Second weekend of September
Where:	Robin Hill Country Park, Isle of Wight
Duration:	3 days
Tel:	020 7379 3133
Website:	www.bestival.net

Thames Festival

A great way to end the summer

FREE

The Mayor's Thames Festival is one of a number of contenders claiming to be 'London's greatest free party'. So what's its claim based on? Well, there are two days of open-air arts, pyrotechnics, illuminations, street theatre, massed choirs, music, crafts and fantastic food. Past events have included high-wire walking across the Thames, al fresco ballrooms, floating stages in the river, themed banquets on Southwark Bridge and a night carnival. Streets and bridges are closed to traffic and transformed, and festival-goers are encouraged to participate rather than spectate. As free parties go, it does take some beating.

When:	Second weekend of September (Sat/Sun)
Where:	Along the Thames from Tower Bridge to Westminster Bridge
Duration:	2 days
Tel:	020 7928 8998
Website:	www.thamesfestival.org

Windsor Festival

Exclusive entertainment in Windsor and Eton

£?

Founded in 1969, with Yehudi Menuhin as an artistic adviser, the Windsor Festival has a strong line-up of choral, orchestral and chamber music, as well as opera, jazz, literature and film. There are also organised walks and tours, and events for families. A large part of the attraction is in the venues, which provide opportunities to snoop around Windsor Castle and Eton College. Friends and benefactors enjoy exclusive access to the Dungeon Club, and exclusive and atmospheric temporary bistro in the dungeon of Curfew Tower in Windsor Castle.

When:	Last two weeks of September
Where:	Windsor and Eton
Duration:	2 weeks
Tel:	01753 714364
Website:	www.windsorfestival.com

Isle of Wight Folk and Blues Festival

The spirit of 1968 lives on in Ventnor

As if the Isle of Wight didn't already have an embarrassment of festivals, here's a 'relaxed, rambling weekend' of folk and blues, old and new. Set in and around Ventor, the island's hippest town, it harks back to the first Isle of Wight Festival in 1968, both in its non-corporate feel and strong, diverse line-up. 'Rambler tickets', for the day or weekend, allow you access to all venues; you can also buy tickets for individual concerts or take in open-mic sessions at the free entry Folk and Blues Village. There's no on-site camping, so you'll need to sort out your own accommodation.

When:	Third weekend of September
Where:	Ventnor, Isle of Wight
Duration:	3 days
Tel:	01983 856200
Website:	www.iowfolkblues.co.uk

Goodwood Revival

A celebration of the glory days of motor racing

The Revival features hundreds of gorgeous classic racing and sports cars from the 1950s and before. It's far more than just a motoring event though. The organisers go to huge lengths to create the authentic period detail (even the plants around the grounds are native species to avoid any anachronistic imports). The air displays feature Spitfires and Hurricanes, there's a traditional funfair and old-fashioned catering stalls. Participants and visitors dress in the fashions of the 1950s and early 1960s, making the whole weekend a fantastic piece of theatre.

When:	Late September (Fri–Sun)
Where:	Goodwood, Chichester, West Sussex
Duration:	3 days
Website:	www.goodwood.co.uk/revival

Moon Lantern Festival

Moonlit traditional celebration in the heart of Chinatown

[£?] [🚶]

This is the other big event in the Chinatown calendar, coming eight lunar months after Chinese New Year, when the full moon is at its brightest. Also known as the Mid-Autumn Festival Celebration, it usually falls around late September, and is a legacy of ancient Chinese moon worship dating back several millennia. Expect dragons, lions and vast red and gold lantern displays, as well as stalls and performances by Chinese artists. There are lantern- and fan-making workshops and Chinese painting sessions for children.

When:	Around late September
Where:	Chinatown, London W1
Duration:	1 day
Tel:	020 7851 6686
Website:	www.chinatownchinese.co.uk

Costermongers Pearly Harvest Festival

See the costermongers out in all their finery

[FREE] [🚶]

Cockney costermongers were originally apple-sellers, though the name came to apply to other street traders. Though poor, they demonstrated their pride through charitable work and by decorating their clothes with mother-of-pearl buttons. In 1875, a young orphan costermonger called Henry Croft took the idea a stage further. He collected enough buttons to cover a whole suit, which he wore as he collected tirelessly for charity, and persuaded other costermongers to join him. Before long every London borough had its own 'Pearly Family' – a bit like the mafia, only dedicated to charitable works and with better outfits. The Pearly Harvest Festival is a chance to see all the pearly royalty in their flamboyant finery as they parade through the streets to gather for a service of thanksgiving in the Church of St Martin-in-the-Fields.

When:	First Sunday in October
Where:	St Martin-in-the-Fields, Trafalgar Square, London WC2
Duration:	1 day

South East

Raindance Film Festival

Celebrating independent British cinema

The Sundance Festival, in Utah, is the leading independent film festival in the US. You might expect Raindance, its British equivalent, to be a poor relation, and when it was first held, in 1993, British film-making was certainly in a parlous state. Since then, though, it's played an inspirational part in the British film revival, giving a big career boost to the likes of Christopher Nolan (*Memento*) and Shane Meadows. *Pulp Fiction* and *The Blair Witch Project* are among the notable films to have their British premieres here. With dozens of features and even more shorts from the UK and around the world, plus masterclasses and panel discussions, there's far more original film-making to be found here than in any multiplex. It's not a festival about big stars (though there's a fair few around) – but you may find yourself sharing a drink with the stars of the future.

When:	Beginning of October
Where:	Cineworld, Haymarket/Cineworld, Shaftesbury Avenue/Rex Cinema, Rupert Street, London
Duration:	12 days
Tel:	0207 287 3833
Website:	www.raindance.co.uk

Dance Umbrella

Keeping the dance establishment on its toes

Dance Umbrella has been at the forefront of the vibrant contemporary dance scene for 30 years, and their annual festival is widely regarded as one of the most important dance festivals in the world. Performers range from established names to exciting new talents, but all are pushing the boundaries of performance possibilities (this isn't a place for tutus and pirouettes). Venues include Sadler's Wells, the Barbican and the Southbank Centre, while recent festivals have also included free outdoor events. Talks, films and installations run alongside the performance programme.

When:	October
Where:	London, various venues
Duration:	6 weeks
Tel:	020 8741 4040
Website:	www.danceumbrella.co.uk

Guildford Book Festival

A diverse line-up, and half-term fodder for young bookworms

[£?] [🚶]

The Guildford Book Festival celebrates the written word in all its forms over two weeks at the end of October. The varied line-up includes best-selling authors, comedians, broadcasters and crime writers. During half-term week, there's a packed children's programme, including storytelling sessions, workshops and interactive events.

When:	End of October
Where:	Guildford
Duration:	2 weeks
Website:	www.guildfordbookfestival.co.uk

London Film Festival

The best films from the best film festivals

[£?]

The UK's largest public film event, the London Film Festival, offers a choice of 300 films from 60 countries. Although it's attended by numerous industry insiders, and always unearths a few new gems, the festival is aimed at the general public. It's been described as a 'festival of festivals', presenting films from Venice, Cannes, Berlin and elsewhere that might not otherwise receive a cinema release in the UK. Cinephiles particularly enjoy the question-and-answer sessions with actors, directors, writers and other people involved with the film that follows many of the screenings. Professional liggers head for the opening and closing gala performances.

When:	End of October
Where:	London, various cinemas
Duration:	2 weeks
Tel:	020 7255 1444
Website:	www.bfi.org.uk/lff

Lewes Fire Festival

Twisted firestarters

FREE

Some towns are content to celebrate 5 November with a fireworks display and a bonfire. Not Lewes. The East Sussex town is home to a spectacular and slightly scary festival of fire. Seven local bonfire societies organise their own fires, and many more from across Sussex join in flamboyant flame-filled processions through the streets, going to great lengths to create the most impressive costumes and dramatic tableaux. As well as celebrating the uncovering of the Gunpowder Plot, Bonfire Night in Lewes commemorates 17 protestant martyrs who were burnt at the stake in the town during the reign of Bloody Mary. Seventeen flaming crosses are carried through the streets in their memory. Effigies of Pope Paul V (the Pontiff at the time of the plot) are still burnt alongside Guy Fawkes and more contemporary hate figures. Another grizzly feature is the display of heads of 'Enemies of Bonfire' impaled on pikes, and a flaming barrel is ceremonially dumped into the River Ouse (the fate that befell the magistrates who tried to stop the 'bonfire boys' having their fun back in 1847).

There are several organised fireworks displays, but firecrackers are often let off in the streets too. There's a genuinely anarchic streak which is all too rare these days, and unexpected in a little county town in Sussex. Around 80,000 people crowd into Lewes for the night, which means the town really is full, and outsiders aren't particularly welcome (though many inevitably show up). The event is certainly not recommended for young children.

When:	5 November
Where:	Lewes, East Sussex
Duration:	1 day
Website:	www.lewesbonfirecouncil.org.uk

Bonfire societies are active all over East Sussex, and neighbouring parts of Kent and West Sussex. Towns and villages across the region from Rye to Littlehampton have impressive carnivals with torchlit processions, fancy dress ('Red Indians' are popular, for obscure reasons), big bonfires and firework displays. They tend to take place on different nights, rather than close to 5 November, as members of the various societies travel to join in each others' events. While none are on the scale of Lewes, many offer a more family-friendly atmosphere.

Bachfest

The best of J. S. Bach

 £?

The London Bach Society has been promoting live performances of the music of J. S. Bach for over 60 years, and the annual Bachfest is a highlight of their programme. The festival, featuring the music of Bach and his contemporaries, has plenty to delight Bach fanatics – often including unusual works and period instruments – as well as curious newcomers.

When:	Mid-November
Where:	Various venues, London
Duration:	10 days
Tel:	01883 717372
Website:	www.bachlive.co.uk

St Ceciliatide International Festival of Music

Celebrating the patron saint of music

 £?

St Cecilia is the patron saint of music, and her feast day (22 November) is marked with this six-day celebration at the Stationers' Hall in the City of London – a grand old livery hall little changed from when Henry Purcell performed here in the 1690s. Orchestra-in-residence Fiori Musicali and other world-class performers present a series of evening concerts, including a canapé reception, champagne in the interval and the option of a full-blown banquet afterwards. There are also daytime recitals, choral works at nearby St Bride's Church and the prestigious St Cecilia lecture.

When:	Around St Cecilia's Day (22 November)
Where:	Stationers' Hall, Ave Maria Lane, London EC4
Duration:	6 days
Tel:	01327 360931 (box office)
Website:	www.st-ceciliatide.com

Haddenham Festival

Bound to keep you on your toes

For four decades, the Buckinghamshire village of Haddenham has run ceilidhs (deluxe barn dances with extra music and song), usually on the first Saturday of the month. The December ceilidh has now grown into a day-long festival, complete with carols and a real ale bar. Hugh Rippon, one of the best callers in the country, keeps the dancers on their toes.

When: First Saturday in December
Where: Haddenham Village Hall, Haddenham, Aylesbury, nr Bucks.
Duration: 1 day
Tel: 01296 485995
Website: www.haddenhamceilidhs.co.uk

London New Year's Eve

See in the New Year with a bang

Since the Millennium, London has been going in for New Year's Eve in a big way. Trafalgar Square is the traditional street party venue, and gets hugely crowded. Recently, the London Eye has become the focus of the night thanks to a jaw-droppingly amazing fireworks display after Big Ben chimes. To give you some idea of the scale, a team of 30 pyrotechnicians were working from Boxing Day onwards for the 2007/8 event, and fireworks were detonated from three barges moored on the Thames, as well as on the Eye itself. The ten-minute display costs more than £100,000 a minute. Waterloo and Westminster Bridges and the north embankment are the best places to watch, but get very crowded, you'll need to arrive by 9 p.m. to be sure of a place. Because of their scale and height, though, the fireworks can be seen from high ground all over London. Public transport is free (Free! In London!) all night, although the most congested stations, like Trafalgar Square, are closed. The New Year's Day Parade is one of the largest of its kind, with 10,000 performers and around a million spectators (there's ticket-only seating at the start and end of the route). The two-mile route starts off in Parliament Square, Westminster, and heads via Whitehall, Trafalgar Square, Regent Street and Piccadilly to Green Park.

When: New Year's Eve/New Year's Day
Where: Trafalgar Square/South Bank, London
Website: www.london.gov.uk/newyearseve

Wales

Llanwrtyd Wells Saturnalia

Don't forget your toga

At the Roman winter festival of Saturnalia, slaves reversed roles with their masters in a riot of misrule and indulgence. Something of that anarchic spirit lives on in Llanwrtyd Wells, with this delightfully silly festival of food and fun. The warming winter beers, Roman-themed wines and even the lethal Absinthium Romanum are needed to wash down some of the traditional Roman recipes. *Lumbuli Assi Ita Fiunt*, anyone? (Though if you don't like lambs' testicles, there is more palatable fare on the menu too.) Other events include bike chariot racing (teams of three – two on bikes pulling one in the chariot) and rambling in the Cambrian mountains.

When:	Second Saturday in January
Where:	Llanwrtyd Wells, Powys
Duration:	1 day
Website:	www.llanwrtyd-wells.powys.org.uk

St David's Day

The feast day of the patron saint of Wales, on 1 March, has been a festival for centuries. Traditionally, children had the day off school, and although it's no longer an official holiday, many schools close so children can show off their singing, dancing, musicianship and recitation skills in *eisteddfodau*. Parades are held across the country – the largest is in Cardiff – and while only a few people dress up in traditional costume, the Welsh emblems, the leek and the daffodil, are ubiquitous. In a recent poll, 87 per cent of Welsh people wanted St David's Day to be a Bank Holiday, with most of them happy to sacrifice an existing day off instead.

Llandudno Victorian Extravaganza

Pretend to be a nineteenth-century European aristocrat

Purpose-built in 1850, Llandudno was once a chic resort for the European aristocracy, with the likes of Napoleon III and Otto von Bismarck coming to north Wales to take the waters – though the bucket-and-spade brigades soon moved in from Cheshire and Merseyside. Now every May, street entertainers, town criers and steam organs fill the street while elegantly dressed Victorians stroll along the promenade for this popular Victorian Extravaganza. There's a daily midday carnival parade, and all sorts of Victorian entertainment on offer (with a few anachronistic extras), as well as an extensive vintage transport festival, featuring traction engines and the earliest motor cars and omnibuses.

When:	May Day Bank Holiday weekend (Sat–Mon)
Where:	Llandudno, Conwy, North Wales
Duration:	3 days
Website:	www.victorian-extravaganza.co.uk

Eisteddfod Yr Urdd

Come and hear the bards and minstrels of the future

The youth eisteddfod is one of the largest young people's festivals in Europe, with 15,000 competitors aged 7–24, an audience of 100,000 and another million watching on TV. Classes range from recitations and folk dancing to rock songs, disco dancing (strictly to a Welsh-language soundtrack) and original drama, art, design and technology. The event moves around different areas of Wales, although it comes back to Cardiff every four years. On the *maes* (field), there are the usual stalls and crafts, as well as workshops, sporting events, funfair rides and a climbing wall. Camping and caravan sites are available for the week.

When:	Last week of May (Mon–Sat)
Where:	Venue varies (Sir Conwy 2008, Cardiff Bay 2009)
Duration:	6 days
Tel:	01248 672100
Website:	www.urdd.org/eisteddfod

Fishguard Folk Festival

Friendly folk and Celtic connections

This thriving event features concerts and dance displays, and a welcoming atmosphere – 'meet the artists' events, workshops and plenty of busking and pub sessions blur the boundaries between audience and professionals. The Celtic influence is strong, with performers from Cornwall, Brittany and Scotland joining the Welsh, Irish and English.

When:	Spring Bank Holiday weekend
Where:	Fishguard, Pembrokeshire
Duration:	4 days
Tel:	01348 875183
Website:	www.pembrokeshire-folk-music.co.uk

Hay Festival

'The Woodstock of the mind' – Bill Clinton

Hay-on-Wye, just inside the Welsh border on the fringes of the Brecon Beacons National Park, is a bibliophile's paradise. Despite having a population of less than 2,000, the town supports some 30 bookshops, most of them second-hand treasure troves. The self-styled 'town of books' makes a natural (and idyllic) setting for the world's leading literary festival. So well-known and well-established is the Hay Festival that it's hard to believe it's only been going since 1988, when it attracted a thousand visitors. Festival-goers now number 150,000, and the literary line-up is a heavyweight roll call of Nobel Laureates, Booker Prize winners and opinion formers. There are readings and talks, lectures and debates, seminars and masterclasses. Ideas are tossed, floated and wrestled, wits pitted and polished, intellects stretched and shaped. Bookish they may be, but the Hay folk know how to party too, and there's no shortage of literary gossip. The festival now includes live music and film premieres as well as a kids' festival, Hay Fever. Admirably, Hay also offers free tickets to students.

It doesn't take a Steven Hawking lecture to establish that 150,000 visitors don't fit into a town of 2,000, and accommodation within a 30-mile radius gets booked up well in advance. Even if there's no room in the inn, though, there are opportunities to sleep in stables, or camp on farms, or stay with families. The festival runs a 'find a bed' service between January and June for £10 a booking, or you can try the Hay tourist board on 01497 820144. If all else fails, head for Columbia, where there's a sister festival in the World Heritage city of Cartagena.

When:	End of May–June
Where:	Hay-on-Wye, Powys
Duration:	10 days
Tel:	0870 990 1299 (box office)
Website:	www.hayfestival.com

St David's Cathedral Festival

Join the pilgrimage to Britain's smallest city

£?

St David's is Britain's smallest city, with a population not much larger than the average village and set entirely within the Pembrokeshire Coast National Park. Its beautiful cathedral, a shrine to the sixth-century patron saint of Wales, has been a place of pilgrimage for centuries – and remains so today, as music lovers flock here for the annual festival. The stunning nave provides a peerless acoustic for a week of concerts; the diverse programme takes in jazz as well as classical choral, orchestral and chamber works. Most concerts begin at 7 p.m., but there are late-night recitals at 10.15 p.m. on several evenings – you can enjoy a glass of wine and informal music in the cloisters in between. There are also a handful of lunchtime concerts, while the soaring voices of the cathedral choir can be heard in sung Eucharist and Evensong services during the week.

When:	End of May–June
Where:	St David's Cathedral, St David's, Pembrokeshire
Duration:	9 days
Tel:	01437 720199/720204
Website:	www.stdavidscathedral.org.uk

Great Welsh Beer and Cider Festival

Ales of Wales

The biggest event of its kind in Wales lays on 170 cask ales and a huge range of cider and perry. As you might expect, there's a particular emphasis on Welsh brews. The admission charge includes a free souvenir tankard and programme with tasting notes. There's hot and cold food available, and even a family room (though children are expected to be accompanied, not abandoned). The Cardiff International Arena is a ten-minute walk from the main train and bus stations, so thankfully there's no reason to drive.

When:	Mid-June
Where:	Cardiff International Arena
Duration:	3 days
Website:	www.gwbcf.org.uk

Escape into the Park

Sweaty fun in the sun

Wales' biggest dance music event is a red letter day in any clubber's calendar, as old skool and nu ravers alike don their day-glo and head for Singleton Park, Swansea. Top DJs and live acts supply non-stop beats from midday to midnight as 25,000 writhing bodies shed gallons of sweat – some climatic quirk means that Escape in the Park invariably takes place on the sunniest day of the year. Bring plenty of water.

When:	Second or third Saturday in June
Where:	Singleton Park, Swansea
Duration:	1 day
Tel:	0870 042 4442
Website:	www.escapefestival.com

Gŵyl Gregynog Festival

One of Wales' best-kept secrets

The vast black-and-white beamed country house of Gregynog makes a magnificent venue for one of the UK's oldest and, for those in the know, most special music festivals. In the 1930s, the owners Gwendoline and Margaret Davies not only established one of Wales' finest collections of Impressionist art but also a music festival attracting the likes of Ralph Vaughan Williams, Gustav Holst and Adrian Boult. The festival has continued, in various incarnations, ever since, and big names from clarinettist Emma Johnson and Northumbrian pipe star Kathryn Tickell to the King's Singers continue to perform in the intimate surroundings of the historic music room. The festival caters for catholic tastes, but the quality is always high – and the weekend Young Musician of the Year competition is no exception. Tea, coffee and a bar are available from an hour before the performances, and the 750-acre grounds are open for walks and picnics. Festival rover tickets, covering all the concerts, are available as well as tickets for individual shows.

When:	Mid-June
Where:	Gregynog, Tregynon, Newtown, Powys
Duration:	10 days
Tel:	01686 625007 (box office)
Website:	www.gwylgregynogfestival.org

Gŵyl Ifan

Traditional dancing in the capital

Gŵyl Ifan is a major festival of traditional Welsh dance, with expert dance displays and plenty of opportunity to join in. Held over a long weekend, events include a barn dance, a grand procession through the city centre on Saturday morning, massed dance displays and workshops. Dancing is held at various venues throughout Cardiff city centre and Cardiff Bay, and Saturday culminates in a Taplas (dinner and dancing – tickets need to be bought in advance). As well as Welsh folk dancing, an overseas troupe or two visits every year to show off their own native dances.

When:	Third weekend of June (Fri–Sun)
Where:	Cardiff
Duration:	3 days
Tel:	029 2056 3989
Website:	www.gwylifan.org

Gŵyl Criccieth Festival

Choirs, Celtic harps, kites and a castle

With its ruined castle on the headland, the small resort of Criccieth on Cardigan Bay makes a fine festival destination. The programme offers something for everybody, with music from opera and choirs to Celtic harps and jazz, and other events from folk dancing to kite building. There's an annual David Lloyd George Memorial Lecture in honour of the town's most famous resident. The festival culminates in a striking fireworks display over Criccieth Castle.

When:	Third week of June
Where:	Criccieth, Gwynedd
Duration:	8 days
Tel:	01766 522778
Website:	www.cricciethfestival.co.uk

North Wales Bluegrass Festival

Conwy reverberates to the sounds of Kentucky for this finger-pickin' good festival

This festival features the best of bluegrass from the UK and beyond. As well as scheduled concerts and dances in Conwy Civic Hall and the Festival Marquee, most of the friendly festival-goers bring their own instruments and join 'picking sessions' across the site. The campsite is in the grounds of Conwy Cricket Club, only a few minutes' walk from the town centre and looming Conwy Castle, and you're rarely more than a few feet away from somebody picking a banjo. Sessions are also held in the Malt Loaf pub on Thursday and Sunday evenings, and there are instrumental workshops on Saturday morning.

When:	First weekend of July (Fri–Sun)
Where:	Conwy, north Wales
Duration:	3 days
Website:	www.northwalesbluegrass.co.uk

Llangollen International Musical Eisteddfod

The world comes to Llangollen

First held in 1947, the International Eisteddfod was born out of a belief in the unifying power of music in a world torn apart by war – the point was poignantly proved in only the second year of the festival when a choir from Lubeck in Germany received an enthusiastic reception. Over the years, musicians from dozens of countries have come together in the small Welsh town of Llangollen. A galaxy of stars has appeared: Pavarotti first came here in 1955 with a male voice choir from his home town of Modena (they won their class), and it was the venue of Placido Domingo's first UK appearance in 1968. Along with evening concerts from internationally renowned musicians, there are daytime competitions featuring musicians and dancers from all over the world. Each day has a different theme – international, Celtic, children's, youth – and as many as 5,000 competitors take part, in front of a weekly audience of 50,000. The world spills out onto the streets of Llangollen in the colourful Parade of Nations on Tuesday afternoon, and the Eisteddfod Ground is always full of international crafts, food and drink, workshops and impromptu performances. You can buy tickets for individual events, day season tickets for all daytime sessions or full season tickets which cover the evening events as well – and you get to keep the same seat all week.

When:	Second week of July
Where:	Llangollen, Denbighshire
Duration:	6 days
Tel:	01978 862001 (Tickets)
Website:	www.international-eisteddfod.co.uk

Cardiff Festivals

A spectacular summer of free festivals

[£?] [♦]

For much of the summer, Cardiff is in festive mode. The Cardiff Festival claims to be the UK's largest free outdoor festival. It's actually a series of several separate festivals. The Big Weekend, held at the end of July or beginning of August, is very big indeed: crowds 200,000-strong throng the grounds of the Cardiff Convention Centre. There are big-name live bands and singers, a gigantic funfair, and all the colour and charisma of the Cardiff MAS, the West Indian-style carnival that culminates at the Big Weekend.

The Big Weekend is only part of it, though. At the International Food and Drink Festival, Welsh produce holds its own against the tastiest treats from around the world. There are major concerts at St David's Hall for the Welsh Proms, and open-air theatre at Cardiff Castle and from the Everyman Theatre. The Children's Festival, at Coopers Field behind Cardiff Castle, is a great start to the summer holidays, with circus and theatre shows, workshops, games, sports, music and much more. Down at Cardiff Bay, the Outdoor Action Show features all sorts of land and water-based activities, from canoeing to skateboarding, WOW on the Waterfront presents breathtaking street theatre spectaculars, and the Mermaid Quay Cardiff Harbour Festival offers nautical fun for all ages (wear your pirate costume). Keep an eye out for fringe events, too. And not an entry fee in sight.

When:	July/August
Where:	Cardiff, various venues
Duration:	throughout the summer
Tel:	029 2087 2087
Website:	www.cardiff-festivals.com

Wakestock

Europe's biggest wakeboarding festival

£ £ £ £ £

What snowboarding is to skiing, wakeboarding is to waterskiing. It is the fastest growing water sport in the world – about two thirds of its three million adherents are under 24, and too cool for words. Wakestock Abersoch is held on the Llyn Peninsula, with views across Cardigan Bay and up to Snowdonia. It's a weekend of high octane thrills as the world's boldest and best wakeboarders show off their skills. Amateurs can enter trials for a place in the pro-event. There are also three days of eclectic live music and DJs, ranging from drum and bass to indie (past acts include Mark Ronson, Soul II Soul and The Enemy). A festival campsite is available, though camping's not included in the basic ticket price.

From 2008, Wakestock is also being held at Blenheim Palace, near Oxford. See South Midlands section.

When:	First weekend of July (Fri–Sun)
Where:	Abersoch, Llanengan, Gwynedd
Duration:	3 days
Tel:	01758 710000
Website:	www.wakestock.co.uk

The Small Nations Festival

Small countries, great music

£ £ £ £

As Wales itself proves, a country doesn't have to be big to produce its own great music – and small festivals can have big ideas, too. This miniature festival – numbers are limited to 1,500 – presents great music from Wales and other small and minority language countries. Artists from Madagascar, Bulgaria, Guinea, Cuba and Polynesia have all found their way to the remote farmland site in the Cambrian mountains. There are DJs, a handful of food and drink and trade stalls, a field to camp in and some lovely, big-hearted people.

When:	Second weekend of July
Where:	Cilycwm, Llandovery, Carmarthenshire
Duration:	3 days
Website:	www.cilycwm.com/smallnations

Gower Festival

Chamber music in ancient churches

The gorgeous Gower peninsula was the first part of Britain to be declared an Area of Outstanding Natural Beauty. Tiny first millennium churches, dedicated to ancient Welsh saints (St Teilo, St Cattwg, St Illtyd), are dotted around its rolling green hills. These provide the venues for a series of intimate chamber and choral music concerts, held nightly over the last two weeks of July. The standard of musicianship is exceptionally high (a young Bryn Terfel performed here in 1988), but the unique pleasure is in stepping outside in the interval, enjoying a glass of wine and listening to the sound of the sea, then heading home as the sun sets.

When:	Last 2 weeks of July
Where:	Gower peninsula, various venues
Duration:	2 weeks
Website:	www.gowerfestival.org

Fishguard International Music Festival

Quality music on the Pembrokeshire coast

Sometimes seen as just a hopping-off point for ferries to Ireland, Fishguard becomes a destination in its own right for this annual music festival. It's known for high-quality and relatively low ticket prices. Classical music forms the mainstay of the programme, with John Eliot Gardiner, Tasmin Little and Peter Donohoe among recent highlights. As well as various venues in Fishguard town, festival concerts are held in St David's Cathedral and the superb country mansion of Rhos-y-Gilwen.

When:	End of July–beginning of August
Where:	Fishguard, Pembrokeshire
Duration:	8 days
Tel:	01348 875538
Website:	www.fishguardmusicfestival.co.uk

Royal Welsh Show

Not just sheep

Wales' leading agricultural show attracts 200,000 people a year. All sorts of breeds of livestock are on show – around 8,000 animals – and there are all manner of other agricultural displays and exhibits. More than a thousand trade stands offer everything from antiques to wheelbarrows, and there's a huge offering of food and drink, including the best selection of Welsh produce you'll find anywhere. Other entertainment ranges from airborne motorbike stunts to the Shetland Pony Grand National and riding displays from Ukrainian Cossacks, though none can compete with Meirion Owen and The Quack Pack – if you've ever wanted to see ducks herded by a sheepdog (and who hasn't?), here's your chance.

The Royal Welsh Agricultural Society also runs a Smallholder and Garden Festival in May and a Winter Fair in December.

When:	Fourth week of July (Mon–Thurs)
Where:	Llanelwedd, Builth Wells, Powys
Duration:	4 days
Tel:	01982 553683
Website:	www.rwas.co.uk

The Big Cheese

History comes to life by one of Europe's largest castles

Caerphilly boasts one of the world's great castles, which dominates the skyline behind this fabulous free fair. Street entertainers, live music, dancing, living history encampments with falconry and minstrels and a traditional funfair are just a few of the attractions on offer. There are craft stalls, a huge local produce market (yes, you will be able to taste some authentic Caerphilly cheese) and a fireworks display on the Friday night. Around 80,000 people attend each year.

When:	Last weekend of July (Fri–Sun)
Where:	Caerphilly Castle, Caerphilly
Duration:	3 days
Tel:	029 2088 0011 (visitor centre)
Website:	www.caerphilly.gov.uk/bigcheese

National Eisteddfod of Wales

The gathering of the bards

£? ⚐ ▲

In 1176, Prince Rhys ap Gruffydd held a gathering of the finest poets and musicians in Wales at his castle in Cardigan. A chair at the Lord's table was awarded to the finest poet and musician – and the tradition of the *eisteddfod* (es-teth-fod, from the Welsh word for 'sit') was born. The National Eisteddfod has been held annually since 1880, alternating between north and south Wales and attracting around 150,000 visitors. It remains a competitive festival, with around 6,000 bards, musicians and, these days, film-makers, artists and even scientists hoping to be honoured. The bardic crown (for free verse) and the bardic chair (for metrical poetry) are presented in a solemn ceremony presided over by the Archdruid. Druidic rituals are an important part of the modern-day Eisteddfod: their historical roots are dubious, to say the least, but white-robed bards, dancing maidens, the horn of plenty and a stone circle make a fine spectacle (even if the latter is usually hastily erected out of plastic stones these days).

The Eisteddfod is a Welsh language event, which can be a little bewildering for people who like their vowels, but there's plenty for non-Welsh speakers to enjoy – and Welsh is one of the world's most poetic languages, even if you don't understand a word. The *maes* (field) is full of tents, stands and pavilions with a huge range of exhibitions and trade stalls. Music, dance and drama events take place on the maes and in other nearby venues, and the action from the main pavilion is relayed on big screens outside. Entertainment is certainly not limited to traditional acts, although the Super Furry Animals famously had to hum their English-language songs (they gave out booklets with the lyrics so the audience could sing instead). The Eisteddfod used to have a no-alcohol policy, but this was relaxed in 2004, and alcohol can now be bought on site, along with plenty of other refreshments. Day tickets are available, though many people choose to stay and camp for the whole week.

When: First week of August (Sat–Sat)
Where: Venue varies (Cardiff 2008, Meirion 2009)
Duration: 8 days
Tel: 01352 705201
Website: www.eisteddfod.org.uk

Tapestry Goes West

'Very strange and beautiful' – The Guardian

Tapestry used to hold a festival on a Wild West theme park in Cornwall, and everyone came along in cowboy hats. Then they moved to a deer park on the Welsh coast and had to find a new theme. The ruined abbey on the site, along with tales of dragons, King Arthur and the like, got them thinking along medieval lines – but this is the most cutting-edge medieval festival you'll ever come across. The sophisticatedly hip musical line-up only makes the medieval costumes, jousting, archery displays, mead tents and lords and ladies football match more bizarre. You'll think you dreamt it all when you take the iron horse back east, but what a dream.

When:	Second weekend of August (Fri/Sat)
Where:	Margam Country Park, Margam, Port Talbot, West Glamorgan
Duration:	2 days
Tel:	01639 721795 (Tourist Information)
Website:	www.tapestrygoeswest.com

Brecon Jazz Festival

'One of the Top 5 jazz festivals in Europe'

The population of Brecon increases ten times over each August as 70,000 people descend upon the Powys market town for one of the world's great jazz festivals. There are three programmes of diverse music on offer (even jazz agnostics will find plenty to get into). The Concert Programme comprises some of the world's leading jazz musicians; tickets (sometimes pricey) need to be bought separately for each concert. The Stroller Programme includes dozens of concerts in smaller indoor and outdoor venues; a single wristband (with day and weekend options available) allows access to all of them, and is the best-value way to see some great music while soaking up the ambience. Finally, there's free Street Music in the bandstand in the temporarily traffic-free town centre. There are various campsites around the town – the rugby field is the liveliest – and stunning walking in the Brecon Beacons National Park right on the doorstep.

When:	Second weekend of August (Thurs–Sun)
Where:	Brecon, Powys
Duration:	3–4 days
Tel:	01874 611622 (box office)
Website:	www.breconjazz.co.uk

Green Man

Black Mountains magic for psychedelic folk

£ £ £ £ £ 🧍 🔺

This is a 'folk' festival in the loosest sense of the word. You won't find anyone singing about 'faire maides' with a finger in their ear – though you will spot the odd fantastic beard among the crowd of 10,000 lovely people. You will, though, experience extraordinary genre-defying music – the likes of Joanna Newsom, Devendra Banhart and Tunng have headlined in the past – and a magical atmosphere. The Black Mountains provide a stunning backdrop. Green Man has been growing year on year, but manages to maintain a defiantly alternative, anti-corporate feel and an other-worldly atmosphere. For the many discerning disciples who return every year, it's a nigh on perfect weekend.

When:	Mid-August
Where:	Glanusk Park, Brecon Beacons
Duration:	3 days
Website:	www.thegreenmanfestival.co.uk

Women in Tune Music Festival

Sisters are doing it for themselves

£ £ £ £ £ 🧍 🔺

Women in Tune is a festival run by women, for women, with a week's camping in a beautiful part of west Wales. There's a programme of live music – heavy on singer-songwriters, but also including a range of bands, and DJs in the dance tent. The aim is to provide an inspiring and supportive atmosphere where anyone will feel she can get up on stage and perform. Numerous workshops take place throughout the week, from salsa and storytelling to t'ai chi and theatre. There's also a special Girls Zone, where kids can learn to make dreamcatchers or improve their juggling and poi skills. The campsite is open from Wednesday to the following Tuesday morning. There's a vegetarian/vegan cafe selling mostly organic food, but bring your own plates and cutlery, as these aren't provided – an effective way of cutting down on waste.

When:	Week before August Bank Holiday (Weds–Mon)
Where:	Llanfair Clydogau, Lampeter, Ceredigion
Duration:	6 days
Tel:	01558 650831
Website:	www.womenintune.co.uk

Llandrindod Wells Victorian Festival

Take the waters in true Victorian style

Llandrindod Wells was a popular spa resort in the Victorian era, and now hosts the UK's premier Victorian festival. The elegant architecture in the town centre, its bandstands and bowling greens are largely unspoilt, so it doesn't take too much imagination to turn the clock back. Nonetheless, the transformation during this nine-day festival is astonishing; shops create Victorian window displays, horses and carts drive cars from the streets and almost everyone wears painstakingly authentic period costume. There's street theatre throughout the week, daily costumed parades and all sorts of other organised entertainment: music hall, tea dances, town crier competitions, exhibitions, workshops and themed events (watch out for protesting suffragettes). Evening entertainment includes male voice choir concerts and a variety of balls. Llandrindod, with a population of around 5,000, welcomes some 40,000 visitors during the festival. A spectacular fireworks display over the town's picturesque lake rounds things off in style.

When:	Week leading up to August Bank Holiday
Where:	Llandrindod Wells, Powys
Duration:	9 days
Tel:	01597 823441
Website:	www.vicfest.co.uk

World Bog Snorkelling Championship

The undoubted highlight of the bog snorkelling calendar

Forget the World Cup, Wimbledon and the Olympics. For true athletic prowess and sporting spirit, the only place to be is Waen Rhydd peat bog on the outskirts of Britain's smallest town, Llanwrtyd Wells. Here, elite athletes from as far away as Russia and New Zealand compete for the prestigious title of World Bog Snorkelling Champion by wiggling their way through a 60-yard trench in the bog. They wear snorkels and flippers, but are not allowed to use conventional swimming strokes. Phillip John, an international marine swimmer, holds the world record of 1 minute 35 seconds. There are also classes for ladies, juniors and locals, and the sporting spectacle attracts quite a crowd. For dedicated bog-sport aficionados, mountain bike bog snorkelling and a triathlon are held earlier in the summer.

When:	August Bank Holiday
Where:	Llanwrtyd Wells, Powys
Duration:	1 day
Website:	www.llanwrtyd-wells.powys.org.uk

Wales

Tenby Arts Festival

See out the summer by the seaside

The walled seaside town of Tenby gets a new lease of life at the end of the summer season with this week-long festival. Some renowned classical performers (Julian Lloyd-Webber, Katherine Jenkins) have appeared along with Welsh male voice choirs and local performers. As well as music, there are drama, literary events and exhibitions in Tenby's several art galleries. The festival begins with a carnival parade through the town and there's a sandcastle competition on the beach.

When: Fourth week of September
Where: Tenby, Pembrokeshire
Duration: 8 days
Website: www.tenbyartsfest.co.uk

North Wales Music Festival

Acoustic perfection in the UK's smallest cathedral

St Asaph (population 3,491) promotes itself as the 'City of Music', although despite its ancient cathedral it no longer has city status. Welsh composer William Mathias chose St Asaph Cathedral – the UK's smallest cathedral – as the venue for this music festival in 1972 as he believed it had the finest acoustics in North Wales. Over the years, audiences and performers have tended to agree with him. The festival comprises a week of evening concerts from leading Welsh and international singers, instrumentalists and orchestras, including male voice choirs, harpist Catrin Finch (a patron of the festival) and the BBC National Orchestra of Wales. There are also lunchtime talks, recitals and workshops.

When: Last week of September
Where: St Asaph, Denbighshire
Duration: 8 days
Tel: 01745 584508
Website: www.northwalesmusicfestival.co.uk

Porthcawl Elvis Festival

The King's not dead

Porthcawl is a drowsy Welsh seaside town for most of the year, but for one weekend in September it turns into a surreal parallel universe, inhabited by thousands of Elvis impersonators. In just a few years, it's grown into Europe's largest Elvis festival (yes, there are others!), attracting lookalikes, tribute acts and fans of the King. Some of the world's leading Elvis impersonators compete in the 'Elvies', and also perform in local pubs. Other events over the years have included Elvis cruises, an Elvis 'It's a Knockout', Elvis weddings and a display of Elvis horsemanship. Tickets are available for individual events or there are VIP passes for the whole weekend. The town gets busy with all those Elvises, so book early to avoid hotel heartbreak.

When: Last weekend of September (Fri–Sun)
Where: Porthcawl, Glamorgan
Duration: 3 days
Website: www.elvies.co.uk

Swansea Festival of Music and the Arts

One of Wales' leading arts festivals

Swansea Festival celebrated its 60th birthday in 2008. It's one of the largest arts festivals in Wales. There's a high-class programme of music (mainly classical, but also jazz and other surprises), opera from the Welsh National Opera, theatre, visual arts, dance and more. Brangwyn Hall in the Guildhall is the main venue for concerts, along with the Grand Theatre and the university's Taliesin Arts Centre.

When: First 2 weeks of October
Where: Swansea, various
Duration: 2 weeks
Tel: 029 2062 6998
Website: www.swanseafestival.com

Dylan Thomas Festival

Swansea honours its favourite son

Dylan Thomas called Swansea an 'ugly lovely town', and the city returns the compliment with this annual festival dedicated to its most famous resident. It begins on his birthday, 27 October, and ends on 9 November, the day he died. The two weeks are packed with readings, talks, drama, concerts and other events, including Dylan tours (don't try to keep up with the drinking), many held at the Dylan Thomas Centre, which used to be Swansea's Guildhall. Alongside the official festival is the open-access Dylan Thomas Fringe, which does a good line in singer-songwriters and comedians; the likes of Paul Merton and Arthur Smith appeared early in their careers.

When:	27 October–9 November
Where:	Dylan Thomas Centre and other venues, Swansea
Duration:	2 weeks
Tel:	01792 474051
Websites:	www.dylanthomas.org
	www.swanseafringe.com

Calennig in Cardiff

New Year's Eve by Cardiff Castle

Bute Park by Cardiff Castle is the place to head on New Year's Eve for this free outdoor show. Circus acts, acrobatics and fire shows make a fantastic spectacle for all the family. There's also live music and a family funfair around the Civic Centre, part of a series of midwinter events. The events attract around 15,000 people, and there's a fine fireworks display when the clock strikes midnight. The council lays on free buses from the city centre till the early hours of the morning.

When:	31 December
Where:	Bute Park/Cardiff Civic Centre, Cardiff
Duration:	1 day
Website:	www.cardiffswinterwonderland.com

The Mari Llwyd

In Wales, the mythological Mari Llwyd, a scary skull-faced grey mare, used to put in an appearance on New Year's Eve. Groups of revellers hidden inside their horse costume would prance from door to door, accompanied by a local bard. In a sort of trick-or-treat/poetry-slam hybrid, the Mari Llwyd party would exchange songs and rhyming insults with the residents, and demand food and drink. The custom all but died out with the Industrial Revolution, but is enjoying something of a revival: look out for her in Llangynwyd, Llanwrtyd Wells and parts of Glamorgan and Gwent.

Wales

West Midlands

St Patrick's Day

Europe's biggest outside Dublin

FREE

Birmingham's huge Irish community comes out in force for the city's St Patrick's Day parade, reportedly the largest in the world after Dublin and New York. Crowds of 130,000 dressed in green, shamrocks and leprechaun costumes line the streets to watch the parade, which has dozens of floats and hundreds of participants. It's the culmination of a week of Irish themed festivities. Music fills the pubs, the craic is wonderful, and a canal's worth of Guinness is drunk.

When:	Sunday closest to 17 March
Where:	Birmingham city centre
Duration:	1 day
Website:	www.stpatricksfestival.co.uk

The Big Apple

Seasonal celebrations of English apples and cider

£?

Bordeaux has its grapes; Herefordshire has apples. The apple trees, and the delicious cider they produce, are best appreciated during the 'Big Apple' events in the wonderfully named villages of the Marcle Ridge – Aylton, Little Marcle, Much Marcle, Munsley, Pixley, Putley and Woolhope. During Blossomtime, at the beginning of May, there are guided tours of the blooming orchards; cider, perry and single-variety apple juice tastings; talks and teas. The harvest can be sampled during the Autumn Event, at the beginning of October, with tastings and sales of cider and juices as well as eating apples. There are more talks, tours and demonstrations of traditional cider making, and you can bring along that mysterious fruit from the old tree in your aunt's garden for expert apple identification.

When:	Blossomtime: first weekend of May; Autumn Event: second weekend of October
Where:	Blossomtime: Putley, Ledbury, Herefordshire; Autumn Event: March Marcle, Ledbury, Herefordshire
Duration:	2 days
Website:	www.bigapple.org.uk

Leek Arts Festival

Music and much more

For a small place, the market town of Leek puts on an impressive month-long programme for its annual arts festival, which has now been running for over 30 years. An array of local talent supports some bigger names, and there's a diverse musical programme – folk figures prominently, but there are also classical recitals, jazz, funk, brass bands and a day-long open-air concert, the Bank Holiday Bash, featuring local bands. Arts trails around the town's many galleries, poetry readings, ghost walks, floral displays and outdoor events create a festive atmosphere all month long.

When:	May
Where:	Leek, Staffs.
Duration:	1 month
Tel:	01538 483743 (Tourist Information)
Website:	www.leekartsfestival.org

Birmingham Pride

Outrageous fun and queer goings-on

[FREE]

One of the UK's largest Pride festivals, and all free, Birmingham warms up with some live music, parties and street markets on Friday night and Saturday, before Sunday's Village Pride day. The parade sets off from Victoria Square at 2 p.m. New Street is the best place to watch as it prances its way to Hurst Street in Birmingham's Gay Village. In the village, there's a huge range of live music on offer. As well as big names on the main stage, there's the WOW (Women On Women) stage, Tricky Dicky's Over-18s Stage, Jack and Jones Carbaret Stage, the DV8 Dance Arena and two other live music stages. There are funfair rides, food stalls and trade stands, as well as an over-18s area and a bear pit (no, not really bears. If you have to ask...). The village streets are licensed for the event, but this means you're not allowed to bring in your own alcohol. Music and other events continue on Monday, and a concurrent Queer Arts Festival is expanding all the time.

When:	Spring Bank Holiday weekend (Fri–Mon)
Where:	Birmingham Gay Village (around Hurst Street)
Duration:	4 days
Website:	www.birminghampride.org

Elgar Festival

A musical celebration of Worcester's greatest son

This week-long festival celebrates local lad Sir Edward Elgar, whose music was inspired by the landscapes of his youth. It takes place around his birthday (2 June). The programme features the music of Elgar and others, with concerts by top performers including the English Symphony Orchestra and The Royal Liverpool Philharmonic Orchestra. There are evening and lunchtime recitals, a young musicians' concert and guided Elgar-themed walks around the places that shaped his life and music.

When:	Late May/early June
Where:	Malvern, Worcs.
Duration:	1 week
Tel:	01684 892289
Website:	www.elgar-festival.com

Malvern Fringe

Lots to do at this alternative festival with a community feel

The Malvern Fringe has been going since the late 1970s, offering a more community-focused and popular alternative to the Elgar Festival. There is music, comedy, theatre, street performance, poetry slams, lectures and workshops. The Malvern Fringe also runs a folk weekend during Malvern's October festival in the middle of the month.

When:	Late May/early June
Where:	Malvern, Worcs.
Duration:	4 days
Website:	www.malvernfringe.co.uk

BASS Music Festival

The sound of the streets

BASS stands for Birmingham Art and Street Sounds Festival, a five-week celebration of urban music and arts. Though centred around Birmingham, events are held in venues across the Midlands, including Nottingham, Leicester and Derby. The music ranges from hip-hop to Asian groove, dubstep to drum and bass, reggae to roots – the likes of Sway, Goldie and Lethal Bizzle have been involved in previous years. There are film screenings, dance productions and street art exhibitions, as well as MC masterclasses, performance poetry workshops and other educational events aimed at young people.

When:	End of May–June
Where:	Birmingham and regionally
Duration:	5 weeks
Tel:	0121 224 7444
Website:	www.bassfestival.co.uk

Deva Dubs 'n' Rods

A laid-back VW and Hot Rod show

Admire some audacious automobiles (or 'show 'n' shine' your own), find that rare 1956 Karmann Ghia engine component you needed at the autojumble, or join in the 'It's A Knockout'-style family-friendly fun on the Saturday. There are also trade stalls, comedy on the Friday night and music on the Saturday. VW clubs are encouraged to camp together, but are asked to display at least five of their vehicles in return (there are prizes for the best displays).

When:	Second weekend of June
Where:	Shrewsbury Showground, Shrewsbury, Shropshire
Duration:	2 days
Tel:	01244 535470
Website:	www.devadubshow.co.uk

Leamington Peace Festival

Creating the spirit of community

[£?] [⚘]

From the radical 1970s, through the greedy 1980s and the apathetic 1990s into the fearful noughties, the Leamington Peace Festival has endured as a beacon of hope. This free festival promotes peace and equality, and aims to show how the people of the world can live together in harmony with each other and with nature. There's live music – local and international – and performances in two entertainment areas, a children's tent, workshops and over a hundred stalls. You'll meet charities and activists, all sorts of religious and philosophical groups, artists and craftspeople, and ethically traded food and drink. It's very much a community event, and something of its alternative spirit has seeped into Leamington life over the years.

When:	Second weekend of June (Sat/Sun)
Where:	Pump Room Gardens, Leamington Spa, Warwicks.
Duration:	2 days
Tel:	0845 388 4207
Website:	www.peacefestival.org.uk

Linton Festival

Why go to the music when you can bring the music to you?

[£££] [⛺]

So, the regulars at the Alma Inn, Linton, Herefordshire are planning to drive to a gig in Poole, Dorset. They're thinking of hiring a minibus, till they work out it would actually be cheaper to get the band to come to them. What the hell, why not get a few more bands to come along as well, get some beers in and make a weekend of it? That's how the Linton Festival began in 2001. It's now a popular annual event, attracting major international blues artists, but retains a friendly party feel. There are basic camping facilities nearby, and a wide selection of real ales to wash the blues away.

When:	Third weekend of June
Where:	The Alma Inn, Linton, Ross-on-Wye, Herefordshire
Duration:	3 days
Website:	www.lintonfestival.org

ChickenStock

Watch the bands perform on stage, then get down with them on the dance floor

£ £ £ £ | ⚥ | ▲

Groan-inducing name apart, this is an impeccable (im-peck-able? Sorry...) little festival near Malvern. The idea is simply to have some fun in a field with some friends – which is pretty much Essence of Festival – and all profits go to charity. It's driven by the performers and has a very friendly atmosphere – you might not have heard of the bands playing, but you could end up having a drink with them afterwards. As well as an anything-goes music policy, there's drama, DJs, late-night film screenings, poetry, juggling and whatever else festival-goers come up with. There's an organic hog roast (and plenty of veggie alternatives), and camping on the site.

When:	Third weekend of June (Sat/Sun)
Where:	The Cow Pasture, Lower Howsell Road, Malvern Link, Worcs.
Duration:	2 days
Website:	www.chickenstock.co.uk

Oliver Cromwell Jazz Festival

A weekend of mellow jazz and laid-back fun down by the riverside

£ £ £ | ⚥ | ▲

Oliver Cromwell and his army crossed the River Severn at Upton on their way to the Battle of Leicester – though whether he'd approve of jazz, or festivals, is another matter. The less puritanical can enjoy a weekend of 'New Orleans, Hot Club, Dixieland, Comedy, Traditional and Swing' styles of jazz from bands both international and local. The festival is centred around the Fish Meadow, on the banks of the Severn, where there are three marquees, a jazz bar, stalls and camping. Events also take place in town, accessible with day tickets and weekend stroller tickets. There's a Saturday morning parade with bands and 'energy dancers' and a Sunday jazz parade, as well as musical riverboat trips for ticket holders only.

When:	Last weekend of June
Where:	Fish Meadow, Upton-upon-Severn
Duration:	3 days
Tel:	01684 593254
Websites:	www.uptonjazz.co.uk
	www.uptonfolk.org
	www.uptonbluesfestival.org.uk

Wakestock

Europe's biggest wakeboarding festival: mk II

£ £ £ £ £

In the wake of the well-established Wakestock Abersoch (in the Wales section), the world's coolest water sport (think snowboarding on water) powers into Blenheim Palace, birthplace of Winston Churchill. Yes, Oxfordshire is landlocked, but the majestic 2,100-acre gardens boast a vast lake, a perfect setting for the world's finest wakeboarders. Away from the waterborne action, there are three days of music from the hottest bands and DJs around across three stages.

When:	Last weekend of June (Fri–Sun)
Where:	Blenheim Palace, Woodstock, Oxon.
Duration:	3 days
Tel:	01758 710000
Website:	www.wakestock.com

Ludlow Festival

The Bard at his best in the open air

£?

This two-week summer festival is centred around a professional production of a Shakespeare play in the glorious setting of Ludlow Castle. Shakespeare's plays were written to be performed on an open-air stage in front of a festive audience, and work brilliantly in this setting. The outer bailey is open for picnics from 6.30 p.m. before the performance. Picnics are also an integral part of the Firework Finale, with a popular concert in the castle. It's not just about Shakespeare though; throughout the fortnight there are various musical, literary and dance events around Ludlow, as well as walks, talks and coach tours.

When:	Last week of June–first week of July
Where:	Ludlow Castle, Ludlow, Shropshire
Duration:	2 weeks
Tel:	01584 872150
Website:	www.ludlowfestival.co.uk

The Royal Show

'Europe's premier agricultural fair'

Organised by the Royal Agricultural Society, the Royal Show at Stoneleigh Park is one of the largest agricultural shows in the country. It's aimed at promoting British farming (about 18,000 of the 160,000 visitors come from overseas) and there's plenty of opportunity for working farmers to tackle technological, economic and political issues, but there's plenty more to enjoy. Choose from over 200 rural craft stands, livestock and equine exhibits, a British food and drink market, 40 acres of agricultural machinery, Europe's largest flower marquee and the prestigious Tractor Driver of the Year competition.

When:	First weekend of July (Thurs–Sun)
Where:	Stoneleigh Park, Warwicks.
Duration:	4 days
Tel:	024 7669 6969
Website:	www.royalshow.org.uk

Banbury Hobby Horse Festival

Ride a cock horse to Banbury Cross…

In medieval times, hobby horses, Jacks-in-the-Green, straw men, giants and dragons – usually giant puppets operated by several people – were common features of carnivals and civic processions. Since the turn of the millennium, many of these beasts – ancient, revived and modern – have been coming to Banbury for this festival's procession. Most are connected with morris teams, and the weekend includes dancing and ceilidhs as well as general horseplay and much drinking of the local Hook Norton beer.

When:	First weekend of July
Where:	Banbury, Oxon.
Duration:	3 days
Tel:	01295 259855 (Tourist Information)
Website:	www.hobbyhorsefestival.co.uk

Cornbury Music Festival

'The only rock festival for all ages' The Word

£££££

This is one for everybody, from toddlers to great-grandparents. Cornbury Park, on the edge of Wychwood Forest, has held country fairs for centuries – attracting crowds of 50,000 in the nineteenth century. Today, it holds a charming festival that manages to be both cool and cosy. The eclectic musical line-up has seen headline performances from the likes of Robert Plant, Blondie and The Feeling, alongside some of the best new bands you've never heard of. Beyond the music, Cornbury still has something of the country fair about it, with an arts and crafts trading village, fantastic food and drink stalls, street performers and a large fairground. You can also book hot air balloon flights, weather permitting. There's no shortage of workshops and other entertainment to keep the kids happy – Rupert Bear and Postman Pat have both appeared among the bands on stage.

When:	Saturday/Sunday early July
Where:	Cornbury Park, nr Charlbury, Oxfordshire
Duration:	2 days
Tel:	020 7229 2219
Website:	www.cornburyfestival.com

Ledbury Poetry Festival

'The best in the country' – Andrew Motion

£?

Ledbury is the birthplace of William Langland, author of 'Piers Plowman', one of the first poems in the English language. It's now home to the country's biggest poetry festival, and according to Andrew Motion, also the best (as the Poet Laureate, he should know). More than 50 events take place over ten days, including readings by some of our leading poets, lectures and learned conversations, as well as performance poetry and open-access poetry slams. There are also workshops, outdoor events, concerts, stand-up comedy, films, exhibitions, walks and plenty to keep intelligent kids engaged. An international poetry competition, judged by the annual poet-in-residence, attracts a high standard of entries in both the adult and children's categories.

When:	Early July
Where:	Ledbury, Herefordshire
Duration:	10 days
Tel:	0845 458 1743
Website:	www.poetry-festival.com

Lichfield Festival

High-class arts festival with a few surprises in store

Lichfield, with its unique three-spired cathedral and well-preserved historic buildings, delivers everything you want from a cathedral city – and surpasses itself with this wonderful multi-arts festival. A diverse and sometimes challenging programme presents artists of the highest calibre from all over the world, alongside a lively line-up of community events and local participation. The festival usually throws up a coup or two – Philip Glass performed his only UK solo concert here during his 70th-birthday year. Performances include drama, dance, cinema, literature, visual art, jazz, folk, classical and world music, packing 75 events into ten days. Performance venues include Lichfield Cathedral and the Garrick Theatre (actor David Garrick was a local lad), as well as non-traditional spaces. Free community events include a Medieval Market and the Festival Fireworks. There are marquees selling food and drink on the cathedral lawn, and free live music at the Green Room bar in the Garrick Theatre.

When:	Early July
Where:	Lichfield, Staffs.
Duration:	11 days
Tel:	01543 306270
Website:	www.lichfieldfestival.org

Fuse: The Event in a Tent

Marquee music

Lichfield Arts organises this free fringe event over a long weekend during the Lichfield Festival. It's actually an event in two tents – a main tent and an acoustic tent – in Beacon Park. The eclectic musical line-up, featuring local and international acts, aims to offer something for everybody, and attracts thousands of people. There are also workshops, ranging from belly dancing to circus skills, and street theatre performers.

When:	Second weekend in July (Fri–Sun)
Where:	Lichfield, Staffs.
Duration:	3 days
Tel:	01543 262223
Website:	www.lichfieldarts.org.uk

Birmingham International Jazz Festival

The biggest and best free jazz party in the UK

Birmingham promises 'more jazz per square metre than New Orleans' during this ten-day summer festival. Around 200 concerts are squeezed in, and all but a handful are free. Dozens of venues of all shapes and sizes are pressed into service. You'll hear live jazz coming out of cafes and restaurants, sports clubs and pubs, stations and high street shops, outdoors in the markets and even in the supermarket. Performers come from all over the world, meaning there's a huge variety of sounds and styles to sample.

When:	Early/mid-July
Where:	Birmingham and surrounds
Duration:	10 days
Tel:	0121 454 7020
Website:	www.birminghamjazzfestival.com

Godiva Festival

A big free festival – worth a peep

Coventry's most famous resident lends her name to one of the biggest free festivals around. Corporate sponsorship and council support delivers a decent musical line-up, with big-name headliners and local acts, as well as a local history fair, dance and displays, a skate park and plenty for the kids. The carnival procession features a great range of floats and fancy dress, though (un)dressing as Lady Godiva isn't encouraged. No tickets required, but if you're not local you'll need to arrange your own accommodation for the weekend.

When:	Mid-July (Fri–Sun)
Where:	Memorial Park, Kenilworth Road, Coventry, Warwicks.
Duration:	3 days
Tel:	024 7629 4525
Website:	www.godivafestival.co.uk

> Lady Godiva was an Anglo-Saxon noblewoman. According to legend, she pleaded with her husband to lift the heavy taxes he'd imposed on the people of Coventry. He eventually agreed, on the condition that she ride through the town naked. This she did – having first arranged that everyone would stay in doors and not look. All except one 'Peeping Tom' obeyed.

Latin American Festival

Latin America comes to Birmingham

FREE

Established over 15 years ago, Birmingham's Latin American Festival is the biggest event of its kind in the UK. Throughout the day, Latin American bands take to the stage in Victoria Square, with music ranging from Afro-Cuban to mariachi to samba, while dancers strut their stuff in salsa, tango and other styles. There are salsa and other dance workshops during the day, and you're invited to join in a giant public conga; even the most inhibited English audience members can't stop themselves from dancing by the end of the day. Latin food and cocktails are available to keep your energy up. After the free event, take your dancing feet off to the after party in the Ipanema Club on Broad Street.

When:	Third Sunday in July
Where:	Victoria Square, Birmingham
Duration:	1 day
Tel:	0121 449 3090
Website:	www.abslatin.co.uk

Festival at the Edge

Tales round the campfire and a magical adventure

Once upon a time, a group of story lovers from Bridgnorth decided to create a unique and fantastical festival. Festival at the Edge is the first and, to date, only weekend festival devoted to the art of storytelling. British and international storytellers tell their tales – some specially commissioned for the event – through performance, music, comedy, poetry and related arts. If you have a tale to tell yourself, there are workshops, 'story-rounds' and story sessions that run late into the night – and yes, the all-important campfire is provided. There's a special programme for children, a craft fair, on-site catering and a CAMRA real ale bar. The site itself is in an Area of Outstanding Natural Beauty on Wenlock Edge, a perfect place to camp.

When:	Third weekend in July (Fri–Sun)
Where:	Stokes Barn, Much Wenlock, Shropshire
Duration:	3 days
Tel:	01939 236626
Website:	www.festivalattheedge.org

Truck Festival

Glastonbury meets The Archers

£ £ £ | ▲

Not a festival of truckers (though the main stage consists of three flat bed trucks) but a bite-sized Glastonbury – half-a-dozen stages, a wide range of live bands and DJs, theatre and stand-up comedy, all on a working farm. The sounds of drum and bass and the aroma of manure make for a strangely alluring combination in the Barn Stage on Saturday night. Cutting edge music aside, Truck could be straight out of *The Archers* – the Rotary Club runs the food stall and the local vicar serves ice creams. Rather than increase the capacity of Truck Festival – and risk losing what makes it special – the organisers have decided to support other small festivals that share similar values. Check out Two Thousand Trees in the South West section.

When:	Third weekend of July
Where:	Hili Farm, Steventon, Oxon.
Duration:	2 days
Tel:	01235 821262
Website:	www.thisistruck.com

Global Gathering

Hedonistic highs for party people

£ £ £ £ £ | ⫩ | ▲

Some 55,000 gather for Britain's biggest dance music festival – over half of them camp, too, snatching what sleep they can between the punishing party schedule (5 p.m.–2 a.m. Friday, 2 p.m.–6 a.m. Saturday). If sets from the world's top DJs don't give you enough of a rush, there's an 'adrenaline village' for bungee jumping and extreme rides, dodgems, a fairground and hot air balloon rides... Alternatively, you might prefer to take a break in the chill-out village. Either way, you'll probably want to take Monday morning off work.

When:	Last weekend of July
Where:	Long Marston Airfield, Stratford-upon-Avon, Warwicks.
Duration:	2 days
Website:	www.globalgathering.co.uk

Warwick Folk Festival

Music, morris, mumming and much more

Over three decades, the Warwick Folk Festival has established itself as one of the leading events on the folk circuit. There are some big-name headliners (like festival stalwarts Oysterband and Bellowhead), but also a great deal of music-making by the festival-goers. The site is in the grounds of Warwick School. There are acoustic concerts in the school's Bridgehouse Theatre, ceilidhs and workshops in the Guy Nelson Hall and larger concerts in the main marquee. There are plenty of craft and catering stalls and a family-friendly atmosphere, and camping is attached. Events like morris dancing, mummers' plays and concerts are also held in the town centre, a short walk or free shuttle bus ride away.

When:	Last weekend of July (Fri–Sun)
Where:	Warwick School, Warwick
Duration:	3 days
Tel:	024 7667 8738
Website:	www.warwickfolkfestival.co.uk

Three Choirs Festival

One of the oldest music festivals in the world

The Three Choirs Festival has been held each year since the beginning of the eighteenth century, making it one of the oldest music festivals in the world. Uniquely, it rotates annually between the cathedral cities of Gloucester, Worcester and Hereford – and a healthy sense of competition between the three hosts keeps it constantly fresh. The highpoints of the festival are the grand choral concerts held in the cathedral, featuring the Festival Chorus and major international artists and ensembles. There's also a programme of chamber music, organ recitals, opera, theatre, talks, exhibitions and other events running throughout the festival week.

When:	First week of August
Where:	Gloucester, Worcester or Hereford
Duration:	8 days
Tel:	Gloucester: 01452 529819; Worcester: 01905 616200
Website:	www.3choirs.org

Worcester Festival

Affordable fun for all ages

No shortage of things to keep the kids occupied during the summer holidays in Worcester: the city's festival is packed full of children's shows, bizarre street theatre, craft workshops, live music and dance. There's plenty for adults too, of course, including a wide range of concerts, comedy, craft shows, drama and horticultural events. It's a non-profit-making venture, and the majority of events are free or under a fiver. The festival ends with a fireworks display from the main bridge over the River Severn on Bank Holiday Monday.

When:	August
Where:	Worcester, various venues
Duration:	2/3 weeks
Tel:	01905 619958 (Worcester Live box office)
Website:	www.worcesterfestival.co.uk

The Big Chill

Shiny happy people

There can be few more lovely festival experiences than a Big Chill when the sun shines – which, mysteriously, it usually does for this event. Nestling beneath the bewitchingly beautiful Malvern hills, the huge expanse of Eastnor Castle Deer Park, complete with lakes and woodland, plays host to possibly the happiest festival of them all. The Big Chill's dance culture beginnings have grown into a unique musical mix that takes in everything from world to electronica, cutting-edge techno to high kitsch – from 808s to ukuleles and much more besides. As well as the music there's a plethora of art, film, comedy, multimedia and holistic pursuits; all served up with some great food in a genuinely relaxing family-friendly atmosphere of laid-back sophistication. The smiley punters snap up tickets quickly, so book early to avoid disappointment.

When:	First weekend of August (Fri–Sun)
Where:	Eastnor Castle, Ledbury, Herefordshire
Duration:	3 days
Tel:	020 7685 0525
Website:	www.bigchill.net

Bulldog Bash

Europe's no. 1 biker party

Having begun life as a small Hell's Angels gathering, the Bulldog Bash is now one of Europe's premier motorbike festivals, revving up crowds of 50,000. There's high velocity action on the drag strip, including 'Run What Ya Brung' races, pro demos and rocket bikes reaching speeds of over 220 mph. There are thousands of bikes to drool over, including the UK's biggest custom bike show. Live music blasts from two stages – headliners have included such biker favourites as Status Quo and The Damned – and there's a pounding dance tent. Other on-site entertainment includes wrestling, fairground rides, a Wall of Death, tattoo and piercing stalls and good old-fashioned sexist fun in the form of wet T-shirt contests and topless bike washes. There's on-site camping and free bike parking. The cuddly Hell's Angels provide security – there are no police on site – and the festival is considered one of the safest around.

When:	Second weekend of August (Thurs–Sun)
Where:	Long Marston Airfield, nr Stratford-upon-Avon, Warwicks.
Duration:	4 days
Website:	www.bulldogbash.com

Fairport's Cropredy Convention

'If you really mean it, it all comes round again'

Folk-rock institution Fairport Convention have been running this annual reunion in the village of Cropredy, near Banbury, since the 1970s. It's grown into a three-day festival attracting some 20,000 people – a fair proportion of whom must have been in the band at one time or another. There's a strong line-up of folk-rock and blues, but the highlight is Fairport's own appearance on Saturday night, where band members past and present and numerous special guests come together for a four-hour marathon concert. It reaches a near religious climax as the crowded stage and the packed field sing along to the closing anthem 'Meet on the Ledge'. The atmosphere is relaxed and friendly – with no backstage bar, it's not unusual to see the performers downing Wadsworth 6X along with the punters. There are also friendly village pubs to retreat to and festival campsites nearby – although many festival-goers moor up in their narrowboats along the canal.

When:	Second full weekend of August (Thurs–Sat)
Where:	Cropredy, Banbury, Oxon.
Duration:	3 days
Website:	www.fairportconvention.com/cropredy.php

Shrewsbury Flower Show

The world's oldest flower festival

[£?] [👤]

Visitors have flocked to the world's longest-running horticultural show in Shrewsbury's beautiful Quarry Park, with its famous sunken gardens, since 1875. Each year, 75,000 visitors come to admire the pick of the bunch from professional growers and green-fingered amateurs, as three giant marquees bloom with three million flowers. Admire floral arts exhibitions, browse the gardening stalls or get some tips from gardening experts. Flowers are only part of the fun, though – there's live music (usually of the light classical variety), massed military bands, show jumping, celebrity chef demonstrations, sheepdog displays, a children's area and a firework finale.

When:	Second weekend of August (Fri–Sat)
Where:	Quarry Park, Shrewsbury, Shropshire
Duration:	2 days
Tel:	01743 234050
Website:	www.shrewsburyflowershow.org.uk

V Festival

Corporate but quality

[£ £ £ £ £] [A]

The 'V' stands for Richard Branson's Virgin group, and this is as slick and commercial as festivals come, well stocked with mobile phone charge points and unlikely to cause many spiritual epiphanies. That's not altogether a bad thing, though – it's a well-organised affair, with a clean, non-threatening feel. It was also the first festival to be held simultaneously in two locations, Chelmsford and Staffordshire, with the same bands, give or take, playing on alternate days. It always attracts a decent line-up, with a sprinkling of poppier headliners (Girls Aloud, McFly) to spice up the usual indie suspects on the two main stages, along with the edgier third stage and a new bands tent.

When:	Penultimate weekend of August
Where:	Hylands Park, Chelmsford, Essex; Weston Park, Staffs.
Duration:	2 days
Website:	www.vfestival.com

Towersey Village Festival

The perfect end to the summer holidays

For five decades, festival-goers have descended on the Oxfordshire village of Towersey for a long weekend of folk music, dancing and laid-back fun. There's something special about Towersey that keeps people coming back year after year – some who came as kids back in the early days are now bringing their grandchildren. It's a very family-focused festival – in fact, there's a whole Children's Festival with crafts, music, dancing, singing, puppets, storytelling, face painting and all sorts of other fun in three marquees. There's also a special programme for the many young people aged 12–25 at The Hive. The music kicks off on Thursday evening and keeps on till the night of Bank Holiday Monday. It's become a tradition to dress in drag on Sunday, though thankfully this isn't obligatory.

When:	Towersey, Thame, Oxon.
Where:	August Bank Holiday weekend
Duration:	5 days
Tel:	01629 827016 (box office)
Website:	www.towerseyfestival.com

Shrewsbury Folk Festival

The folk festival that just keeps growing

Having outgrown Bridgnorth and moved to Shrewsbury, this popular folk festival now seems at home at the West Midlands Showground, about half an hour's walk from town. It's a friendly event and a happy summer holiday for many families. There are three marquees with seating – a huge one for main stage acts (a broad range of folk, folk-rock and other rootsy acts from around the world), one for dance (with a proper dance floor) and another that hosts open-mic events and singarounds. There's a good range of catering outlets including a well-stocked real ale bar, crafts and shopping stalls on site. Music, dancing, crafts and circus skills workshops are popular, and there are special programmes for children and 'youths'. The campsite is arranged into quiet, late night and family zones, and the free hot showers are very welcome. Unusually for an arena festival you can bring your dog, though you're expected to take it out of the marquee if it starts barking during a performance.

When:	August Bank Holiday weekend (Fri–Mon)
Where:	West Midlands Showground, Berwick Road, Shrewsbury, Shropshire
Duration:	4 days
Tel:	01746 768813
Website:	www.shrewsburyfolkfestival.co.uk

BunkFest

Music, dance, steam and beer...

If you've ever wished for a folk festival that would hold jam sessions on working steam railways and concerts on river boats, then BunkFest is the one for you. The local steam railway – the Bunk – is a branch off the Great Western Railway that runs from Cholsey to Wallingford, and there are regular sessions on 'The Singing Train'. Half a dozen riverboat concerts take place each day on a Thames cruiser. There are also performances in more conventional venues around Wallingford, a late-night festival club, storytelling sessions and dance displays. A craft fair takes place in the market place, and there are food stalls alongside the town's hostelries. There's no festival camping, but there are a number of campsites nearby.

When:	Weekend after August Bank Holiday (Fri–Sun)
Where:	Wallingford, Oxon.
Duration:	3 days
Website:	www.bunkfest.co.uk

Ross Cider and Music Festival

Cider-fuelled festivities on the farm

This takes place at Broome Farm, a large cider farm just outside Ross-on-Wye that grows over 70 different varieties of cider apple and perry pear trees. You can sample the cider made from many of these, and other local farms, while stomping along to live folk music in the barn. There are cider-making demonstrations, a large craft fair and farmers' market, and a terrific tipsy atmosphere.

When:	First weekend of September
Where:	Broome Farm, Peterstow, Ross-on-Wye, Herefordshire
Duration:	2 days
Tel:	01989 567232
Website:	www.rosscider.com

Abbots Bromley Horn Dance

Eight centuries of horned madness

FREE

The Horn Dance is one of the oldest surviving traditional dances in the country. Records show it was performed at Barthelmy Fair in 1226, though radio carbon dating on one of the sets of reindeer horns used in the dances showed them to be over a thousand years old. There are 12 dancers, six carrying antlers, plus a hobby horse, Maid Marion, a fool and a bowman, with musical accompaniment provided by melodeon and triangle. The horns are collected from the parish church at 8 a.m., and the dancers visit various pubs and other locations around the village. Many locals and visitors follow the well-lubricated walk, which lasts all day and is about ten miles, and there's also a fair on the village green.

When:	Wakes Monday (Monday after first Sunday after 4 September)
Where:	Abbots Bromley, Staffs.
Duration:	1 day
Website:	www.abbotsbromley.com

Birmingham ArtsFest

See the city centre transformed in this huge free arts weekend

FREE

ArtsFest promises 'the magical, the mystical and the momentous all made in the Midlands!' Five outdoor stages in the city centre present performances ranging from theatre to jazz, pop to ballet, and there are exhibitions and installations in many civic and cultural buildings and spaces. Over 1,500 artists are involved, and the free event attracts more than 100,000 people. Travel round by canal boat for the full Venice-of-the-Midlands experience.

When:	Second weekend of September
Where:	Birmingham city centre
Duration:	3 days
Tel:	0121 464 5678
Website:	www.artsfest.org.uk

West Midlands

Bromyard Folk Festival

Music in the marches

Held in beautiful countryside in the Welsh marches, the longstanding folk festival packs over 170 hours of entertainment into a long weekend. The focus is on traditional music from the British Isles, and many leading folk musicians perform here. As with most folk festivals, there's also plenty of participation – many morris teams attend, and each evening concludes with a late-night club session and singaround. There are also ceilidhs, workshops, dancing, children's entertainment and a high-quality craft fair. Most events take place on site, where there's camping, a real ale bar and a good range of food, but there are also concerts and dance displays in the town.

When:	Second full weekend of September (Fri–Sun)
Where:	Bromyard, Herefordshire
Duration:	3 days
Website:	www.bromyard-folk-festival.org.uk

Blenheim Horse Trials

The equine elite compete in the Duke of Marlborough's back garden

Blenheim Palace, one of the finest stately homes in the country, is home to a suitably high-class equestrian event, attracting many of the world's best riders and thousands of spectators. Dressage takes place on Thursday and Friday, with the Palace providing a splendid backdrop. There's cross-country around the parkland on Saturday, and the show jumping finale on Sunday. Away from the eventing action, there are competitions for Pony Clubs and Riding Clubs, displays of classic cars and sports cars, and more than 200 trade stands selling country clothing, pearls, fine art, overseas property and the like. Well-behaved dogs and children are welcome, and there's a play area with bouncy castles and climbing walls.

When:	Second weekend of September (Thurs–Sun)
Where:	Blenheim Palace, Woodstock, Oxon.
Duration:	4 days
Tel:	01993 813335
Website:	www.blenheim-horse.co.uk

Burton Beer Festival

Get a taste of Britain's brewing capital

Burton-on-Trent is the capital of the British brewing industry, thanks to the quality of its gypsum-rich water. You can smell brewing on the air (the Marmite factory adds to the aroma). The town remains home to several large brewers, which have swallowed up some of its most famous beers (Bass, Ind Coope's Burton Ale), but in the last couple of decades new microbreweries have revived the town's traditions. This popular CAMRA (Campaign for Real Ale) festival showcases the distinct Burton style, along with more than a hundred other beers, ciders and country wines. There's also live music, food and bar snacks in the shape of the famous real pork scratchings.

When:	Mid-September
Where:	Burton Town Hall, King Edward Place, Burton-On-Trent, Staffs.
Duration:	2 days
Website:	www.burtoncamra.org.uk

Stratford on Avon Music Festival

Music and more in Shakespeare country

Stratford puts on a strong and varied programme of concerts for this autumn festival, with classical concerts alongside jazz, folk, world music and cabaret (there's usually a play or two going on in the town at the same time, it being some old playwright's birthplace). The festival 'rover' ticket allows you access to almost everything, and works out very good value if you're thinking of attending a number of concerts. The festival runs a busy education programme, with many of the performers running workshops in local schools, and family concerts at the weekends.

When:	Mid-October
Where:	Stratford-upon-Avon, Warwicks.
Duration:	9 days
Tel:	01789 207100 (box office)
Website:	www.stratfordmusicfestival.com

Autumn in Malvern Festival

High-class arts in the Malverns

Each October, some of the world's most prestigious musicians, poets, writers, film makers and other artists head for the Malvern Hills. Classical concerts in the Priory, touring theatre and literary walks on the hills are among the highlights.

When:	October
Where:	Malvern, Worcs.
Duration:	1 month
Tel:	01684 892289
Website:	www.malvernfestival.co.uk

South West

Gloucester International Cajun and Zydeco Festival

The sounds of Louisiana at Gloucester Guildhall

£?

For one weekend every year, the River Severn stands in for the swamps of Louisiana as the UK's largest Cajun and Zydeco festival lurches into Gloucester. Top bands from New Orleans, as well as France, Germany and the UK, show off their sweet, sweaty, swampy sounds, and it's almost impossible not to dance. There are afternoon jam sessions, Cajun cooking and an atmosphere more Mardi Gras than Cotswolds.

When:	Last weekend of January
Where:	Guildhall, Gloucester
Duration:	3 days
Tel:	01452 522232
Website:	www.gloucester.gov.uk

Bath Literature Festival

Not just Jane

£?

Long famous in literature, thanks largely to former resident Jane Austen, Bath has more recently gained a reputation for its literature festival. An intensive programme of more than a hundred events in just over a week brings an array of novelists, journalists, poets, politicians, actors, comedians, scriptwriters and biographers for readings, talks, performances and discussions. Keen to provoke debate, the festival organises events around a number of themes; topical issues in the past have included human rights, women and society, and Britishness. There are also family events, workshops, walks and free storytelling shows at the Library.

When:	February–March
Where:	Bath, Somerset
Duration:	9–10 days
Tel:	01225 463362
Website:	www.bathlitfest.org.uk

Vibraphonic

One city under a groove

Exeter gets its groove on with this fortnight of reggae, soul, jazz, funk, blues, hip-hop, drum and bass, grime, house, dub and whatever else is cooking. There's an impressive range of DJs and performers: think Mr Scruff and Gilles Peterson, but also Humphrey Lyttleton and the Basquiat Strings. As well as concerts at various venues, there are workshops, dance performances, films and graffiti art.

When:	March
Where:	Exeter, Devon
Duration:	2–3 weeks
Website:	www.vibraphonic.co.uk

Cheltenham Festival

The leading racing meet in the National Hunt calendar

With 25 races run over four days, this equestrian event has a great atmosphere, helped by the large Irish contingent (especially when it coincides with St Patrick's Day). The Cheltenham Gold Cup is the ultimate steeplechase, requiring a higher level of skill and finesse than the mêlée of the Grand National. The beautiful setting of Prestbury Park, carved out of the Cotswolds Hills, makes it an ideal spot for a spring day out.

When:	March
Where:	Cheltenham
Duration:	4 days
Website:	www.cheltenhamfestival.net

All Tomorrow's Parties

Cutting-edge alternative sounds – and a proper bed to sleep in

£ £ £ £

A love of leftfield indie music doesn't necessarily go together with a love of sleeping in tents and getting muddy. That realisation led indie treasures Belle and Sebastian to put together the Bowlie Weekender in 1999 in the comfortable surroundings of Pontin's holiday camp at Camber Sands, East Sussex. As well as enjoying a great line-up, hand-picked by the band, punters got to sleep in proper beds in chalets, with showers and stoves and electricity points. The idea proved so popular that it grew into All Tomorrow's Parties, which now holds three festivals a year in the UK, as well as similar events in the States. The main venue has now moved to Butlin's in Minehead, although it has come back to Camber Sands a few times. The premise remains the same: a band (Dinosaur Jr, Sonic Youth, Portishead) curates the festival, putting together their own dream line-up. Sometimes more than one collaborate, and actors (Vincent Gallo), artists (the Chapman brothers) and fans have also contributed. This always ensures a musical line-up with a few surprises – certainly not just the usual festival suspects. Meanwhile, fans enjoy holiday camp comforts, a beach and an intimate atmosphere. There are two spring weekends, and a winter one – The Nightmare Before Christmas. As the capacity is limited to 6,000, tickets sell out quickly.

When:	April/May (two separate weekends) and December
Where:	Butlin's, Minehead, Somerset (sometimes Pontin's, Camber Sands, East Sussex)
Duration:	2 days
Website:	www.atpfestival.com

Nailsworth Festival

A small town with big ideas

£?

The small Cotswold town of Nailsworth boasts a thriving festival, with an enviable programme of music, theatre, exhibitions, walks and talks. The festival also incorporates Nailstock, a community-run free music festival, where every band has to have at least one member from the GL5 or GL6 postal districts.

When:	Last week of April/beginning of May
Where:	Nailsworth, Stroud, Glos.
Duration:	2 weeks
Tel:	01453 833270
Website:	www.nailsworthfestival.org.uk

Padstow Obby Oss

Pagan horseplay

FREE

Long before Rick Stein and co made it a Mecca for foodies, Padstow was famous for its Obby Oss (Hobby Horse). Thousands converge on the town for one of the oldest May Day festivals in the country, celebrating the Celtic festival of Beltane, which marked the return of the sun god Bel. The hobby horse is a not entirely benevolent caped creature with a snapping-jawed mask. Its origins are uncertain, but horse deities were worshipped in many Celtic societies. The day starts at midnight, with singers making their way around the town. By morning, the old streets and the maypole are garlanded with wildflowers and greenery, and the people of the town turn out in colourful costumes with flowers in their hair. The morning's dancing gets under way with a number of junior Osses, before the Blue Ribbon Oss and the black-clad Old Oss appear. They cavort through the town to the beat of drums and accordions, attended by followers in coloured costumes. Unsuspecting maidens are dragged beneath the horse's cape – a relic of an ancient fertility rite, it apparently means they'll become pregnant within the year. Festivities continue late into the night.

When:	1 May (or the following Monday if this is a Sunday)
Where:	Padstow, Cornwall
Duration:	1 night
Website:	www.blueribbonoss.org.uk

Dot-to-Dot Festival

Join up the dots as you party your way around the city

£ £

See East Midlands section for full description.

When:	Spring Bank Holiday weekend (Sat/Sun)
Where:	Bristol and Nottingham
Duration:	2 days
Tel:	08713 100000
Website:	www.dottodotfestival.co.uk

Cornwall International Male Voice Choral Festival

Showcasing the very best in male voice singing

£?

Traditional male voice choirs are still found in many Cornish towns and villages, and this competitive biennial festival brings over 3,000 singers together in the cathedral city and capital of Truro. Previous festivals have also included choirs from England, Wales, Holland, Germany, Italy, Hungary, Estonia, Latvia, Switzerland, Finland, Eire, the Faroe Islands and Jersey. Many of the concerts take place in the impressive Truro Cathedral, but there are also events in churches and halls in and around the capital, including the Eden Project. Look out for impromptu open-air performances.

When:	First week of May, odd years
Where:	Truro, Cornwall
Duration:	1 week
Website:	www.cornwallintmalechorfest.co.uk

Cheltenham Festivals
'The list of nationally significant events staged in Cheltenham has lengthened by the year, to the point where it could justifiably be called the festival capital of Britain.' That's what *The Times* says, and who are we to argue? Cheltenham's four main festivals clock up annual ticket sales of over 125,000 and attract artists of international renown. As if that's not enough, the town also boasts a February folk festival at the town hall (see www.cheltenhamtownhall.org.uk) and the Wychwood Festival in May.
www.cheltenhamfestivals.com

Cheltenham Jazz Festival

'I'm at the Cheltenham Jazz Festival. The music is fabulous, the crowds are great and I am having a ball.' Michael Parkinson

£?

This is one of the country's leading jazz festivals, with jazz legends, cutting-edge innovators from around the world and popular Radio 2-friendly stars. Over 50 concerts take place during the week, including free music in the Jazz Marquee all day and performances from young musicians supported by the Jerwood Charitable Foundation. The concurrent Fringe offers a lively mix of jazz and other musical genres, as well as dance, comedy, cabaret, literature, visual art and photography.

When:	First week of May
Where:	Cheltenham
Duration:	1 week
Tel:	01242 774400
Website:	www.cheltenhamfestivals.com

South West

Paignton Bike Festival

Leathers, loud music and charitable deeds by the sea

FREE

The Hell's Angels provided heavy-handed security at the infamous Altamont concert of 1969. BMAD (Bikers Make A Difference) in the West Country prefer to organise festivals to raise money for the Devon Air Ambulance and a local children's hospice. Good causes aside, anyone venturing down to Paignton can look forward to a multitude of motorbikes, lots of leather, stunts, displays and three days of proper loud rock bands on the seafront.

When:	First weekend in May
Where:	Paignton seafront, Devon
Duration:	3 days
Website:	www.bmad.co.uk

Helston Furry Day

See in the spring with this ancient fertility dance

£?

The Furry, Flora or Faddy dance is unique to the Cornish town of Helston, and is one of the oldest festive traditions in the country. It probably derives from a pagan fertility ritual celebrating the passing of winter into spring, and the colourful spectacle attracts huge numbers of visitors. The day kicks off early: the first dance takes place at 7 a.m., and there's a children's dance at 10 a.m., featuring over a thousand school kids wearing white with colour-coordinated flowers. The Furry Dance itself is at midday. The men of the town are decked out in top hats and tails and the women wear their poshest frocks. All wear lilies of the valley, the town's traditional flower. They process through the steep, narrow streets of the town, even making their way through shops, gardens and houses. An evening dance takes place at 5 p.m. The Hal-an-Tow, a mummers' play involving St George and the Dragon, is also performed. There's a carnival atmosphere throughout the day and carousing in the pubs late into the night.

When:	8 May (unless this is a Sunday or Monday, in which case it will be the preceding Saturday)
Where:	Helston, Cornwall
Duration:	1 day
Website:	www.helstonfloraday.org.uk

Daphne du Maurier Festival

Celebrating Cornwall's favourite novelist

Daphne du Maurier lived and wrote in her beloved Cornwall, and its people and places inspired her most famous novels: *Jamaica Inn*, *Frenchman's Creek* and *Rebecca*. This Festival of Arts and Literature celebrating her life and work is centred around a 'festival village', complete with theatre, bookshop and restaurant, erected each year in the grounds of Fowey Hall Hotel, which overlooks the Fowey estuary. While du Maurier is the focus of the festival, there's a general arts programme with walks and talks, music and theatre, boat-trips and plenty of location-spotting. There is an abundance of accommodation in the fishing village of Fowey and throughout the 'Cornish Riviera', which is worth taking the time to explore.

When:	Mid-May
Where:	Fowey Hall Hotel, Fowey, Cornwall
Duration:	10 days
Tel:	0845 094 0428 (box office)
Website:	www.dumaurierfestival.co.uk

Run to the Sun

Bring your board and your Bug

There seems to be a natural affinity between surfers and VW Beetles and Campervans. Newquay is chock-full of Volkswagens at any time, but never more so than at the end of May, when a veritable customised procession heads west for Run to the Sun. The first event, in 1987, attracted around 70 cars; now, up to 100,000 people descend on Travelgue Holiday Park for three days of clubbing, surfing and general VW-related mayhem. Try to catch the 'cruise' on the way down: it convenes at Helston services on the M4, picks up other cars at various service stations along the way, and pulls into Newquay a thousand cars strong and five miles long. Don't bring a water pistol – following complaints from residents, they're now banned.

When:	Spring Bank Holiday weekend
Where:	Travelgue Holiday Park, Newquay, Cornwall
Duration:	4 days
Tel:	01637 851851
Website:	www.runtothesun.co.uk

World Pilot Gig Championships

Oar and wonder

FREE

Six-oared pilot gigs were originally used on the Isles of Scilly for rowing local navigators out to passing ships to steer them through the treacherous waters – though they were also often called into action as lifeboats when other ships were wrecked on the rocks. These days, they're used for sport, and the World Championships are the highlight of the gig racing season. 'World' is a bit of a misnomer – Cornwall, with the odd boat from Holland and the Faroe Islands would be more accurate – but the races are fiercely contested and the hundred-odd brightly painted wooden gigs make for a stunning spectacle. Barbecues on the beach and much post-race carousing in harbourside pubs add to the occasion.

When:	Spring Bank Holiday weekend
Where:	Isles of Scilly
Duration:	3 days
Tel:	01720 422000
Website:	www.worldgigs.co.uk

Cooper's Hill Cheese Rolling

Chase a cheese down a hill – try not injure yourself

FREE

Britain has a fine tradition of inventing sports. Football, cricket, rugby, golf and, of course, cheese rolling. This venerable athletic pursuit reaches its apogee at Cooper's Hill, near the village of Brockworth in the Cotswolds. It's a simple game. Competitors hurl themselves down the stupidly steep slope (a 1:1 incline in places) after a wheel of Double Gloucester cheese. The person who catches it wins the cheese – although since the cheese can reach speeds of 70 mph, this is virtually impossible, so it becomes instead a race to the bottom. There are five races (one is women-only), and anyone is free to enter, but be warned – it's a rare year where nobody requires hospital treatment afterwards. Cheese has been rolled at Cooper's Hill for at least two centuries and the event always attracts large crowds. The Cheese Rollers pub in nearby Shurdington is the place to go for pre-roll doping and to dissect proceedings afterwards.

When:	Spring Bank Holiday, 12 noon
Where:	Cooper's Hill, Brockworth, Glos.
Duration:	1 day
Website:	www.cheese-rolling.co.uk

Chippenham Folk Festival

Four days of the best in folk song, music, dance and traditions in the heart of Wiltshire

£ £ £ £ 👤 🔺

This folk festival outgrew its roots in the village of Lacock years ago, and now takes over the town of Chippenham for a long weekend. Over 200 events take place – main concerts and ceilidhs are held in a park by the river, where there are also craft and catering stalls. Virtually every pub and other possible venue in the town is commandeered for sessions, concerts and workshops. Street theatre, dance displays, processions and buskers cram the pedestrianised high street and market square, and there's a large street fair on the Bank Holiday Monday. Season ticket holders can stay in special camping and caravan sites in the town centre beside the River Avon.

When:	Spring Bank Holiday weekend (Fri–Mon)
Where:	Chippenham, Wilts.
Duration:	4 days
Tel:	01249 657190
Website:	www.chippfolk.co.uk

Wychwood Festival

Roots at the racecourse

£ £ £ £ £ 👤 🔺

Imagine a 'bijou Glastonbury' (*The Independent*) or 'an excellent hybrid of the Big Chill, WOMAD and The Cambridge Folk Festival' (*Time Out*). That's the Wychwood Music Festival – a fusion of world, folk, dance and indie with the common message that 'music can unite us all'. If that sounds a little woolly in theory, it's powerful in practice – the festival has a wonderfully civilised atmosphere (the venue, Cheltenham Racecourse, and its immaculate toilets probably help). Regularly running up multiple nominations at the UK Festival Awards, Wychwood is fast becoming a favourite on the festival circuit.

When:	Last weekend of May
Where:	Cheltenham Racecourse, Prestbury Park, Cheltenham, Glos.
Duration:	3 days
Tel:	01993 772580
Website:	www.wychwoodfestival.com

Fal River Festival

Events on the estuary

A fortnight of festive fun around Falmouth and the beautiful Fal estuary, with events on and off the water. Maritime activities include canoe trips up the river and heritage cruises, gig racing, tall ships and sailing races in traditional boats, including oyster dredgers and gaff-rigged ketches. A busy arts programme includes open artists' studios, exhibitions, music and drama. There's also a number of family events – don't miss the chance to make mud sculptures on the creek...

When:	Last week of May–first week of June
Where:	Various venues in and around Falmouth, Cornwall
Duration:	2 weeks
Tel:	01872 862090
Website:	www.falriverfestival.co.uk

The Hunting of the Earl of Rone

Bizarre stuffed earl abuse

Here's a random one. The Earl of Rone (Tyrone) was forced to flee from Ireland in 1607 and, according to local legend, was shipwrecked off the coast of North Devon. He hid out in the woods, surviving on ship's biscuits, before being captured by local grenadiers. It's a strange story, as the historical Earl of Rone, one Hugh O'Neill, actually reached Spain and lived the rest of his days there – there's no evidence for his Devon escapades. Nevertheless, every Spring Bank Holiday the villagers of Combe Martin re-enact the 'Hunting of the Earl of Rone'. Over the preceding weekend, costumed grenadiers, a hobby horse, a fool and other villagers hunt through the village for the unfortunate Earl. His masked, straw-stuffed effigy is finally found in the woods on the Monday night, mounted back-to-front on a donkey and paraded through the village to the sea. Along the way he is frequently shot by the grenadiers, revived by the hobby horse and fool, remounted, then shot again. Around sunset, he's finally shot on the beach and thrown into the sea. The hunt was banned in 1837 for 'licentiousness and drunken behaviour' (it was traditional for the procession to stop at every pub en route which, in the nineteenth century, was rather a lot), but revived in 1974. It now attracts thousands of onlookers, and guesthouses can get booked up early.

When:	Spring Bank Holiday Monday
Where:	Combe Martin, Devon
Duration:	1 day
Website:	www.earl-of-rone.org.uk

Brixham Heritage Festival

Historical happenings at the home of the trawler

This week-long festival kicks off with a musical, featuring traditional folk songs and sea shanties, that tells the story of a Brixham smuggler and the Great Gale of 1866. There follows a week of concerts, classic car rallies, crab-catching contests and street entertainments. The port of Brixham is the birthplace of the trawler industry, and trawler races have been held here since 1851. The Brixham Heritage Race, held at the beginning of the festivities, is a popular feature in the sailing calendar, with trawlers and other traditional sailing boats competing in a variety of classes.

When:	Whitsun half-term (Heritage Race on the first Saturday)
Where:	Brixham, Devon
Duration:	1 week
Tel:	01803 522207
Website:	www.holidaytorbay.co.uk

Cotswold Olimpicks

Predating the modern Olympics by three centuries

London 2012 may grab the headlines, but in the same year Chipping Camden in the Cotswolds will be celebrating the 400th anniversary of its own Olympick (sic) Games. Robert Dover beat Pierre de Courbetin to the idea of reviving the ancient games by some three centuries, and they've continued annually ever since. The Games are held on Dover's Hill, with magnificent views across the Vale of Evesham and the Welsh marches. The most prestigious title is the 'Champion of the Hill', awarded to the top performer in the traditional events of Standing Jump, Putting the Shot, Throwing the Sledgehammer, and Spurning the Barre (a form of caber-tossing). Athletes, all amateur and doped with nothing stronger than cider, also compete in cross-country races, wrestling and the ever-popular shin-kicking, while morris dancing, Punch and Judy, pipe bands and falconry add to the spectacle. The day is rounded off with a bonfire, fireworks and a torchlit procession into Chipping Camden. Floodlit dancing in the town square kicks off at 11 p.m. and goes on till late, with all the surrounding pubs and hotels staying open.

When:	Friday after Spring Bank Holiday
Where:	Dover's Hill, Chipping Camden, Glos.
Duration:	1 day
Tel:	01384 274041
Website:	www.olimpickgames.co.uk

Bath International Music Festival

Musical innovation from classical to contemporary

A centre of culture for centuries, Bath doesn't disappoint with its annual music festival. The diverse programme includes orchestral, chamber and contemporary classical music, contemporary jazz and world music and, since Joanna McGregor took over as artistic director, cutting-edge electronica. The festival has a history of innovative programming, including a now-famous collaboration between Yehudi Menuhin and Ravi Shankar, or more recently a concert in Bath Abbey with Brian Eno, Bath Camerata and McGregor herself. The 17-day festival also includes lunchtime recitals, talks, masterclasses, free outdoor events and children's concerts.

When:	Late May–early June
Where:	Bath, Somerset
Duration:	17 days
Tel:	01225 463362 (box office)
Website:	www.bathmusicfest.org.uk

Bath Fringe

Artistic bedlam late into the night

Since 1981, the Bath Fringe has run alongside the original festival. It's grown hugely in recent years, and now features a frenetic programme of gigs, theatre, cabaret, comedy, dance, visual arts, street theatre, kids' shows and the odd unclassifiable happening. The Fringe includes a three-day street art festival, the Bedlam Fair. There's no shortage of places to hang out, with three late-night festival clubs and all the glamour of the Art Deco Spiegeltent.

When:	Late May–early June
Where:	Bath, Somerset
Duration:	17 days
Tel:	01225 463362 (box office)
Website:	www.bathfringe.co.uk

Salisbury International Arts Festival

Artistic excellence in historic settings

Salisbury is garnering a growing reputation for one of the country's best multi-arts festivals. It attracts artists of international calibre from the worlds of music, theatre, opera and dance, including such luminaries as Ravi Shankar, Peter Brook and the Beijing National Opera. The festival commissions innovative original work, notably an ambitious four-year collaboration between author Vikram Seth and composer Alec Roth, which has attracted rave reviews. There's a strong line-up of literary events and other speakers, arthouse films at Salisbury Arts Centre (a deconsecrated medieval church) and outdoors at Old Sarum hill fort and unique site-specific performances. Salisbury makes full use of a number of superb venues, including the incomparable cathedral, Stonehenge and Wilton House, where the Globe Theatre Company have performed Shakespeare in the gardens. There are also free events including street theatre in the medieval market square, spectacular outdoor sculptures and community projects.

When:	May–June
Where:	Salisbury, Wilts.
Duration:	17 days
Tel:	01722 332977
Website:	www.salisburyfestival.co.uk

North Devon Festival

Exmoor and more

North Devon celebrates its vibrant cultural scene in over 200 events that take place at 80 indoor and outdoor venues in towns and villages across the area. They cover a comprehensive range of tastes and interests from the Festival at the Theatre, which brings world-class musicians, comedians and speakers to the Landmark Theatre, Ilfracombe and Barnstaple's Queen's Theatre, to classic cars and the National Sandcastle Competition. Touring theatre companies and fairs travel to towns and villages around the region, and many communities hold their own events. Concerts and exhibitions abound, and there's a plethora of nature walks and other country pursuits. The lively Barnstaple Fringe runs at around the same time, and the North Devon Festival enjoys an association with various other events. If you're planning a trip to this part of the world in June, you're sure to find something of interest.

When:	Throughout June
Where:	All over North Devon
Duration:	1 month
Tel:	01271 324242
Website:	www.northdevonfestival.co.uk

Cheltenham Science Festival

Breaking the mould when it comes to science

This lively festival was launched in 2002 and attracts 15,000 visitors a year. There are lectures, debates and presentations on a broad range of up-to-the-minute and controversial scientific issues, and plenty of hands-on stuff in the interactive Discover Zone to keep the kids and the less cerebral entertained. As an extra bonus, many of the events are free.

When:	First week of June
Where:	Cheltenham
Duration:	1 week
Tel:	01242 774400
Website:	www.cheltenhamfestivals.com

Cheltenham Music Festival

Pioneering programming since the end of the war

This fortnight-long event has been running since 1945, continuously producing exciting and innovative programmes of classical music, inspired by an annual theme. International stars and up-and-coming artists perform in orchestral and chamber concerts, and there are talks, masterclasses, community participation and free outdoor events.

When:	First two weeks of June
Where:	Cheltenham
Duration:	2 weeks
Tel:	01242 774400
Website:	www.cheltenhamfestivals.com

Heritage Bristol Volksfest

A friendly festival for VW enthusiasts, with a decidedly chilled vibe

Admire Vee-Dubs of all shapes and sizes or show off your own in the show-and-shine at this weekend Volkfest. There's a beach party, live music, off-road races, an auto-jumble, a traders' area that rivals the town centre in size and random events like a dog agility contest. The whole weekend has a real family feel, and camping is available on site on Friday and Saturday nights.

When:	First weekend of June
Where:	North Somerset Showground, Wraxhall, nr Nailsea, Bristol
Duration:	3 days
Tel:	01275 330425
Website:	www.bristolvolksfest.co.uk

Sunrise Celebration

Hippy heaven

Come and see in the summer at this socially committed and environmentally sustainable Somerset celebration. You can expect organic-only food, recycling facilities, renewable energy and more compost toilets per person than any other festival (well, they can't be worse than portaloos, can they?). Entertainment, events and edification take place across a number of different arenas, laid out in a sacred mandala design and based around themes like green innovation, permaculture, tipis and spiritual healing. You could try astrological speed dating, take a gong bath, join in a tribal ceremony, drink some chai tea or groove to psy-trance. Yes, it's all very New Age-y, but if the June do on that other Somerset farm has become too commercial for you, this is the perfect alternative.

When:	First weekend of June
Where:	Bearley Farm, Yeovil, Somerset
Duration:	3 days
Tel:	0845 009 6347 (Information Line)
Website:	www.sunrisecelebration.com

Wimborne Folk Festival

Traditional music by the Minster

££££ ⛺ ▲

First held in 1980, this annual folk festival now attracts thousands of people from across the UK and abroad to the historic Dorset town of Wimborne Minster. There are big-name performers from the field of traditional English and Celtic music, ceilidhs and a Festival Club where anyone is free to perform. The streets fill with morris teams and market stalls, and jam sessions spill from the pubs. Camping is provided at a site less than ten minutes' walk from the town centre.

When:	Second weekend of June
Where:	Wimborne, Dorset
Duration:	3 days
Tel:	01202 623740
Website:	www.wimbornefolkfestival.co.uk

Beach Break

Roll out the beach and roll on the tunes

££££ ▲

This is effectively a big student beach party, with some top DJs, bands, indie films, theatre and emerging student talent. An impressive pitch on *Dragons' Den* had the dragons competing for a slice of the action, although in the end the young organisers decided to turn elsewhere for investment. As it's aimed at students during the non-stop party period between the end of exams and the start of the summer vacation, it takes place mid-week. Surfing, canoeing, paintball, swimming and games on sandy Polzeath Beach add to the fun. Just pray for sunshine...

When:	Monday–Wednesday, mid-June
Where:	Polzeath Beach, North Cornwall
Duration:	3 days
Website:	www.beachbreaklive.com

Golowan Community Arts Festival

Have an amazing mazey time

Golowan was founded in 1990 as a revival of the ancient celebration of the feast of St John (Goelyowann – a Christianised version of a pagan summer solstice celebration) that had died out in the Penzance area in the late Victorian era. It's grown into one of the UK's largest community festivals, attracting 60,000 visitors from all over the world, and perhaps the most significant celebration of Cornish culture. The ten-day programme blends Cornish traditions with a diverse programme of music, street theatre, storytelling, stalls, fireworks, torchlit processions and the like. There's a strong strand of community involvement (thousands of children take part) and a true festive atmosphere. Events culminate with the parades and pageantry of Mazey Day ('mazey' being a useful local word meaning 'a bit dazed and confused').

When:	Mid-June
Where:	Penzance, Newlyn and Mousehole, Cornwall
Duration:	8 days
Tel:	01736 332211
Website:	www.golowan.com

Exeter Summer Festival

Arts, entertainment and the ancient Lammas Fair

Devon's capital presents a wealth of artistic events over its fortnight-long festival, featuring leading international artists. The festival begins with a bang, with live music, street entertainment and fireworks on The Quay. Another popular free event is the Lammas Fair procession, led by the Lord Mayor, which dates back nearly a thousand years. There's a strong spread of theatre, comedy, dance, classical and contemporary music, film and art exhibitions in various venues across the city, including the cathedral.

As if that's not enough, they do it all again in November, though the Autumn Festival focuses more on artists from Exeter and the West Country.

When:	Last two weeks of June
Where:	Exeter, Devon
Duration:	2 weeks
Website:	www.exeter.gov.uk

South West

Glastonbury

The earth mother of all festivals

It's hard to believe that, not so long ago, Glastonbury belonged to the counter-culture. While there's no doubt that Glastonbury is now hugely commercialised, it would be wrong to suggest that it's become sanitised or homogenised. For one long weekend it becomes the largest and most diverse city in Somerset, and arguably the most culturally vibrant on Earth.

For a start, there's the beautiful pastoral setting on the edge of the Mendip Hills. This is an area steeped in myth and it's a sorry soul that remains unmoved as the sun sets behind Glastonbury Tor.

The music, meanwhile, is second to none. Bands consider it an honour to play here, and many pull out career-defining sets – Oasis in 1994, Pulp in 1995, Radiohead in 1997... Choose from the world's top bands on the Pyramid Stage, the coolest alternative acts on the Other Stage or cutting-edge DJs in the Dance Village (yes, Village – why settle for one dance stage when you can have seven?). For a more laid-back atmosphere, head to the Acoustic Tent or the Jazz-World Stage, or check out something innovative on the John Peel Stage.

Planning a superstar-spotting itinerary and rushing from one arena to the next is not, however, the best way to enjoy the Glastonbury experience. In fact, you could spend an amazing weekend without seeing a single name band. There are dozens of smaller stages, tents and spaces – you might stumble upon salsa dancing, a Celtic ceilidh, freeform jazz or even opera.

You can shop till you drop in some of the quirkiest markets imaginable and eat fine food from all over the world. You'll find enough fringe theatre here to rival the Edinburgh Festival. Circus, cabaret, comedy, crazy costumes – and that's just the audience.

It would be easy to laze away the whole festival exploring alternative cultures in the Green Fields, taking a shamanic journey, joining in craft workshops or just sipping tea in a tipi. Ducking into random tents, watching the headphone-wearing dancers partying quietly till dawn at the Silent Disco or joining a bevy of bongo players in the stone circle as the midsummer sun rises – it's the moments of random serendipity that make the Glastonbury experience unique.

When:	Third weekend of June (though every four years or so there's a fallow year)
Where:	Worthy Farm, Pilton, Shepton Mallet, Somerset
Duration:	3 days
Tel:	0844 412 4626
Website:	www.glastonburyfestivals.co.uk

Stonehenge Solstice

The oldest festival in the book

Stonehenge has been the venue for some sort of solstice festival for several millennia. The stone circle dates back to around 2200 BC, and it's widely assumed that druids held rituals here, though nobody really has a clue what these were. Neo-druids have been re-enacting solstice ceremonies here in the late nineteenth century.

In 1974, they were joined by five hundred hippies at the first Stonehenge Free Festival. 'Wood fires, tents and tipis, free food stalls, stages and bands, music and magic...' in the words of organiser Jeremy Ratter, who later founded the very un-hippy punk band Crass. 'Old friends met new, hands touched, bodies entwined, minds expanded and, in one tiny spot on our Earth, love and peace had become a reality.'

Ten years later, the Stonehenge Festival had grown into Britain's largest free festival, attracting crowds of 70,000 in 1984. The following year, though, love and peace were in short supply. 'New-age travellers' had become public enemy number one, and the police moved in to prevent a convoy of 300 from reaching the stones in a notoriously brutal operation.

The following year, Margaret Thatcher's government introduced the 1986 Public Order Act, which included the draconian provision that: 'Two people proceeding in a given direction can constitute a procession and can be arrested as a threat to civil order'. This and the later Criminal Justice Act put paid to the likes of the Stonehenge Free Festival – until another piece of legislation came to the rescue. The European Court of Human Rights has ruled that members of any recognised religion have a right to worship in their own church – and in 1999, the various neo-druids and pagans who claim Stonehenge as their temple were allowed back.

Today, up to 30,000 revellers of all ages gather for impromptu music, dancing and midsummer merrymaking. It's fair to say only a small proportion attach any religious significance to it – but the sunrise can't fail to provide an uplifting spiritual moment (and a great picture on your camera-phone). Being in among the stones is a privilege, too – tourists have to pay to look at them from behind a fence. As no one sleeps, there's no camping at the site; people looking to camp in lay-bys and unofficial sites do get moved on.

When: Summer Solstice (20/21 June)
Where: Stonehenge
Duration: 1 day

For a more laid-back solstice celebration, head up the road to Avebury – an equally evocative and far more extensive ancient site. It's become the preferred option for many practising pagans, and a few thousand other people drawn by the atmosphere. Strict druids and hardened partygoers also head to Stonehenge for the winter solstice and at the equinox.

Pilton Festival

The revenge of the pagans

Not to be confused with Michael Eavis' original name for his Glastonbury shindig, this festival takes place in Pilton, Barnstaple and is also known as Green Man Day. The Green Man was a pre-Christian symbol of nature and fertility, and was a prominent figure in many medieval festivals (although the one at Pilton is a relatively recent reinvention). Despite his pagan nature, the Green Man is often depicted in church carvings – there's a fine example in Pilton's own parish church. The Church's co-option of the old religion is re-enacted in the festival's central pageant, an encounter between the Green Man and the Pilton Prior. Throughout the day there's a festival market with crafts and produce, music, street entertainers, storytellers, sideshows and more.

When:	Third Saturday in June
Where:	Pilton, Barnstaple, Devon
Duration:	1 day
Tel:	01271 375776
Website:	www.piltonfestival.co.uk

3 Wishes Faery Fest

Away with the fairies for a midsummer night's dream

What better way to spend midsummer's eve than to be spirited away by the fairies (or, as they prefer to be known, faeries)? On Bodmin Moor, in the heart of Celtic Cornwall, you'll find a little slice of fairyland in this unique and fantastically fey festival. There's music from the likes of the Mediæval Bæbes and Daughters of Gaia, mystic marquees, unicorn rides, fairy fashion shows, fire faeries, storytelling, wing workshops and more elfin types than you can shake a wand at. Your children are safe with the faeries here, and will find plenty of magical adventures. Remember, faeries have a Puckish sense of humour – don't take it all too seriously.

When:	Midsummer weekend (Fri–Sun)
Where:	Colliford Lake Park, nr Liskeard, Bodmin Moor, Cornwall
Duration:	3 days
Tel:	01736 330201
Website:	www.3wishesfaeryfest.co.uk

South West

Mevagissey Feast Week

A fishing port that knows how to have fun

The old fishing port of Mevagissey, once the centre of the Cornish pilchard industry, celebrates its Feast Week at the end of June every year. It's a lively traditional festival with concerts on the quay (listen out for the renowned Mevagissey Male Voice Choir), a carnival and dancing in the streets. There's a fishing boat race around the bay and a fancy dress raft race, preceded by an anarchic flour and water fight. The people of Meva know how to party hard – anyone expecting a quiet seaside holiday may get more than they bargained for.

When:	Last week of June
Where:	Mevagissey, Cornwall
Duration:	1 week
Website:	www.mevagissey.net

Frome Festival

Somerset's largest community festival

This thriving community festival packs more than 160 events into ten days. Most events are products of Frome's thriving artistic scene, but there's also a smattering of famous national and international names. Music ranges from classical and choral to jazz, folk, indie and world music. Comedy, dance and drama, an extensive literary programme, exhibitions, walks and talks, craft stalls and a farmer's market add to the occasion. There are artistic workshops for children, families and adults and a youth cafe where teenagers can hang out or join in free workshops.

When:	Early July
Where:	Frome, Somerset
Duration:	10 days
Tel:	01373 453889
Website:	www.fromefestival.co.uk

Larmer Tree Festival

The original boutique festival and still the best-kept secret

£££££

This little gem of a festival promises five days of music and mellow vibes hidden away in beautiful ornamental gardens laid out by eccentric Victorian archaeologist General Pitt-Rivers. There's an eclectic blend of music from over 70 local and established acts – previous headliners included Jools Holland, Billy Bragg and Dreadzone – plus street theatre, a huge programme of creative workshops for children and adults, and award-winning toilets. Performers have to compete with the vocal talents of the free-range peacocks and macaws.

When:	Mid-July
Where:	Larmer Tree Grounds, Tollard Royal, nr Salisbury, Wilts.
Duration:	5 days
Tel:	01725 552300
Website:	www.larmertreefestival.com

Tewkesbury Medieval Festival

Re-enact the end battle of the Wars of the Roses

£

Ever fancied watching a pitched battle between 2,000 knights on horseback, archers and men-at-arms? Want to camp in medieval style for the weekend? Need a new embroidered gown or a cooking pot? And be entertained by jesters and minstrels? Then don't miss Europe's biggest medieval spectacular, which attracts serious re-enactors and thousands of other curious onlookers. Enjoy a hog roast and a goblet of mead, and watch out for the dragons. The event takes place on the site of the Battle of Tewkesbury, the final battle of the Wars of the Roses in 1471 (Lancastrians beware – there will be beheadings, though apparently not fatal ones). The day ends with a compline (night prayer) service in the Abbey. There are no facilities for camping on site – see the website for accommodation options nearby.

When:	Second weekend of July
Where:	Lincoln Green Lance, Tewkesbury, Glos.
Duration:	2 days
Tel:	01684 295027 (Tourist Information)
Website:	www.tewkesburymedievalfestival.org

South West

Tolpuddle Martyrs Festival

The workers united will never be defeated

The transportation of six Dorset farm labourers to Australia to form a trade union put the village of Tolpuddle on the map, and marked the birth of the trade union movement in the UK. Their legacy is commemorated in this right-on left-wing festival. There are speeches from TUC leaders and politicians and, more interesting perhaps, the likes of Mark Thomas and other comedians and activists. There's a strong folk-rock musical line-up – Billy Bragg is, unsurprisingly, a fixture – with an opening night ceilidh and democratic open-mic sessions in the Workers Beer tent. Entry to the festival is free – you pay for parking and to stay at the festival campsite.

When:	Second weekend of July (Fri–Sun)
Where:	Tolpuddle, Dorchester, Dorset
Duration:	3 days
Tel:	01305 267992 (Tourist Information)
Website:	www.tolpuddlemartyrs.org.uk

Marlborough Jazz Festival

Waking up Wiltshire

The elegant Wiltshire market town of Marlborough may seem an unlikely home for one of the country's hippest jazz festivals. For 362 days of the year, it's a sleepy sort of place, but for one weekend in July, the joint is most definitely jumping, as some of the hottest world stars and new talents descend on the town. The festival has a particularly strong record of booking up-and-coming artists, and audiences are invited to vote in the 'best newcomer' award. Concerts are up close and personal, and musicians relish playing here – many return year after year. There's more than you could possibly hope to catch in one weekend, but stroller tickets allow you to come and go as you please – definitely good value if you're staying for the duration.

When:	Second weekend of July (Fri–Sun)
Where:	Marlborough, Wilts.
Duration:	3 days
Tel:	01672 515095
Website:	www.marlboroughjazz.co.uk

South West

Lawfrowda Festival

Community celebration near Land's End

St Just, just a few miles from Land's End, is the first/last town in England, and is the venue for this celebration of community arts. A week-long festival of events showcasing local creative talent culminates in Lafrowda Day, which features three impressive processions – a children's procession in the morning, the Community Procession in the afternoon and a lantern procession at 10 p.m. The giant puppets are truly spectacular. There's 12 hours of free entertainment to suit every taste, as well as street performers, stalls and a wonderful atmosphere.

When:	Third Saturday in July (Lawfrowda Day) and preceding week
Where:	St Just, Cornwall
Duration:	9 days
Tel:	01736 888160
Website:	www.lafrowda-festival.co.uk

Gloucester Festival

A fortnight's free fun

Gloucester's fortnight of festivities is one of the best municipal festivals around. It kicks off with a great carnival procession, and there are plenty of free events every day and night. Expect live music, street performers, family events, cultural diversity, outdoor theatre, comedy and exhibitions, as well as sporting events and a fireworks display. A family funfair runs in Gloucester Park for most of the duration.

When:	Last two weeks of July
Where:	Gloucester
Duration:	2 weeks
Website:	www.gloucester.gov.uk

South West

International Brick and Rolling Pin Throwing Contest

Stroud's strange sporting spectacle

[FREE] [🏃]

One of the lesser-known championships in international sport, Brick and Rolling Pin Throwing have been contested annually in Stroud since 1960, when the visiting Mayor of Stroud, Oklahoma, mentioned his town's peculiar sporting event (it was just bricks to begin with – rolling pins were a later addition for the womenfolk). The Gloucestershire town now competes against its namesakes in Oklahoma, Australia and Canada, which hold the contest simultaneously, give or take a few hours' time difference.

> **When:** Third Saturday of July
> **Where:** Stroud Showground, Glos.
> **Duration:** 1 day

Port Eliot LitFest

Not your typical literature festival

[£ £ £ £] [🏃] [⛺]

The *enfant terrible* of the literary festival circuit, Port Eliot makes other literature festivals look a little staid and stuffy in comparison. Though there are literary heavyweights reading and speaking, Port Eliot feels more like a boutique music festival – there's enough music, cabaret, films and multimedia happenings to keep less bookish types enthused. There's a complete absence of intellectual snobbery, and plenty of surprises hidden away in the landscaped gardens. Kids will be entertained and even educated in the House of Fairy Tales, and teenagers get in on the act with poetry slams and camera-phone movies. The grounds of Port Eliot on the St Germans estuary are beautiful, the atmosphere simultaneously invigorating and relaxing, and the homemade cakes superb. Anyone not keen on conventional camping can hire a luxury 'podpad' (complete with reading light) or tipi, or there are numerous guest houses and self-catering cottages in the area.

> **When:** Third weekend of July
> **Where:** Port Eliot, St Germans, Cornwall
> **Duration:** 3 days
> **Tel:** 01503 232783
> **Website:** www.porteliotlitfest.com

Two Thousand Trees

It's ethical, it's green, it's musical…

Disillusioned by the rampant commercialism of mainstream festival, the organisers of Two Thousand Trees came up with this alternative. Limited to 2,000 people, it's a laid-back weekend of local and bigger-name bands, back-to-nature vibes, deliberately uncommercial, affordable and environmentally switched-on (the recycling and renewable energy rates put most local authorities to shame). The emphasis is on having fun in a field, and the site on the edge of the Cotswolds is a glorious place to camp.

When:	Saturday/Sunday, third weekend of July
Where:	Upcote Farm, Withington, Cheltenham, Glos.
Duration:	2 days
Website:	www.twothousandtreesfestival.co.uk

WOMAD

There's a whole world of music out there

Founded by Peter Gabriel, WOMAD (World of Music, Arts and Dance) aims 'to bring together and to celebrate many forms of music, arts and dance drawn from countries and cultures all over the world'. The festival features a globe-trotting line-up ranging from ancient traditional instruments to futuristic electronic beats – often within the same act. The leading lights of world music headline – Youssou N'Dour, Nitin Sawhney, Annoushka Shankar and the Gotan Project to name but a few – but the joy is often in the random discoveries from incredible musicians, or even countries, you've never heard of.

For its 25th anniversary in 2007, WOMAD moved from Reading to the far more appealing surroundings of Charlton Park in the Wiltshire countryside. Wonderful atmosphere, and very family-friendly: under-14s go free, and there's a huge range of music, dance, craft and cookery workshops.

WOMAD sometimes also holds events at the Eden Project, and organises regular festivals around the world.

When:	Last weekend of July
Where:	Charlton Park, Malmesbury, Wilts.
Duration:	3 days
Website:	www.womad.org

Trowbridge Village Pump Festival

A beautiful site and a unique atmosphere

£££££

This friendly festival, featuring leading names in folk and roots music from the UK and around the world, is held in the picturesque surroundings of Stowford Manor Farm in west Wiltshire. It's a nicely manageable size, but with plenty going on across three marquee stages, along with a children's tent, three beer tents and a good range of trade stalls selling food and drink, craft, clothes, musical instruments and other items from all over the world. For a festival that began life in a pub garden, it's attracted some impressive acts over the years, with recent headliners including Ralph McTell, the Be Good Tanyas, Suzanne Vega and Bellowhead. Free on-site camping is available.

When: Last weekend of July (Thurs–Sun)
Where: Stowford Manor Farm, Trowbridge, Wilts.
Duration: 4 days
Tel: 01225 769132
Website: www.trowbridgefestival.com

Bristol Harbour Festival

Entertainment on shore and on the water

£?

Bristol's historic harbour is the scene of a large free festival – attracting around 180,000 people over the course of the weekend – with events on and off the water. There's live music, including a dance stage, street theatre and circus and a continental market. In the harbour itself are hundreds of colourful boats, historic tall ships and water displays. Saturday night erupts with a huge fireworks display that makes the most of the cranes and other industrial features of the port.

When: End of July/beginning of August (Fri–Sun)
Where: Bristol Harbourside, Avon
Duration: 3 days
Website: www.bristol.gov.uk

South West

Gloucester International Rhythm and Blues Festival

Enjoy (Severn) Delta blues

Gloucester becomes more Deep South than south west at this annual festival. There are concerts from blues heavyweights, smaller-scale gigs in pubs, clubs and restaurants, open-mic sessions and a free outdoor event. Bring your harmonica.

When:	End of July/beginning of August
Where:	Gloucester
Duration:	8 days
Tel:	01452 412828
Website:	www.gloucesterblues.co.uk

Guiting Festival

World-class musicians in a village hall

For four decades, world-class classical and jazz musicians have been lured to the beautiful Cotswold village of Guiting Power, near Stow-on-the-Wold to perform in the village hall in this week-long festival. One of these, innovative pianist Joanna McGregor, is now the festival's president; the chance to see artists of her calibre performing in such an intimate, friendly setting should be grabbed with both hands.

When:	Last week of July/August
Where:	Village Hall, Guiting Power, Stow-on-the-Wold, Glos.
Duration:	8 days
Tel:	01242 603912 (Booking)
Website:	www.guitingfestival.org

Endorse it in Dorset Festival

Silly fun and fine music

£££££ [♦] [▲]

Held on a farm near the village of Sixpenny Handley in deepest Dorset, this three-day, 5,000-capacity festival is one of the happiest and friendliest you're likely to come across. Founded by the legendary (in parts of east Dorset) cowpunk band Pronghorn, Endorse it has quality bands and DJs known and unknown, from ska to dub to hip-hop to bluegrass, plus comedy, theatre, plenty of stuff for the kids and an endearingly homespun feel.

When:	Early August
Where:	Oakley Farm, Sixpenny Handley, Dorset
Duration:	3 days
Website:	www.lgofestivals.com

Three Choirs Festival

One of the oldest music festivals in the world

£?

The Three Choirs Festival has been held each year since the beginning of the eighteenth century, making it one of the oldest music festivals in the world. Uniquely, it rotates annually between the cathedral cities of Gloucester, Worcester and Hereford – and a healthy sense of competition between the three hosts keeps it constantly fresh. The highpoints of the festival are the grand choral concerts held in the cathedral, featuring the Festival Chorus and major international artists and ensembles. There's also a programme of chamber music, organ recitals, opera, theatre, talks, exhibitions and other events running throughout the festival week.

When:	First week of August
Where:	Gloucester, Worcester or Hereford
Duration:	8 days
Tel:	Gloucester: 01452 529819; Worcester: 01905 616200; Hereford: 01432 374200
Website:	www.3choirs.org

Ripcurl Board Masters Festival

Europe's biggest surf, skate and music event

£ £ £

Newquay is the UK's number one surf spot, and this festival is Europe's biggest surf, skate and music event. The professional surfing contests on Fistral Beach make a stunning (free) spectacle, as do the bikini-clad 'Boardmasters Babes', and there's impressive action on dry land too with BMX and skate ramps. There's a beach bar and live music sessions on the beach all week. On Friday and Saturday a music festival, Unleashed, takes place on the cliff tops overlooking Watergate Bay, featuring some top name bands. There's no on-site camping, but there are campsites around Newquay – probably a good idea, as other accommodation in town gets booked up.

When:	First week of August
Where:	Fistral Beach/Watergate Bay, Newquay, Cornwall
Duration:	7 days
Tel:	020 8789 6655
Website:	www.ripcurlboardmasters.com

Sidmouth FolkWeek

A week of non-stop music in the perfect seaside setting

£ £ £ £ £

With its perfect bay enclosed by towering red cliffs, Regency architecture, beaches and rock pools, Sidmouth is the quintessential seaside town. It's the sort of place people come back to year after year, and that's exactly what thousands of folk music fans do every August. The festival began life in 1955 as a morris dancing event, but it now covers a broad range of music, song, dance and crafts. There are performances from top performers, but these are only part of the attraction. Over the course of the week, every empty space in town seems to become a venue for a concert, a ceilidh or a workshop, the streets and the seafront are full of buskers and dancers and impromptu sessions start up in the pubs. There's a busy programme of events for under-16s, and the whole town has a truly festive atmosphere.

A funding crisis almost spelt the end of the festival in 2004, but supporters quickly rallied and a newly formed company has got Sidmouth back on track. There's a choice of tickets; the cheaper season ticket option allows access to all events except the big-name evening concerts. A special FolkWeek campsite is available (just keep the noise down on that accordion…).

When:	First week of August
Where:	Sidmouth, Devon
Duration:	8 days
Tel:	01395 578627 (box office)
Website:	www.sidmouthfolkweek.co.uk

Big Green Gathering

The future's bright, the future's green

£ £ £ £ £

Europe's largest green-themed festival, which attracts up to 20,000 people, grew out of Glastonbury's Green Fields, which had themselves been inspired by previous Green Gatherings in the early 1980s. There are demonstrations of green technology, permaculture and sustainable homes; holistic healing and alternative therapies; esoteric and Eastern spirituality, with no shortage of meditation sessions, t'ai chi workshops and gong massages; eco-friendly and fair-trade crafts and commerce; organic and entirely vegetarian food. If all that sounds rather earnest, don't worry: this isn't a Green Party conference. There's a strong emphasis on celebration and family-friendly fun. There's an eclectic range of music – from Balkan beats and tribal dance to folk, hip-hop and reggae – complete with solar-powered lighting and sound systems, as well as comedy, cabaret and general randomness. The Mendip Hills in Somerset are a fine place to celebrate the natural environment. Make sure you travel by public transport.

When:	Early August
Where:	Fernhill Farm, Mendip Hills, nr Cheddar, Somerset
Duration:	5 days
Tel:	01458 834629
Website:	www.big-green-gathering.com

Bloom

A unique boutique festival with the ultimate show-stopping finale

£ £ £

This boutique festival is set in the grounds of Dyrham Park, a National Trust property outside Bath. The line-up features sophisticated beats across a wide range of music. The organisers are quite particular about their food, hand-picking a selection of local traders who offer organic and ethically produced food, plus a tongue-tingling variety of international cuisines. With Bath Ales on board, you won't be disappointed at the bar, either. With mud sculpting and juggling classes to get stuck into, there's plenty for kids to do, and many of the artists bring their own families along. Expect to stumble upon random acts of fun: in 2007, Bloomers broke the Guinness World Record for the largest game of musical statues. An extra special treat lies in store as the festival winds down – each year it coincides with the Perseid meteor shower, and the site provides a rare, unspoilt view of this celestial phenomenon.

When:	Second weekend of August
Where:	Dyrham Park, Glos.
Duration:	3 days
Website:	www.bloomfestival.com

Falmouth Week

The south west's premier sailing event

Sailing enthusiasts flock to the Fal for this packed week of water-based activities. There's a full programme of races, featuring everything from dinghies to early-twentieth-century superyachts, traditional crafts and working fishing boats. Beginners and families are catered for alongside the ultra-competitive. There are also concerts and other events on shore.

When:	Second week of August
Where:	Falmouth, Cornwall
Duration:	1 week
Website:	www.falmouthweek.co.uk

Bristol Balloon Fiesta

More than just a load of hot air

If the sight of a hot air balloon on a summer's evening lifts your heart, then the Bristol Balloon Fiesta will send your spirits soaring. At 6 a.m. and 6 p.m. on Friday, Saturday and Sunday, over 100 hot air balloons float up in a mass ascent. These include numerous odd shapes – elephants, dogs, bagpipers, shopping trolleys and fire extinguishers are among those to have taken off in recent years. These shapes do not fly straight, and are a major test of skills for the pilot. Equally spectacular is the Night Glow, where the tethered balloons illuminate the sky like giant light bulbs in a choreographed *son et lumière* display, followed by stunning fireworks, which attracts crowds of 100,000. Daytime events include aerobatics, parachute descents and motorbike stunts, as well as music and some amazing balloon model-making.

   If you want to experience a hot air balloon ride yourself during the fiesta, you're best off contacting one of the local operators in advance: try Bristol Balloons (0117 963 7858), Bailey Balloons (01275 375300) or First Flight (01934 852875).

When:	Second weekend of August (Thurs–Sun)
Where:	Ashton Court, Long Ashton, Bristol
Duration:	4 days
Website:	www.bristolfiesta.co.uk

South West

Fowey Royal Regatta

Royalty-endorsed racing and giant pasties

One of Britain's premier sailing events sees hundreds of visitors descend on the small town of Fowey; Queen Victoria, Prince Albert and the current Queen are among those to have made the trip during the regatta's long and proud history. There are sailing races every day, but also plenty of events on dry land, including a floral dance, carnival procession and a giant pasty ceremony (the pasty makes its way from Polruan to Fowey by boat), and in the air, where the Red Arrows usually put in an appearance.

When:	Third week of August
Where:	Fowey, Cornwall
Duration:	1 week
Tel:	01726 833573
Website:	www.foweyroyalregatta.co.uk

Weymouth Carnival

A great parade on the Esplanade

The Weymouth Carnival has been going strong for 50 years, and tens of thousands line the Esplanade to watch the procession. Alongside impressive floats and fancy dress, the crowning of the carnival queen and aerobatics from the Red Arrows are quirky events like space hopper racing and sand sculpting on the beach. The fireworks spectacular is one of the best around. Organised by the Round Table, the carnival has raised over £1 million for local charities since 1957.

When:	Third Wednesday in August
Where:	Weymouth Esplanade
Duration:	1 day
Website:	www.weymouthcarnival.co.uk

Beautiful Days

The perfect weekend for nostalgic crusties (and their kids)

[£ £ £] [⚒] [⛰]

During the early 1990s, The Levellers were the archetypal festival band – all dreadlocks, baggy clothes, right-on anti-establishment slogans and catchy fiddle riffs. They've recreated those halcyon days in the sylvan setting of Escot Park in Devon with this friendly, defiantly un-corporate weekender. Madly eclectic music (Radical Dance Faction and Boney M, anyone?) and all-important good vibes galore – especially in the kids' area.

When:	Third weekend of August
Where:	Escot Park, Ottery St Mary, Devon
Duration:	3 days
Website:	www.beautifuldays.org

Bude Jazz Festival

Classic jazz, Cornish style

[£ £ £ £]

New Orleans comes to Cornwall, as the pretty seaside town of Bude goes overboard for jazz. There are around 20 events a day over the eight-day festival, in pubs, halls, hotels and restaurants; a 'stroller ticket' allows you access to almost all of them. The music covers a range of styles from blues to bop, with a particular penchant for old style New Orleans and classic jazz. There's a lot of holiday accommodation available in the town, but it's in great demand over the festival.

When:	Last week of August
Where:	Bude, Cornwall
Duration:	8 days
Tel:	01288 356360
Website:	www.budejazzfestival.co.uk

Royal Torbay Regatta

Two centuries of sailing contests

FREE

The Torbay Royal Regatta has been running since 1803, and the natural amphitheatre of the bay makes a fine racing arena for a variety of sailing races. There's also a 10-km run, from Torquay to Paignton – arguably the most scenic road race in the country. A huge firework display and the Red Arrows add to the spectacle.

When:	Last weekend of August
Where:	Torbay, Devon
Duration:	2 days
Tel:	01803 292006 (Yacht club)
Website:	www.royaltorbayyc.org.uk

> Around the same time, just along the coast, the Dartmouth Royal Regatta also takes place. First held just a couple of decades later in 1822, it gained its royal status following an unscheduled visit from Queen Victoria and family in 1856. There's a similar programme of sailing, air displays and music: see www.dartmouthregatta.org. Nearby Paignton, Brixham and Babbacombe also hold regattas in July and August.

Great Dorset Steam Fair

Let off steam at one of the world's finest gatherings of vintage vehicles

£ £

A farm in Dorset provides the setting for what over the past 40 years has grown into 'the world's leading steam and vintage vehicle preservation event.' Only a small proportion of the 200,000 people who visit the fair every year are traction engine nuts, though – most come to enjoy the spectacle and the atmosphere and for a fascinating window onto a bygone era. The 600-acre showground includes over 2,000 working exhibits, including 200 steam engines and an old-time steam funfair, all swingboats, roundabouts and organ tunes. There's a modern funfair, too – one of the largest travelling shows in the country – as well as live music (this is one of the few places where a Wurzels tribute band feels like just the right thing), exhibitions of rural crafts and tools, a well-stocked Food Hall and other entertainment. The hundred or so heavy horses, groomed to their finest and working the land with traditional agricultural machinery, are always particularly popular, and there's a ploughing match on the Wednesday. Although most visitors come for the day, thousands camp on site; other accommodation in the area gets booked up by June.

When:	Last week of August (Weds–Sun)
Where:	Tarrant Hinton, Blandford Forum, Dorset
Duration:	5 days
Tel:	01258 860361
Website:	www.gdsf.co.uk

Greenbelt Festival

Christianity at its most inclusive

In our secular society, the words 'Christian rock festival' are enough to send all but the most evangelical running for cover. Greenbelt, however, is an exception. For one thing, it has a strong and eclectic musical line-up that includes, but certainly isn't limited to, bands with explicit Christian beliefs. Over the years, U2, Moby, Jamelia, Goldie, Lambchop and Coldcut have all performed along with leading 'Christian rock' bands like Delirious?. With Archbishop of Canterbury Rowan Williams as the festival's patron, there's also a questioning and open-minded philosophy – it's unlikely that Peter Tatchell or Asian Dub Foundation would be on the bill at more fundamentalist gatherings. There are thoughtful talks and panel discussions on topics like social justice and human rights, plus comedy, poetry, performance and visual arts, busking, beats and a folk club. As well as worship and mass hymn singing, there are activities and entertainment specifically aimed at children and teenagers.

When:	August Bank Holiday weekend (Fri–Mon)
Where:	Cheltenham Racecourse, Cheltenham, Glos.
Duration:	4 days
Tel:	020 7374 2760
Website:	www.greenbelt.org.uk

Newlyn Fish Festival

Always something fishy going on

Newlyn, just west of Penzance, remains one of Cornwall's main fishing centres, and celebrates its heritage on August Bank Holiday Monday with the annual Fish Festival. The pretty harbour is filled with fishing boats and other ships of all shapes and sizes, many open to visitors. There's a smorgasbord of locally caught fish on sale at the fish market, as well as other stalls and entertainment around the quay: live music, cooking demonstrations and traditional Cornish maritime craftspeople showing off their skills.

When:	August Bank Holiday Monday
Where:	Newlyn, Cornwall
Duration:	1 day
Tel:	01736 364324
Website:	www.newlynfishfestival.org.uk

Didmarton Bluegrass Festival

Every shade of bluegrass

£ £ £ £ 👤 ⛺

One of the UK's leading bluegrass festivals, Didmarton caters for everyone from banjo-toting aficionados to those who just enjoy live music in a friendly atmosphere. Bands come from across the UK, the US and worldwide. The music can be surprisingly diverse – the bluegrass ranges from 'old time' to 'progressive', and there's a smattering of other folk and country styles thrown in. There's on-site camping and catering, including an amazingly cheap real ale bar.

When:	Weekend after August Bank Holiday
Where:	Kemble Airfield, Cirencester, Glos.
Duration:	3 days
Website:	www.didmarton-bluegrass.co.uk

Widecombe Fair

Traditional Devonshire village fair attracts Old Uncle Tom Cobley and all

£? 👤

First held in the 1850s, this country show attracts visitors from all over the world after being immortalised in song, along with Uncle Tom Cobley and all. Tom Pierce's ill-fated grey mare is resurrected for her annual appearance, alongside displays of livestock and vintage vehicles, trade stands and local produce, and everything from a gymkhana and dog show to bale tossing and a tug of war. Festivities continue into the night with music and dancing on site and in the picturesque Dartmoor village of Widecombe-in-the-Moor.

When:	Second Tuesday in September
Where:	Fair Field, Widecombe-in-the-Moor, Newton Abbot, Devon
Duration:	1 day
Website:	www.widecombe-in-the-moor.com

Stroud Fringe Festival

Artistic types take over the town

For a small town, Stroud attracts a disproportionate number of artists, craftspeople, writers and musicians. Its bohemian inhabitants come out in force for the colourful fringe festival every September. There's an eclectic range of music, crafts, street performances and kids' events, and virtually everything is free. The atmosphere is infectious and you can expect a few spontaneous surprises. In recent years, a campsite has been opened on the edge of town during the festival for those who want to immerse themselves fully in the experience.

When:	Second weekend of September
Where:	Stroud, Glos.
Duration:	3 days
Website:	www.stroudfringe.co.uk

Stroud boasts a number of other festivals, all of which provide a good excuse to sample some Cotswold cafe culture (fair-trade organic coffee from independent outlets only, please – no Starbucks here). May sees the Stroudwater International Textiles Festival (www.stroudwatertextiles.org.uk) celebrate the town's heritage with exhibitions from the world's leading textiles artists. In June, the many artists in the Stroud Valleys open up their studios and run exhibitions (www.sva.org.uk). Stroud also has a good value mixed arts festival (www.stroudartsfestival.org) and a photography festival (www.stroudphotofestival.co.uk) in October.

End of the Road Festival

The perfect way to round off the festival season

Hosted by the same venue as the Larmer Tree Festival earlier in the summer (with the same resident peacocks and parrots), this event is an intimate affair limited to just 5,000 people. There's quality local and organic food, good beer and a refreshing absence of sponsors and advertising hoardings. There's a defiantly left-field music line-up – bands play long sets and genuinely seem to enjoy being there. And who can blame them?

When:	September
Where:	Larmer Tree Grounds, Tollard Royal, nr Salisbury, Wilts.
Duration:	3 days
Tel:	01342 892664
Website:	www.endoftheroadfestival.com

St Ives September Festival

Discover why artists love St Ives

Cornwall's largest arts festival features a diverse musical programme which encompasses folk, jazz, world musical and classical, as well as poetry, literature, films and talks in the archetypal seaside town. St Ives has a long tradition as an artists' colony (there's a branch of the Tate here), making for a particularly high standard of exhibitions and open studios. There are also many free events around the town, including acoustic sessions and open-mic nights in the pubs. Today's thriving festival actually developed out of the festival fringe, which had grown up around the old St Ives Festival. When the main St Ives Festival ran into funding difficulties and folded in 2001, the fringe committee stepped into the breach, and the festival has gone from strength to strength.

When:	Second/third weeks of September
Where:	St Ives, Cornwall
Duration:	15 days
Tel:	01736 366077
Website:	www.stivesseptemberfestival.co.uk

Jane Austen Festival

Celebrating Bath's most famous resident

Miss Austen gets a festival all of her own when Bath reverts to its Georgian heyday in a celebration of her life and works. There's a huge costumed Regency Promenade with music and dancing, a Regency Ball at the Assembly Rooms, walking tours of Austen's Bath, lectures and even bonnet-making workshops. If you're planning on attending the ball, make sure you join in at the Regency dance workshops during the week.

When:	End of September
Where:	Bath, Wilts.
Duration:	10 days
Tel:	01225 443000
Website:	www.janeausten.co.uk/festival

Cheltenham Literature Festival

The world's oldest literature festival

In 1949, a group of friends decided that the solitary pleasures of reading and writing and the conviviality of a festival were not, after all, incompatible. Over 400 writers, including many famous names, and tens of thousands of literature lovers now descend on the town for readings, debates and other events, including a lively fringe and plenty of fun for young bookworms too.

When:	October
Where:	Cheltenham, Glos.
Duration:	10 days
Tel:	01242 774400
Website:	www.cheltenhamfestivals.com

Lowender Peran

Cornwall celebrates its national identity

Cornwall, it should be remembered, is *not* part of England. This festival, founded in 1978, celebrates the ancient kingdom's Celtic connections, with visitors and performers coming from Brittany, Wales, Scotland, Ireland and the Isle of Man. Events include ceilidhs, concerts, dancing, storytelling and traditional dance workshops, and there's a strong emphasis on joining in.

When:	Third week of October
Where:	Perranporth, Cornwall
Duration:	5 days
Tel:	01872 553413
Website:	www.lowenderperan.co.uk

Bridgwater Guy Fawkes Carnival

The biggest Bonfire Night in the West

Few places celebrate Bonfire Night with such gusto as in Bridgwater and other neighbouring Wessex towns. The West Country was a strongly Protestant area, so the failure of the Catholic Gunpowder Plot was enthusiastically commemorated. Bridgwater's bonfire dates right back to 1605, the year of the plot. Over the centuries, the bonfire got bigger, the costumes more extrovert and the homemade fireworks-on-sticks – the Bridgwater Squibs – safer (though the last is a recent development). In the 1880s, an organising committee brought a degree of order to the anarchy and put together the first carnival procession, illuminated by paraffin lamps.

Bridgwater now boasts possibly the biggest illuminated carnival in Europe, with more than a hundred carnival floats, known here as 'carts'. They have themes like fictional characters, historical events or scenes from around the world, with the participants, or 'features', forming moving scenes or static tableaux. Towed by tractors, they're put together by carnival clubs or 'gangs' from across the region, and are the culmination of months of work. The illuminated carts are up to 100 feet long and can each cost thousands of pounds, take thousands of hours to build and glow with thousands of light bulbs. Around 150,000 people come to see the spectacle, some watching from grandstand seating, others enjoying the atmosphere on the street.

When:	Early November (usually Friday nearest 5 Nov)
Where:	Bridgwater, Somerset
Duration:	1 day
Website:	www.bridgwatercarnival.org.uk

Carnival circuits across the West Country

So much artistry and hard work goes into creating the carnival carts that it would be a shame to show them only at Bridgwater. Over the years, a couple of dozen other carnivals have sprung up across the West Country to light up the dark autumn nights from the end of August to late November. Many of these also attract large crowds, and clubs attempt to take their carts around as many of the carnivals on the various circuits as they can manage. The oldest and most popular circuit is the Somerset County Guy Fawkes Carnival Association Circuit. It kicks off in Bridgwater on the Friday, then heads to North Petherton the next day, Burnham-on-Sea on the following Monday, Shepton Mallet on the Wednesday, Wells on Friday, Glastonbury and Chilkwell on Saturday, winding up in Weston-super-Mare on the following Monday.
www.southwestcarnivals.com

Ottery St Mary Tar Barrels

If you play with fire...

At this very moment, there's probably a health and safety committee deep in the bowels of Whitehall discussing what to do about Ottery St Mary and its flaming barrels. This unique Bonfire Night event has been going on in the Devon town since the seventeenth century and remains exhilaratingly untamed, as local people carry barrels of flaming tar through the streets. The event kicks off in the early evening with children carrying mini barrels, with teenagers and women following. Things really heat up when big burly rugby playing types run through the streets with massive 30-kilo barrels – don't get too close. There are 17 barrels in all, and each is traditionally lit outside a different Ottery pub. A huge bonfire, 35 foot high and 50 foot wide, blazes in St Saviour's Meadow, as fairground lights whirl behind. The event is, of course, perfectly safe if everyone acts sensibly (though with the amount of alcohol consumed, this is not a given), but the streets do get very crowded, and bringing children along later in the evening is not recommended.

When:	5 November (unless Sunday)
Where:	Ottery St Mary, Devon
Duration:	1 day
Tel:	01404 813964 (Tourist Information)
Website:	www.otterytarbarrels.co.uk

Montol

Pagan mischief and Cornish carolling

In the week leading up to the winter solstice, Penzance stages a revival of this ancient festival. There's a three-day Montol Market with beautifully decorated stalls and street performances. The solstice itself is celebrated with a lantern procession through the town and a beacon bonfire. Penglaz, the Penzance Obby Oss, appears along with 'geese' or 'guise' dancers – disguised dancers who embody the spirit of misrule. The guise dancers used to go from house to house, gatecrashing parties and 'testing the ale' – these days, they manage to put in an appearance at most of the town's pubs. Singing 'Cornish carols' is also popular. Folklorists 'collected' many of our favourite traditional Christmas carols, including 'I Saw Three Ships' and 'The First Noel', in Cornwall after they had died out in other parts of Britain.

When:	Mid-June
Where:	Penzance, Cornwall
Duration:	8 days
Tel:	01736 332211
Website:	www.montol.co.uk

Tom Bawcock's Eve

Gaze at the Christmas lights and try Stargazy Pie

FREE

Long ago, in the midst of the winter storms, the people of the Penwith fishing village of Mousehole faced starvation. A young man named Tom Bawcock bravely put to sea – and came back with a miraculous catch of fish. The village of Mousehole has celebrated Tom Bawcock's Eve on 23 December ever since – for at least 300 years. An old song tells the story: 'Merry place you may believe, tiz Mouzel 'pon Tom Bawcock's Eve / To be there then who wouldn't wesh, to sup o' sibm soorts o' fish.' The 'seven sorts of fish' are baked in a Stargazy Pie, with their heads protruding through the crust. The Ship Inn on the harbour is the place to go. Tom Bawcock's Eve is also an occasion to admire Mousehole's famous Christmas lights. For more than 40 years, the locals have been decorating houses, streets and even boats with lights – in what is already a picture-book horseshoe harbour, it's a magical sight.

When: 23 December
Where: Mousehole, nr Penzance, Cornwall
Duration: 1 day

Weymouth New Year's Eve

Bring out the fancy dress

£?

The Dorset seaside town of Weymouth is the unlikely venue for arguably the best New Year's Eve party in England. The town turns out in force and fancy dress, with around 20,000 costumed revellers taking to the streets for a night of mayhem and merriment, claimed by some to be 'the world's largest fancy dress party'. No big-name bands or bank-breaking pyrotechnics (though there are fireworks displays and plenty of live music around the town) – just hordes of people of all ages determined to enjoy themselves. It's a great place to see in the New Year.

When: New Year's Eve
Where: Weymouth, Dorset
Duration: 1 day

Festival Survival Tips

1. Camping is part of the fun. You don't need loads of gear – a tent, a sleeping bag, a torch and a water bottle are the essentials. Most tents look alike, so make sure you find a landmark that helps you locate yours (and bear in mind more tents may appear after you've pitched yours) – a flag or a windsock could be a lifesaver when you're stumbling back at midnight. Gazebos, windbreaks and awnings create privacy and space, and lanterns, rugs and furniture give a home-from-home feel – but check with the festival organisers, as not all festivals allow these. Campfires, sadly, are usually a no-no too. Campsites at folk festivals, in particular, often attract impromptu jam sessions – but 11 p.m. is usually curfew time.

2. The weather will make a huge difference to your festival experience – for better or worse. The glorious British weather means you should come prepared for all eventualities. Sun cream and plenty of water are essential when the sun shines – but remember that clear, starry nights are often the coldest, and a thick fleece or jumper is essential. You're probably more worried about the rain, though – Glastonbury's mud baths are especially infamous. Wellies are a godsend, but the trick is not to worry and just go with the flow. Caked in mud? So is everyone else. You can have a shower when you get home.

3. Festival toilets have improved hugely in recent years, but can still be pretty disgusting by Sunday afternoon. Loo paper is usually kept stocked up, but it's a good idea to keep a packet of tissues in your pocket just in case. Use the liquid hand sanitiser provided, or carry your own bottle with you. Showers are a luxury, if you can be bothered with the often enormous queues. Remember, though: it's a festival, and no one's too bothered about your hygiene habits (although a squirt of deodorant never goes amiss).

4. Alcohol has been part of the festive experience since time immemorial. Drunk people do not, however, make pleasant festival company, and tents are not the nicest places to wake up with a hangover, so don't overdo it. Most festivals allow you to take your own alcohol into the campsite, but often don't let you take it into the main arena. They can be quite strict about this, so check beforehand if you don't want your bottle of White Lightning/Chateau Lafayette confiscated.

5. Drugs are no more legal at festivals than anywhere else. That said, marijuana is endemic; if you do plan to smoke a joint, be discreet and respect people who'd rather you didn't smoke around them, particularly those with children. Festivals can be alarming places to experiment with harder drugs – including the sometimes surprisingly powerful 'herbal highs' you'll often find (legally) on

sale. If you do find yourself or your friends freaking out, seek out the St John Ambulance crew, who are all too used to it.

6. Getting lost is surprisingly easy, even at smaller festivals. It's a good idea to arrange a meeting point and times in case you get separated from your friends (e.g. behind the main stage mixing desk, on the hour). Don't just rely on mobile phones: batteries die, reception drops out and ringtones get drowned out by real music.

7. Crime occurs whenever large numbers of human beings are gathered together, though for the most part, festivals are friendly and unthreatening places. Theft can, sadly, be a problem – mainly, though not exclusively, at the larger festivals. Don't leave valuables in your tent – and try not to bring too many with you anyway.

8. Food and drink is one of the great pleasures of festival-going. Unless you're on a really tight budget, there's no need to bring your own Pot Noodles and boil-in-the-bag meals. You can easily eat a different style of global cuisine for every meal, and you'll increasingly find organic, locally sourced and fair-trade ingredients. Prices are usually reasonable, although three meals and a few snacks (late night doughnuts.... mmm....) can quickly add up. On most sites, you don't need to waste money on bottled water – there are taps with drinking water around the site, so fill up your own bottle.

9. Green issues have been a theme of alternative festivals for many years, but now even the mainstream ones are catching up. Most festival sites are fields, parks and gardens for the rest of the year, and should be treated with respect. Recycling facilities are usually good, so use them. There's nothing worse than ending a wonderful festival stuck in a five-mile traffic jam. Share a lift (check some online festival forums) or use public transport – even some of the most remote events lay on shuttle buses from the nearest station.

10. Enjoy! You won't be able to see everything you want to. Bands will clash, your friends will have different tastes, and you might even want an early night. Just enjoy what you can, and don't worry about what you might have missed. Festivals are a great place to discover new bands, new genres or even entire new art forms. Seek out the weird and wonderful, join a drumming circle, get your face painted like a tiger – remember, you have 360 other days to act normal.

Getting in for free

Can't afford to go to all the festivals you want to? Don't try and sneak in under the fence – try these legitimate ways of getting in for free instead.

1. All festivals need stewards, to collect tickets, marshal crowds, direct traffic and so on. Many are crying out for volunteers. You'll have to put in your shift (this varies from festival to festival), but you'll have plenty of play time too. Contact the festival well in advance if you're interested.

2. Charities do a lot of campaigning and fundraising at festivals, and are often on the look-out for people to staff their stalls or collar passers-by. You'll be expected to work around four or five hours a day, mainly during the day time. The rest of the time is yours. Oxfam provides large numbers of entrance stewards at Glastonbury, though demand for volunteer places is always high.

3. The Workers Beer Company is the largest supplier of bars to festivals. Try contacting them if you're interested in pulling pints (www.workersbeer. co.uk). Hundreds of food stalls and other concessions make their way round the festival circuit each summer. It's always worth approaching them to see if they have work available.

4. If you're interested in performing yourself, a lot of festivals are keen to hear from you. Send a CD or a link to your MySpace page (check which they'd prefer). Even the more obscure festivals receive loads of requests though, so don't expect to be offered a headlining slot on the main stage just like that.

5. Festivals rarely hire lighting and sound technicians, stagehands and so on directly. If you have technical experience, try contacting events management companies who provide services to festivals, or entertainment industry recruitment agencies. You'll often be working when everyone else is having fun – but you'll get paid, and it beats being in an office.

Listing by month

This list gives you an overview of what festivals are taking place around the country each month. They are listed in the order that they happen within each month. Flick to the page number given for a full description of each festival.

January

February

March

April

May

June

July

August

September

October

November

December

THE
BIG WALKS
OF GREAT BRITAIN

including South Downs Way, Offa's Dyke Path, The Thames Path,
The Peddars Way and Norfolk Coast Path,
The Wolds Way, The Pembrokeshire Coast Path,
The West Highland Way, The Pennine Way

DAVID BATHURST

The Big Walks of Great Britain

David Bathurst

£9.99

978-1-84024-566-0

From the South West Coast Path to the Great Glen Way, from the Cotswold Way to Hadrian's Wall, and from the Yorkshire Wolds to Glyndwr's Way, there are big walks here to keep you rambling all year round. And what better way to discover the landscapes of Great Britain, from green and gentle dales to majestic mountains and rugged cliffs?

An indefatigable walker, David Bathurst has unlaced his boots to produce this invaluable companion to the 19 best-loved long-distance footpaths. His appreciation of the beauty and history of the British countryside and his light-hearted style will appeal to experienced and novice walkers alike.

- The definitive guide to the national trails of England and Wales and the Scottish National Long Distance Walking Routes

- Detailed descriptions of the trails and a wealth of practical information, including amenities available

- Recommends historic and geographic areas of interest on or near the paths, from ancient burial mounds to flora and fauna

- Routes range in difficulty from the gentle 73-mile Great Glen Way to the massive 628-mile South West Coast Path

www.summersdale.com